UNDERSTANDING LINEAR ALGEBRA
Using MATLAB

Erwin Kleinfeld • Margaret Kleinfeld

University of Iowa

Prentice
Hall

Upper Saddle River, NJ 07458

Executive Editor: George Lobell
Supplement Editor: Melanie Van Benthuysen
Assistant Managing Editor: John Matthews
Production Editor: Wendy A. Perez
Supplement Cover Manager: Paul Gourhan
Supplement Cover Designer: PM Workshop Inc.
Manufacturing Buyer: Lisa McDowell

© 2001 by Prentice Hall
Upper Saddle River, NJ 07458

Printed in the United States of America

10 9 8 7 6 5

ISBN 0-13-060945-5

Prentice-Hall International (UK) Limited, London
Prentice-Hall of Australia Pty. Limited, Sydney
Prentice-Hall Canada, Inc., Toronto
Prentice-Hall Hispanoamericana, S.A., Mexico
Prentice-Hall of India Private Limited, New Delhi
Pearson Education Asia Pte. Ltd., Singapore
Prentice-Hall of Japan, Inc., Tokyo
Editora Prentice-Hall do Brazil, Ltda., Rio de Janeiro

About the Authors

Erwin Kleinfeld and Margaret Kleinfeld are professors of mathematics at the University of Iowa in Iowa City, Iowa. They are the authors of two textbooks on linear algebra, A Short Course in Matrix Theory and Elementary Linear Algebra, published by Nova Science Publishers,Inc.

Contents

Introduction

This book is intended as a supplement to an elementary linear algebra text and is designed to work well with any standard text. Its purpose is to help students taking a first course in linear algebra. It could also be used as a review by someone who has already taken such a course. We introduce some basic MATLAB commands to remove the computational burden and to illustrate the concepts with numerical examples. In our teaching we have noticed that students are impatient with long explanations and have difficulty with abstract concepts. They tell us repeatedly that they prefer to learn by seeing examples and working problems. We are responding by writing this supplement with lots of examples and problems. The examples show some interesting methods, and the problems give the students some practice using them. In the course of working these numerical problems the student will see vectors, subspaces, linear dependence, span, and basis used in a very concrete way.

We begin with the reduced row echelon form (RREF) and row operations. We show how the RREF can be used to solve many problems. The Hermite form, a standard form that was in use before the RREF became fashionable, gives an easy way to find the null space of a matrix. The Hermite form H is readily obtained from the RREF, and a basis of the null space appears as the nonzero columns of $H - I$, where I is the identity matrix. Students appreciate this algorithm, especially for finding linearly independent eigenvectors and for expressing in vector form the complete solution to a system of linear equations.

Our "worksheets" provide an easy and active way to learn MATLAB: Call up the MATLAB program and enter the commands just as they are listed in a worksheet. By observing the output, the student learns what the commands do. It is not necessary to read about the commands before hand. A student could get a good introduction to MATLAB just by going through this book and doing all the worksheets. At the other extreme the student could skip all the MATLAB sections and use the rest as a linear algebra tutorial.

Chapter 1

Reduced Row Echelon Form

1.1   Finding the RREF of a Matrix

If A is a matrix, there are three types of elementary row operations that one can perform on A.

1. Exchange two rows.

2. Multiply a row by a nonzero number.

3. Add a multiple of one row to another.

The matrix A is said to be in reduced row echelon form if it satisfies the following **four** conditions:

1. The first nonzero entry in every row is a 1, called the leading 1 of that row.

2. The leading 1 in row $(i + 1)$ is to the right of the leading 1 in row i.

3. Any column that contains the leading 1 of some row is all zeros elsewhere in that column.

4. The zero rows, if any, come last.

Fact   *Any matrix A can be transformed into one and only one matrix B in reduced row echelon form (RREF) by a sequence of elementary row operations.*

The matrix B is called the reduced row echelon rorm of A, or $\text{RREF}(A)$.

The process of transforming a matrix A into its RREF by a sequence of elementary row operations is called row reduction. We give an example:

1

Example 1.1 *We find the RREF for the matrix*

$$A = \begin{bmatrix} 2 & 2 & 4 \\ 3 & 6 & -3 \\ 5 & 2 & 8 \end{bmatrix}.$$

Start in the upper left hand corner and work down and to the right. The first step is to get a 1 in the 1,1 position. We multiply row 1 by $\frac{1}{2}$ to get

$$\begin{bmatrix} 1 & 1 & 2 \\ 3 & 6 & -3 \\ 5 & 2 & 8 \end{bmatrix}.$$

Now adding multiples of row 1 to the other rows, we produce zeros in the rest of column 1. First we add -3 times row 1 to row 2 to get

$$\begin{bmatrix} 1 & 1 & 2 \\ 0 & 3 & -9 \\ 5 & 2 & 8 \end{bmatrix}.$$

Then we add -5 times row 1 to row 3 to get

$$\begin{bmatrix} 1 & 1 & 2 \\ 0 & 3 & -9 \\ 0 & -3 & -2 \end{bmatrix}.$$

Now we want to get a 1 in the 2,2 position, so we multiply row 2 by $\frac{1}{3}$ to get

$$\begin{bmatrix} 1 & 1 & 2 \\ 0 & 1 & -3 \\ 0 & -3 & -2 \end{bmatrix}.$$

Next use multiples of row 2 to produce zeros in the rest of column 2. We add -1 times row 2 to row 1 to get

$$\begin{bmatrix} 1 & 0 & 5 \\ 0 & 1 & -3 \\ 0 & -3 & -2 \end{bmatrix},$$

and add 3 times row 2 to row 3 to get

$$\begin{bmatrix} 1 & 0 & 5 \\ 0 & 1 & -3 \\ 0 & 0 & -11 \end{bmatrix}.$$

Multiplying row 3 by $-\frac{1}{11}$, we get

$$\begin{bmatrix} 1 & 0 & 5 \\ 0 & 1 & -3 \\ 0 & 0 & 1 \end{bmatrix}.$$

Now adding -5 times row 3 to row 1, and adding 3 times row 3 to row 2 gives

$$\begin{bmatrix} 1 & 0 & 0 \\ 0 & 1 & 0 \\ 0 & 0 & 1 \end{bmatrix}.$$

This is the 3×3 identity matrix I. Thus $\text{RREF}(A) = I$.

Example 1.2 *Find the RREF of the matrix*

$$\begin{bmatrix} 2 & 3 & -1 \\ 4 & 2 & 2 \\ 4 & -1 & 5 \end{bmatrix}.$$

Multiplying row 1 by $\frac{1}{2}$ (equivalently dividing row 1 by 2) gives

$$\begin{bmatrix} 1 & \frac{3}{2} & -\frac{1}{2} \\ 4 & 2 & 2 \\ 4 & -1 & 5 \end{bmatrix}.$$

Multiplying row 1 by -4 and adding to rows 2 and 3, we get

$$\begin{bmatrix} 1 & \frac{3}{2} & -\frac{1}{2} \\ 0 & -4 & 4 \\ 0 & -7 & 7 \end{bmatrix}.$$

Now multiply row 2 by $-\frac{1}{4}$ to get

$$\begin{bmatrix} 1 & \frac{3}{2} & -\frac{1}{2} \\ 0 & 1 & -1 \\ 0 & -7 & 7 \end{bmatrix}.$$

Now 7 times row 2 added to row 3 gives

$$\begin{bmatrix} 1 & \frac{3}{2} & -\frac{1}{2} \\ 0 & 1 & -1 \\ 0 & 0 & 0 \end{bmatrix},$$

and adding $-\frac{3}{2}$ times row 2 to row 1, we get

$$\begin{bmatrix} 1 & 0 & 1 \\ 0 & 1 & -1 \\ 0 & 0 & 0 \end{bmatrix}.$$

This is the RREF of the matrix we started with.

Example 1.3 *Find the RREF of the matrix*

$$A = \begin{bmatrix} 3 & 2 & 4 & 1 & 3 & 4 \\ 0 & -1 & 1 & 4 & 3 & 1 \\ 5 & 4 & 6 & 3 & 7 & 5 \\ 7 & 6 & 8 & -2 & 4 & 0 \end{bmatrix}.$$

First we need to get a 1 in the 1,1 position. We could divide row 1 by 3, but that would produce fractions. This would be OK, but a better choice is to multiply row 1 by 2, and then subtract row 3 from row 1. Multiplying row 1 by 2, we get

$$\begin{bmatrix} 6 & 4 & 8 & 2 & 6 & 8 \\ 0 & -1 & 1 & 4 & 3 & 1 \\ 5 & 4 & 6 & 3 & 7 & 5 \\ 7 & 6 & 8 & -2 & 4 & 0 \end{bmatrix}.$$

Now subtracting row 3 from row 1 (equivalently, adding −1 times row 3 to row 1) gives

$$\begin{bmatrix} 1 & 0 & 2 & -1 & -1 & 3 \\ 0 & -1 & 1 & 4 & 3 & 1 \\ 5 & 4 & 6 & 3 & 7 & 5 \\ 7 & 6 & 8 & -2 & 4 & 0 \end{bmatrix}.$$

The next step is to clear the rest of column 1 by adding multiples of row 1 to the other rows. We add (−5) times row 1 to row 3 to obtain

$$\begin{bmatrix} 1 & 0 & 2 & -1 & -1 & 3 \\ 0 & -1 & 1 & 4 & 3 & 1 \\ 0 & 4 & -4 & 8 & 12 & -10 \\ 7 & 6 & 8 & -2 & 4 & 0 \end{bmatrix}.$$

Next we add (−7) times row 1 to row 4 to obtain

$$\begin{bmatrix} 1 & 0 & 2 & -1 & -1 & 3 \\ 0 & -1 & 1 & 4 & 3 & 1 \\ 0 & 4 & -4 & 8 & 12 & -10 \\ 0 & 6 & -6 & 5 & 11 & -21 \end{bmatrix}.$$

Now we want to get a leading 1 for row 2, so we multiply row 2 by −1 to obtain

$$\begin{bmatrix} 1 & 0 & 2 & -1 & -1 & 3 \\ 0 & 1 & -1 & -4 & -3 & -1 \\ 0 & 4 & -4 & 8 & 12 & -10 \\ 0 & 6 & -6 & 5 & 11 & -21 \end{bmatrix}.$$

We clear the rest of column 2 by adding multiples of row 2 to the other rows. First we add −4 times row 2 to row 3 to obtain

$$\begin{bmatrix} 1 & 0 & 2 & -1 & -1 & 3 \\ 0 & 1 & -1 & -4 & -3 & -1 \\ 0 & 0 & 0 & 24 & 24 & -6 \\ 0 & 6 & -6 & 5 & 11 & -21 \end{bmatrix}.$$

Now adding −6 times row 2 to row 3, we get

$$\begin{bmatrix} 1 & 0 & 2 & 3 & 3 & 2 \\ 0 & 1 & -1 & -4 & -3 & -1 \\ 0 & 0 & 0 & 24 & 24 & -6 \\ 0 & 0 & 0 & 29 & 29 & -15 \end{bmatrix}.$$

We move down one row and over one column to the 3, 3 position, but there is a zero there. If there were a nonzero entry in row 4 column 3, we would exchange rows 3 and 4 to get a nonzero entry in the 3, 3 position. We do not want to move rows 1 or 2, which already have leading 1's. In this situation we move over one more column. The leading 1 in row 3 will now be in the fourth column. We multiply row 3 by $\frac{1}{24}$ to obtain

$$\begin{bmatrix} 1 & 0 & 2 & 3 & 3 & 2 \\ 0 & 1 & -1 & -4 & -3 & -1 \\ 0 & 0 & 0 & 1 & 1 & -\frac{1}{4} \\ 0 & 0 & 0 & 29 & 29 & -15 \end{bmatrix}.$$

Now −3 times row 3 added to row 1 gives

$$\begin{bmatrix} 1 & 0 & 2 & 0 & 0 & \frac{11}{4} \\ 0 & 1 & -1 & -4 & -3 & -1 \\ 0 & 0 & 0 & 1 & 1 & -\frac{1}{4} \\ 0 & 0 & 0 & 29 & 29 & -15 \end{bmatrix}.$$

Next 4 times row 3 added to row 2 gives

$$\begin{bmatrix} 1 & 0 & 2 & 0 & 0 & \frac{11}{4} \\ 0 & 1 & -1 & 0 & 1 & -2 \\ 0 & 0 & 0 & 1 & 1 & -\frac{1}{4} \\ 0 & 0 & 0 & 29 & 29 & -15 \end{bmatrix},$$

and adding -29 *times row 3 to 4 gives*

$$\begin{bmatrix} 1 & 0 & 2 & 0 & 0 & \frac{11}{4} \\ 0 & 1 & -1 & 0 & 1 & -2 \\ 0 & 0 & 0 & 1 & 1 & -\frac{1}{4} \\ 0 & 0 & 0 & 0 & 0 & -\frac{31}{4} \end{bmatrix}.$$

Now multiply the fourth row by $-\frac{4}{31}$ *to get*

$$\begin{bmatrix} 1 & 0 & 2 & 0 & 0 & \frac{11}{4} \\ 0 & 1 & -1 & 0 & 1 & -2 \\ 0 & 0 & 0 & 1 & 1 & -\frac{1}{4} \\ 0 & 0 & 0 & 0 & 0 & 1 \end{bmatrix}.$$

Adding multiples of row 4 to the other rows changes only the last column, so we get

$$\begin{bmatrix} 1 & 0 & 2 & 0 & 0 & 0 \\ 0 & 1 & -1 & 0 & 1 & 0 \\ 0 & 0 & 0 & 1 & 1 & 0 \\ 0 & 0 & 0 & 0 & 0 & 1 \end{bmatrix}.$$

This is the RREF of A.

We now do some more examples of row reduction.

Example 1.4 *Find the RREF of the matrix* $\begin{bmatrix} 1 & 1 & 1 \\ 1 & -1 & 1 \\ 1 & 2 & 4 \end{bmatrix}.$

$$\begin{bmatrix} 1 & 1 & 1 \\ 1 & -1 & 1 \\ 1 & 2 & 4 \end{bmatrix} \rightarrow \begin{bmatrix} 1 & 1 & 1 \\ 0 & -2 & 0 \\ 1 & 2 & 4 \end{bmatrix} \rightarrow \begin{bmatrix} 1 & 1 & 1 \\ 0 & -2 & 0 \\ 0 & 1 & 3 \end{bmatrix} \rightarrow \begin{bmatrix} 1 & 1 & 1 \\ 0 & 1 & 0 \\ 0 & 1 & 3 \end{bmatrix}$$

$$\rightarrow \begin{bmatrix} 1 & 0 & 1 \\ 0 & 1 & 0 \\ 0 & 1 & 3 \end{bmatrix} \rightarrow \begin{bmatrix} 1 & 0 & 1 \\ 0 & 1 & 0 \\ 0 & 0 & 3 \end{bmatrix} \rightarrow \begin{bmatrix} 1 & 0 & 1 \\ 0 & 1 & 0 \\ 0 & 0 & 1 \end{bmatrix} \rightarrow \begin{bmatrix} 1 & 0 & 0 \\ 0 & 1 & 0 \\ 0 & 0 & 1 \end{bmatrix}.$$

Thus $\mathrm{RREF}\left(\begin{bmatrix} 1 & 1 & 1 \\ 1 & -1 & 1 \\ 1 & 2 & 4 \end{bmatrix}\right) = \begin{bmatrix} 1 & 0 & 0 \\ 0 & 1 & 0 \\ 0 & 0 & 1 \end{bmatrix}.$

Example 1.5 *Find the RREF of the matrix* $\begin{bmatrix} 1 & 2 & 3 & 6 \\ 2 & 3 & 4 & 9 \\ 3 & 0 & 2 & 5 \end{bmatrix}.$

This time we sometimes do more than one row operation before rewriting the matrix.

$$\begin{bmatrix} 1 & 2 & 3 & 6 \\ 2 & 3 & 4 & 9 \\ 3 & 0 & 2 & 5 \end{bmatrix} \rightarrow \begin{bmatrix} 1 & 2 & 3 & 6 \\ 0 & -1 & -2 & -3 \\ 0 & -6 & -7 & -13 \end{bmatrix}$$

$$\rightarrow \begin{bmatrix} 1 & 2 & 3 & 6 \\ 0 & 1 & 2 & 3 \\ 0 & -6 & -7 & -13 \end{bmatrix} \rightarrow \begin{bmatrix} 1 & 0 & -1 & 0 \\ 0 & 1 & 2 & 3 \\ 0 & 0 & 5 & 5 \end{bmatrix} \rightarrow \begin{bmatrix} 1 & 0 & -1 & 0 \\ 0 & 1 & 2 & 3 \\ 0 & 0 & 1 & 1 \end{bmatrix}$$

$$\rightarrow \begin{bmatrix} 1 & 0 & 0 & 1 \\ 0 & 1 & 0 & 1 \\ 0 & 0 & 1 & 1 \end{bmatrix}. \text{ This last matrix is the RREF.}$$

1.1.1 Exercises

In problems 1-14, find the RREF of the given matrix.

1. $\begin{bmatrix} 1 & 2 & -3 \\ 3 & 8 & -9 \\ -2 & 9 & 6 \end{bmatrix}$ 2. $\begin{bmatrix} 1 & 3 & 9 \\ 2 & -4 & 8 \\ 3 & -3 & 3 \end{bmatrix}$ 3. $\begin{bmatrix} 2 & 3 & 4 & 9 \\ 3 & 4 & 5 & 12 \\ 4 & 5 & 6 & 15 \end{bmatrix}$

4. $\begin{bmatrix} 1 & 2 & 4 & -6 & 8 \\ 3 & 6 & 1 & 0 & -1 \\ 4 & 8 & 2 & 1 & 0 \\ 2 & 4 & 0 & 0 & 1 \end{bmatrix}$ 5. $\begin{bmatrix} 1 & 2 & 3 & 6 \\ 2 & 3 & 4 & 9 \\ -3 & -4 & -5 & 0 \end{bmatrix}$

6. $\begin{bmatrix} 4 & 1 & 1 & 6 \\ 1 & 4 & 1 & 6 \\ 1 & 1 & 4 & 6 \end{bmatrix}$ 7. $\begin{bmatrix} -2 & 1 & 1 \\ 1 & -2 & 1 \\ 1 & 1 & -2 \end{bmatrix}$

8. $\begin{bmatrix} 1 & 2 & 4 & 0 & 1 \\ 3 & 6 & 12 & 1 & 0 \\ 5 & 10 & 20 & -1 & -1 \end{bmatrix}$ 9. $\begin{bmatrix} 1 & 0 & 2 & 3 & 4 \\ 3 & 0 & 4 & 5 & 12 \\ 2 & 0 & 6 & 8 & 8 \end{bmatrix}$

10. $\begin{bmatrix} 2 & 3 & 4 & 5 \\ 3 & 4 & 5 & 6 \\ 4 & 5 & 6 & 7 \end{bmatrix}$ 11. $\begin{bmatrix} 2 & 2 & 2 \\ 3 & -3 & 3 \\ 4 & 8 & 12 \end{bmatrix}$ 12. $\begin{bmatrix} \frac{1}{2} & \frac{1}{2} & \frac{1}{2} & 1 & 0 \\ \frac{1}{3} & -\frac{1}{3} & \frac{1}{3} & 0 & 1 \\ \frac{1}{4} & \frac{1}{2} & 1 & 0 & 0 \end{bmatrix}$

13. $\begin{bmatrix} 0 & 5 & 4 & 3 & 0 \\ 0 & 1 & -1 & 1 & -1 \\ 0 & 8 & 6 & 4 & 2 \end{bmatrix}$ 14. $\begin{bmatrix} 2 & 5 & 4 \\ 3 & 4 & 1 \\ 5 & 9 & 5 \end{bmatrix}$

In problems 15-24, state whether the given matrix is or is not in RREF, and for those that are not, find the RREF.

15. $\begin{bmatrix} 1 & 5 & 0 \\ 0 & 0 & 0 \\ 0 & 0 & 1 \end{bmatrix}$ 16. $\begin{bmatrix} 1 & 5 & 0 & 8 & 0 \\ 0 & 0 & 1 & 7 & 0 \\ 0 & 0 & 0 & 0 & 1 \end{bmatrix}$ 17. $\begin{bmatrix} 1 & 0 & 0 \\ 0 & 0 & 1 \\ 0 & 1 & 0 \end{bmatrix}$

18. $\begin{bmatrix} 0 & 1 & 0 & 3 & 0 & 0 & 7 \\ 0 & 0 & 1 & 5 & 0 & 9 & 6 \\ 0 & 0 & 0 & 0 & 1 & 8 & 5 \end{bmatrix}$ 19. $\begin{bmatrix} 1 & 2 & 3 & 4 \\ 0 & 0 & 0 & 0 \end{bmatrix}$

20. $\begin{bmatrix} 1 & 1 & 0 & 3 & 0 & 0 & 7 \\ 1 & 0 & 1 & 5 & 0 & 9 & 6 \\ 1 & 0 & 0 & 0 & 1 & 8 & 5 \end{bmatrix}$ 21. $\begin{bmatrix} 0 & 0 & 0 & 0 \\ 1 & 2 & 5 & 0 \\ 0 & 0 & 0 & 1 \end{bmatrix}$

22. $\begin{bmatrix} 1 & 0 & 5 & 6 & 0 \\ 0 & 1 & 0 & 4 & 0 \\ 0 & 0 & 1 & -2 & 0 \\ 0 & 0 & 0 & 0 & 1 \end{bmatrix}$ 23. $\begin{bmatrix} 1 & 4 & 0 & 3 & 0 \\ 0 & 0 & 1 & -2 & 0 \\ 0 & 0 & 0 & 0 & 1 \\ 0 & 0 & 0 & 0 & 0 \end{bmatrix}$

24. $\begin{bmatrix} 0 & 1 & 0 & 5 & 0 & 7 \\ 0 & 0 & 1 & 6 & 0 & 8 \\ 0 & 0 & 0 & -2 & 0 & -4 \\ 0 & 0 & 0 & 0 & 1 & 6 \end{bmatrix}$

1.1.2   Matlab

To enter a matrix in Matlab at the EDU» prompt, type

$$A=[3\ 2\ 4\ 1\ 3\ 4;0\ -1\ 1\ 4\ 3\ 1;5\ 4\ 6\ 3\ 7\ 5;7\ 6\ 8\ -2\ 4\ 0]$$

Remark   *The entries of a row are separated by spaces (as above) or commas.   The semicolon indicates the start of the next row.*

Then the Matlab program will display on screen:

```
A =
    3    2  4    1  3  4
    0   -1  1    4  3  1
    5    4  6    3  7  5
    7    6  8   -2  4  0
```

To have Matlab find RREF(A) and name it B, at the EDU» prompt, type

$$\boxed{\text{B=rref(A)}}$$

Matlab will display the answer on the screen as follows:

$B =$

$$
\begin{array}{cccccc}
1 & 0 & 2 & 0 & 0 & 0 \\
0 & 1 & -1 & 0 & 1 & 0 \\
0 & 0 & 0 & 1 & 1 & 0 \\
0 & 0 & 0 & 0 & 0 & 1
\end{array}
$$

If the Matlab output of an **rref** command has complicated decimal entries, the **rats** command will approximate the decimals with fractions. Remember, however, that Matlab does floating-point calculations, not exact calculations, and the fractions may not be the exact answer.

$$\boxed{\text{rats(A)}}$$

approximates the entries of **A** with fractions.

When entering a matrix, you may enter fractions, in the form 2/3 or decimals such as .25. Matlab will convert the fractions to decimals or decimal approximations.

Example 1.6 *Here are the inputs and outputs from a Matlab session. The inputs are preceded by the EDU» prompt.*

```
EDU» A=[1/2,2/3,1/2;1/3,1/4,4/3]
A =
      0.5000   0.6667   0.5000
      0.3333   0.2500   1.3333
EDU» r=rref(A)
r =
      1.0000        0   7.8571
           0   1.0000  −5.1429
EDU» rats(r)
ans =
      1   0    55/7
      0   1   −36/7
```
You may mix decimals, fractions, and whole numbers in your input.

Example 1.7 *Another example:*

```
EDU» A=[1,5/3,2/4;.5,.65,3]
A =
      1.0000   1.6667   0.5000
      0.5000   0.6500   3.0000
EDU» r=rref(A)
r =
      1.0000        0   25.5000
           0   1.0000  −15.0000
EDU» rats(r)
ans =
      1   0   51/2
      0   1   −15
```

Warning *Do not enter output of the **rats** command in further computations.*

Matlab will also do the row reduction one step at a time using the command **reduce(A)**, but you must acquire the "m-file" named "reduce.m" written by David R. Hill. It is one of several instructional m-files that he has written for Matlab. The tool kit of instructional m-files is available free of charge from his Web site or from the MathWorks Inc., the developers of Matlab.

Warning *Matlab is case sensitive. A and a are two different names.*

Although most books (including this one) usually use capital letters to name matrices, when entering in Matlab it is easier to use lower case and the worksheets in the Matlab exercises usually do so.

When naming things in Matlab, the following rules apply:

The name may contain up to 19 characters.

* .   The name must start with a letter, which can be followed by letters, digits, or underscores.

The name must be a single word, no spaces allowed.

Punctuation characters are not allowed.

Reusing a name automatically clears its old meaning from memory. To find out what letters or words are currently in use as names, type the command

> who

This will give a list of the names currently in use.

Matlab will find the transpose of a matrix using the command **transpose(A)** or **A'**. (The prime is typed using the apostrophe key.) At the EDU» prompt, type

> C=transpose(A)

or

> C=A'

Matlab will return the transpose of A and name it C. (The transpose of A is the matrix whose rows are the columns of A.)

To adjoin more columns (in the form of a matrix B of appropriate size) to a matrix A, at the EDU» prompt, type

> D=[A B]

Matlab will adjoin the columns of B to A at the right and name the resulting matrix D. Note that there is a space between A and B.

To adjoin more rows (in the form of a matrix B of appropriate size) to a matrix A, at the EDU» prompt, type

> E=[A;B]

Matlab will adjoin the rows of B at the bottom of the matrix A and name the resulting matrix E.

To end your Matlab session and close the program, at the EDU» prompt, type

```
quit
```

Before quiting a Matlab session, you can print the current workspace directly from Matlab using the **print** command. You can also copy and paste from Matlab into a word processing program.

If you want to insert a comment in your Matlab session, type % at the prompt:

```
%
```

What follows the % sign is not taken by Matlab as a command.

1.1.3   Matlab Exercises

The first exercise is a worksheet containing input for a Matlab session. Go to your computer or a computer lab and start up the Matlab program. Type in the commands exactly as they appear in the exercise and observe the output. After each command hit the Enter key and observe the output.

Worksheet

```
EDU» a=[1 2 3;4 5 6]
EDU» b=[3 4 5]
EDU» c=[a;b]
EDU» rref(c)
EDU» d=c'
EDU» e=rref(d)
EDU» rats(e)
EDU» a=[-2 3;1 1;6 4]
EDU» b=[1;1;1]
EDU» c=[a b]
EDU» d=rref(c)
EDU» a=[4 2 7;-7 5 8;3 3 3]
EDU» rref(a)
EDU» b=[3 3;4 -5;10 4]
```

EDU» c=[a b]
EDU» rref(c)
EDU» rats(ans)
EDU» who
EDU» a
EDU» ans
EDU» b
EDU» % matlab is fun
EDU» quit

Use Matlab to find the RREF of the following matrices. Use the **rats** command to get your answer translated into fractions.

1. $\begin{bmatrix} \frac{1}{3} & \frac{2}{3} & 1 \\ \frac{1}{4} & \frac{3}{4} & 3 \end{bmatrix}$

2. $\begin{bmatrix} 2 & 3 & 1 & 4 \\ 1 & 4 & 1 & 5 \\ 3 & 7 & 2 & 9 \\ -1 & 1 & 0 & 1 \end{bmatrix}$

3. $\begin{bmatrix} 8 & 7 & 6 & 0 & 4 \\ 7 & 0 & 5 & 4 & 0 \\ 6 & 5 & 0 & 3 & 2 \end{bmatrix}$

4. $\begin{bmatrix} \frac{1}{3} & \frac{1}{5} & \frac{2}{5} & -3 \\ \frac{1}{5} & \frac{2}{5} & \frac{1}{3} & 4 \end{bmatrix}$

5. $\begin{bmatrix} 1 & 0.5 & 3 & 2.5 \\ 2 & 1.5 & 0.5 & 3 \end{bmatrix}$

Use Matlab to check the RREFs you found in the preceding set of exercises.

1.1.4 Optional Matlab: Diary, Save, and Load Commands

The following commands might be useful to you but are not used in what follows.

If you want to save your Matlab work to a file to print out later, you use the **diary** command. When you start your Matlab session, at the EDU» prompt, type

diary filename

The session will be saved to a file named whatever name you have used. (If no filename is specified, the session will be saved to a file named "diary".) If the named file already exists, output is appended to the end of the file. The file will be an ASCII file, which you can print or open in a text editor or word processing program. Where the file will be saved depends on how your system is set up. (If you are using Matlab on your own computer, look in the folder Matlab_SE_5.3\work.) This is a useful command if you are assigned to do some problems in Matlab. You can just save your session to a file, print it, and hand it in. However, you can't call up this file in Matlab and resume working on it.

A useful feature of the **diary** command is that you can suspend it by entering the command **diary off.** You can then do some calculations on Matlab that you don't want included in the file. Typing **diary on** causes the program to resume saving output to the previously named file. Because of these commands you cannot use "off" or "on" as filenames with the **diary** command. The command **diary** alone acts as a "toggle", turning the diary function on if it is off, or off if it is on.

If you just want to save the matrices that you have entered and named so that you can use them again in a later session without entering them again, this is done with the command **save**. At the EDU» prompt, type

save filename

The matrices currently named will be saved to the file. To retrieve these matrices during a later session on Matlab, we use the command **load**. At the EDU» prompt, type

load filename

The matrices saved will be available to Matlab.

1.2   Solving Equations

The system of equations

$$
\begin{array}{rcrcrcr}
3x & + & 2y & + & z & = & 4 \\
x & + & 3y & + & z & = & -3 \\
-x & + & 2y & + & z & = & -4
\end{array}
$$

can be written in vector form as

$$
x\begin{bmatrix} 3 \\ 1 \\ -1 \end{bmatrix} + y\begin{bmatrix} 2 \\ 3 \\ 2 \end{bmatrix} + z\begin{bmatrix} 1 \\ 1 \\ 1 \end{bmatrix} = \begin{bmatrix} 4 \\ -3 \\ -4 \end{bmatrix}
$$

or in matrix form as

$$\begin{bmatrix} 3 & 2 & 1 \\ 1 & 3 & 1 \\ -1 & 2 & 1 \end{bmatrix} \begin{bmatrix} x \\ y \\ z \end{bmatrix} = \begin{bmatrix} 4 \\ -3 \\ -4 \end{bmatrix}.$$

The latter form we often shorten to

$$AX = B.$$

We see that a solution to this system tells us how to write the column vector B as a linear combination of the column vectors of A.

We solve the system by doing row reduction on the augmented matrix $[A \; B]$. The augmented matrix of our system is

$$\begin{bmatrix} 3 & 2 & 1 & 4 \\ 1 & 3 & 1 & -3 \\ -1 & 2 & 1 & -4 \end{bmatrix}.$$

The RREF of this matrix is

$$\begin{bmatrix} 1 & 0 & 0 & 2 \\ 0 & 1 & 0 & -3 \\ 0 & 0 & 1 & 4 \end{bmatrix}.$$

This is the augmented matrix of the system of equations

$$\begin{aligned} x &= 2 \\ y &= 3 \\ z &= 4. \end{aligned}$$

Since elementary row operations don't change the solution set of a system, we conclude that

$$X = \begin{bmatrix} x \\ y \\ z \end{bmatrix} = \begin{bmatrix} 2 \\ -3 \\ 4 \end{bmatrix}$$

is the unique solution to the original system. We have used the following very important fact:

Fact *Elementary row operations on the augmented matrix of a system don't change the solution set of the system.*

In solving linear systems $AX = B$ with m equations and n unknowns, three outcomes are possible:

1. There is a unique solution, as in the preceding example. This case is characterized by t'ie existence of a le ling 1 in every column **except** the **last** of the RREF of $[A \ B]$, the augmented matrix of the system.

.2. There is no solution. This case is characterized by the appearance of a leading 1 in the last column of the RREF of $[A \ B]$.

3. There are infinitely many solutions. This case occurs if in the RREF of $[A \ B]$ there is no leading 1 in the last column and there is at least one other column with no leading 1.

The linear system $AX = 0$, where $B = 0$ (the zero vector), is called **homogeneous**. If $B \neq 0$, the linear system $AX = B$ is called **nonhomogeneous**. For a homogeneous system, $X = 0$ is always a solution, so case 2 (no solution) above does not occur, and the interest lies in determining whether 0 is the only solution or whether there are infinitely many solutions.

Example 1.8 *Find all solutions of the following system of equations:*

$$\begin{array}{rrrrrcl} 3x & + & 2y & + & z & = & 1 \\ x & + & y & + & z & = & 2 \\ 2x & + & y & - & z & = & 4. \end{array}$$

.The augmented matrix of this system is

$$\begin{bmatrix} 3 & 2 & 1 & 1 \\ 1 & 1 & 1 & 2 \\ 2 & 1 & -1 & 4 \end{bmatrix},$$

which has RREF $\begin{bmatrix} 1 & 0 & 0 & -8 \\ 0 & 1 & 0 & 15 \\ 0 & 0 & 1 & -5 \end{bmatrix}$. *Thus there is a unique solution*

$$X = \begin{bmatrix} x \\ y \\ x \end{bmatrix} = \begin{bmatrix} -8 \\ 15 \\ -5 \end{bmatrix}.$$

Example 1.9 *Find all solutions of the following system of equations:*

$$\begin{array}{rrrrrcl} 3x & + & 6y & + & 9z & = & 12 \\ x & + & 2y & + & 3z & = & 4 \\ 2x & + & y & - & z & = & 4. \end{array}$$

The augmented matrix of this system is

$$\begin{bmatrix} 3 & 6 & 9 & 12 \\ 1 & 2 & 3 & 4 \\ 2 & 1 & -1 & 4 \end{bmatrix},$$

which has RREF

$$\begin{bmatrix} 1 & 0 & -\frac{5}{3} & \frac{4}{3} \\ 0 & 1 & \frac{7}{3} & \frac{4}{3} \\ 0 & 0 & 0 & 0 \end{bmatrix}.$$

This matrix represents the system of equations

$$\begin{array}{rcl} x + \quad - \frac{5}{3}z &=& \frac{4}{3} \\ y + \frac{7}{3}z &=& \frac{4}{3}. \end{array}$$

For any choice of z we can solve for x and y in terms of z and get a solution. Thus there are infinitely many solutions. Let $z = t$, where t is any real number. Then

$$X = \begin{bmatrix} x \\ y \\ z \end{bmatrix} = \begin{bmatrix} \frac{4}{3} + \frac{5}{3}t \\ \frac{4}{3} - \frac{7}{3}t \\ t \end{bmatrix}$$

is a complete solution.

Remark *The variables corresponding to columns which have a leading 1 in the RREF are solved for in terms of the variables that do not have leading 1's in the corresponding columns. The latter can be chosen freely and can be considered parameters.*

Example 1.10 *Find all solutions to the following system of equations:*

$$\begin{array}{rcl} 3x + 6y + 9z &=& 1 \\ x + 2y + 3z &=& 2 \\ 2x + y - z &=& 4. \end{array}$$

The augmented matrix of this system is

$$\begin{bmatrix} 3 & 6 & 9 & 1 \\ 1 & 2 & 3 & 2 \\ 2 & 1 & -1 & 4 \end{bmatrix},$$

which has RREF

$$\begin{bmatrix} 1 & 0 & -\frac{5}{3} & 0 \\ 0 & 1 & \frac{7}{3} & 0 \\ 0 & 0 & 0 & 1 \end{bmatrix}.$$

The last line represents the equation

$$0x + 0y + 0z = 1,$$

which is clearly impossible for any numbers x, y, z. Therefore, this system has no solution.

Remark *These examples have all been three equations, three unknowns. The number of equations and unknowns do not have to be equal for the illustrated method of solving them to work. You can still form the augmented matrix, find the RREF, and read off the solution or solutions, or determine that there are none.*

Remark *If there are fewer equations than unknowns, you cannot hope for a unique solution, you have only the possibilities no solution or infinitely many solutions. If you have more equations than unknowns, any of the outcomes is possible. (This is because some of the equations may be redundant or contradictory.)*

Remark *We will revisit the topic of solving linear systems of equations with more examples and problems in Section 2.4, where we use the Hermite form and the relation of the solution set of* $AX = B$ *to the null space of* A.

1.2.1 Exercises

Solve the following systems of linear, nonhomogeneous equations:

1.
$$\begin{aligned}
x + 2y + 3z &= 6 \\
4x + 5y + 6z &= 15 \\
7x + 8y + 9z &= 24
\end{aligned}$$

2.
$$\begin{aligned}
x + y + z &= 3 \\
2x + 3y + 4z &= 9 \\
5x + 6y + 7z &= 12
\end{aligned}$$

3.
$$\begin{aligned}
x + y + z &= 3 \\
x + 2y + 4z &= 7 \\
x + 3y + 9z &= 13
\end{aligned}$$

4.
$$\begin{aligned}
w + x + 2y + z &= 7 \\
2w - x + 3y - 2z &= 3 \\
4w - 3x + 4y - 3z &= 3
\end{aligned}$$

5.
$$\begin{aligned}
v + w - 3x + 2y + z &= 4 \\
3v + 3w - 5x + y - 3z &= 5 \\
x + 4y - 2z &= 3
\end{aligned}$$

6.
$$\begin{aligned}
v + 2w + 3x + 4y + 5z &= 3 \\
2v + 4w + 4x + 3y + 9z &= 6 \\
x + 2y + 2z &= 5
\end{aligned}$$

7.
$$
\begin{aligned}
2x + y + z &= 4 \\
x + 3y + 2z &= 6 \\
3x - 2y + 3z &= 4 \\
-x - y + 5z &= 3
\end{aligned}
$$

8.
$$
\begin{aligned}
v + w - 3x - 5y + 7z &= 12 \\
w + 2x \qquad\quad - 5z &= 7
\end{aligned}
$$

9.
$$
\begin{aligned}
w + 5x - 4y + z &= 10 \\
3w - x + y - 3z &= 7 \\
9w + 13x - 10y - 3z &= 42
\end{aligned}
$$

10.
$$
\begin{aligned}
2w + x + y + z &= 5 \\
3w + 2x - y - z &= 7 \\
16w + 9x + 3y + 3z &= 35 \\
w + 2x + y + z &= 5 \\
w + x + 2y - z &= 6
\end{aligned}
$$

11.
$$
\begin{aligned}
w - x + y - z &= 3 \\
w + x + y + z &= 5 \\
w + 2x + 4y + 8z &= 15 \\
w + 3x + 9y + 27z &= 41
\end{aligned}
$$

12.
$$
\begin{aligned}
4w - 3x + 2y - z &= 2 \\
w + 2x + 3y + 4z &= 3 \\
2w - x + y - 2z &= 6
\end{aligned}
$$

For each of the systems of equations above, find the solution if the right-hand side of the equation is replaced by all zeros (in other words, solve the homogeneous system with the same coefficient matrix as the given system).

1.2.2 Matlab

You can use Matlab to find the RREF as in the preceding section.

In Matlab you can enter the augmented matrix directly, with spaces separating the entries of a row and semicolons to start a new row. In the preceding example we would have entered at the EDU» prompt:

$$C = [3\ 6\ 9\ 1; 1\ 2\ 3\ 2; 2\ 1\ -1\ 4] \qquad \text{(Matlab would print)}$$

$$
C = \begin{array}{cccc}
3 & 6 & 9 & 1 \\
1 & 2 & 3 & 2 \\
2 & 1 & -1 & 4
\end{array}
$$

Then we would enter $D = rref(C)$ (Matlab would print)

$$D = \begin{array}{cccc} 1 & 0 & -\frac{5}{3} & 0 \\ 0 & 1 & \frac{7}{3} & 0 \\ 0 & 0 & 0 & 1 \end{array}.$$

If you had already entered the coefficient matrix as A and the column vector B, you could enter

$C = [A \; B]$ and Matlab would print

$$C = \begin{array}{cccc} 3 & 6 & 9 & 1 \\ 1 & 2 & 3 & 2 \\ 2 & 1 & -1 & 4 \end{array}.$$

Some new commands:

$$\boxed{\text{A*B}}$$

returns the matrix product of A and B.

$$\boxed{\text{X=A(:,4)}}$$

captures the fourth column of A and names it X.

Example 1.11 *Here we solve $AX = B$ by finding $C = rref([A \, B])$.*

```
EDU» A=[2 -1 3;1 1 0;3 2 -1]
A =
     2   -1    3
     1    1    0
     3    2   -1
EDU» B=[3;3;6]
B =
     3
     3
     6
EDU» C=[A B]
C =
     2   -1    3   3
     1    1    0   3
     3    2   -1   6
```

```
EDU»D= rref(C)
D=
      1  0  0  1
      0  1  0  2
      0  0  1  1
```

Remark *We can capture the last (fourth) column of the matrix D using the command X=D(:,4).*

```
EDU» X=D(:,4)
X =
      1
      2
      1
```

Remark *We check by finding the product A times X.*

```
EDU» A*X
ans =
      3
      3
      6
```
So we see that A*X = B, and we have the solution.

1.2.3 Matlab Exercises

The first exercise is a worksheet containing input for a Matlab session. Go to your computer or a computer lab and start up the Matlab program. Type in the commands exactly as they appear below and observe the output.

Worksheet

```
EDU» a=[1 1 1;1 2 4;1 3 6]
EDU» b=[1;0;1]
EDU» c=rref([a b])
EDU» x=c(:,4)
EDU» a*x
EDU» a=[3 2 1;1 -1 2;0 4 -4]
EDU» b=[-2;5;1]
EDU» c=rref([a b])
EDU» a
EDU» b=[-1;3;-8]
EDU» c=rref([a b])
EDU» x=c(:,4)
EDU» a*x
```

EDU» quit

Use Matlab to check your solutions to the systems of equations in
Exercises 1.2.1.

1.3   The Inverse of a Matrix

Fact   *Let A be a square matrix and B another matrix of the same size such
that $AB = BA = I$, where I is the identity matrix of the same size.   Then
A is invertible, and B is the inverse of A.   We write $B = A^{-1}$.*

Example 1.12

$$\begin{bmatrix} 1 & 2 & 2 \\ 2 & 1 & 3 \\ 1 & 0 & 1 \end{bmatrix} \begin{bmatrix} 1 & -2 & 4 \\ 1 & -1 & 1 \\ -1 & 2 & -3 \end{bmatrix} = \begin{bmatrix} 1 & 0 & 0 \\ 0 & 1 & 0 \\ 0 & 0 & 1 \end{bmatrix} = I$$

and

$$\begin{bmatrix} 1 & -2 & 4 \\ 1 & -1 & 1 \\ -1 & 2 & -3 \end{bmatrix} \begin{bmatrix} 1 & 2 & 2 \\ 2 & 1 & 3 \\ 1 & 0 & 1 \end{bmatrix} = \begin{bmatrix} 1 & 0 & 0 \\ 0 & 1 & 0 \\ 0 & 0 & 1 \end{bmatrix}.$$

Therefore,

$$\begin{bmatrix} 1 & 2 & 2 \\ 2 & 1 & 3 \\ 1 & 0 & 1 \end{bmatrix}^{-1} = \begin{bmatrix} 1 & -2 & 4 \\ 1 & -1 & 1 \\ -1 & 2 & -3 \end{bmatrix}$$

and

$$\begin{bmatrix} 1 & -2 & 4 \\ 1 & -1 & 1 \\ -1 & 2 & -3 \end{bmatrix}^{-1} = \begin{bmatrix} 1 & 2 & 2 \\ 2 & 1 & 3 \\ 1 & 0 & 1 \end{bmatrix}.$$

Another example is

$$\begin{bmatrix} 2 & 1 & -1 \\ 1 & 0 & 1 \\ -2 & 1 & 3 \end{bmatrix} \begin{bmatrix} \frac{1}{8} & \frac{1}{2} & -\frac{1}{8} \\ \frac{5}{8} & -\frac{1}{2} & \frac{3}{8} \\ -\frac{1}{8} & \frac{1}{2} & \frac{1}{8} \end{bmatrix} = \begin{bmatrix} 1 & 0 & 0 \\ 0 & 1 & 0 \\ 0 & 0 & 1 \end{bmatrix}$$

and

$$\begin{bmatrix} \frac{1}{8} & \frac{1}{2} & -\frac{1}{8} \\ \frac{5}{8} & -\frac{1}{2} & \frac{3}{8} \\ -\frac{1}{8} & \frac{1}{2} & \frac{1}{8} \end{bmatrix} \begin{bmatrix} 2 & 1 & -1 \\ 1 & 0 & 1 \\ -2 & 1 & 3 \end{bmatrix} = \begin{bmatrix} 1 & 0 & 0 \\ 0 & 1 & 0 \\ 0 & 0 & 1 \end{bmatrix},$$

so that

$$\begin{bmatrix} 2 & 1 & -1 \\ 1 & 0 & 1 \\ -2 & 1 & 3 \end{bmatrix}^{-1} = \begin{bmatrix} \frac{1}{8} & \frac{1}{2} & -\frac{1}{8} \\ \frac{5}{8} & -\frac{1}{2} & \frac{3}{8} \\ -\frac{1}{8} & \frac{1}{2} & \frac{1}{8} \end{bmatrix}$$

and

$$\begin{bmatrix} \frac{1}{8} & \frac{1}{2} & -\frac{1}{8} \\ \frac{5}{8} & -\frac{1}{2} & \frac{3}{8} \\ -\frac{1}{8} & \frac{1}{2} & \frac{1}{8} \end{bmatrix}^{-1} = \begin{bmatrix} 2 & 1 & -1 \\ 1 & 0 & 1 \\ -2 & 1 & 3 \end{bmatrix}.$$

Fact *Not every square matrix has an inverse.*

Example 1.13 *For any 3×3 matrix B*

$$\begin{bmatrix} 1 & 3 & 1 \\ 4 & -1 & 3 \\ 0 & 0 & 0 \end{bmatrix} B = \begin{bmatrix} * & * & * \\ * & * & * \\ 0 & 0 & 0 \end{bmatrix} \neq \begin{bmatrix} 1 & 0 & 0 \\ 0 & 1 & 0 \\ 0 & 0 & 1 \end{bmatrix}.$$

Thus a matrix with a zero row cannot be invertible.

It is easy to check whether or not a given matrix B is the inverse of another given matrix A. In fact, you only need check one of the products AB or BA, for although it is not obvious, if one of them is I, the other must be also. However, it is not always easy to find A^{-1} given A. A method for finding A^{-1} (if it exists) is based on the following facts.

Fact *If A is invertible, then $\mathrm{RREF}(A) = I$.*

Fact *If A is not invertible, then $\mathrm{RREF}(A)$ has the last row a zero row.*

Fact *If A is invertible, the same row operations that change A into I will change I into A^{-1}.*

Procedure *To find A^{-1} or show that it is not invertible, start with the "superaugmented" matrix $[A\ I]$, and do elementary row operations until A becomes I. Then you will have $[I\ A^{-1}]$. If at any point you get a row that is all zeros in the A part, stop! The matrix is not invertible.*

Example 1.14 *Find the inverse of the matrix*

$$A = \begin{bmatrix} 1 & 2 & 2 \\ 2 & 1 & 3 \\ -3 & -2 & -5 \end{bmatrix}.$$

We form the superaugmented matrix

$$[A\ I] = \begin{bmatrix} 1 & 2 & 2 & 1 & 0 & 0 \\ 2 & 1 & 3 & 0 & 1 & 0 \\ -3 & -2 & -5 & 0 & 0 & 1 \end{bmatrix}.$$

We now row reduce this matrix until the first three columns are in RREF. Adding multiples of row 1 to rows 2 and 3 gives

$$\begin{bmatrix} 1 & 2 & 2 & 1 & 0 & 0 \\ 0 & -3 & -1 & -2 & 1 & 0 \\ 0 & 4 & 1 & 3 & 0 & 1 \end{bmatrix}.$$

At this point we could divide row 2 by −3, but a smarter way to get a 1 in the 2, 2 position is to add row 3 to row 2

$$\begin{bmatrix} 1 & 2 & 2 & 1 & 0 & 0 \\ 0 & 1 & 0 & 1 & 1 & 1 \\ 0 & 4 & 1 & 3 & 0 & 1 \end{bmatrix}.$$

Now using the leading 1 in the second row to clear the second column, we get

$$\begin{bmatrix} 1 & 0 & 2 & -1 & -2 & -2 \\ 0 & 1 & 0 & 1 & 1 & 1 \\ 0 & 0 & 1 & -1 & -4 & -3 \end{bmatrix}.$$

Add −2 times the last row to the first row to get

$$\begin{bmatrix} 1 & 0 & 0 & 1 & 6 & 4 \\ 0 & 1 & 0 & 1 & 1 & 1 \\ 0 & 0 & 1 & -1 & -4 & -3 \end{bmatrix}.$$

We conclude that

$$A^{-1} = \begin{bmatrix} 1 & 6 & 4 \\ 1 & 1 & 1 \\ -1 & -4 & -3 \end{bmatrix}.$$

We check by multiplying:

$$\begin{bmatrix} 1 & 2 & 2 \\ 2 & 1 & 3 \\ -3 & -2 & -5 \end{bmatrix} \begin{bmatrix} 1 & 6 & 4 \\ 1 & 1 & 1 \\ -1 & -4 & -3 \end{bmatrix} = I.$$

Thus

$$\begin{bmatrix} 1 & 2 & 2 \\ 2 & 1 & 3 \\ -3 & -2 & -5 \end{bmatrix}^{-1} = \begin{bmatrix} 1 & 6 & 4 \\ 1 & 1 & 1 \\ -1 & -4 & -3 \end{bmatrix}.$$

Fact   *When A is invertible, the system of equations $AX = B$ has a unique solution for every column matrix B with the same number of rows as A. You can find this solution by multiplying B on the left by A^{-1}. The unique solution is $X = A^{-1}B$.*

Example 1.15 *Solve the system*

$$\begin{bmatrix} 1 & 2 & 2 \\ 2 & 1 & 3 \\ -3 & -2 & -5 \end{bmatrix} \begin{bmatrix} x \\ y \\ z \end{bmatrix} = \begin{bmatrix} 4 \\ -3 \\ 2 \end{bmatrix}.$$

We found the inverse of the coefficient matrix in the preceding example, so we have

$$\begin{bmatrix} x \\ y \\ z \end{bmatrix} = \begin{bmatrix} 1 & 2 & 2 \\ 2 & 1 & 3 \\ -3 & -2 & -5 \end{bmatrix}^{-1} \begin{bmatrix} 4 \\ -3 \\ 2 \end{bmatrix}$$

$$= \begin{bmatrix} 1 & 6 & 4 \\ 1 & 1 & 1 \\ -1 & -4 & -3 \end{bmatrix} \begin{bmatrix} 4 \\ -3 \\ 2 \end{bmatrix} = \begin{bmatrix} -6 \\ 3 \\ 2 \end{bmatrix}.$$

To check we compute that

$$\begin{bmatrix} 1 & 2 & 2 \\ 2 & 1 & 3 \\ -3 & -2 & -5 \end{bmatrix} \begin{bmatrix} -6 \\ 3 \\ 2 \end{bmatrix} = \begin{bmatrix} 4 \\ -3 \\ 2 \end{bmatrix}.$$

Remark   *If you have to do the computations without the aid of a computer, it is easier to solve the system by row reducing the augmented matrix $[A\ B]$ as we did in the preceding section rather than computing A^{-1}, but once you have A^{-1}, you can solve $AX = B$ for any B just by matrix multiplication.*

1.3.1   Exercises

Find the inverse of each of the following matrices or show why they cannot be inverted by giving their RREF.

1. $\begin{bmatrix} 1 & 2 \\ 2 & 3 \end{bmatrix}$ 2. $\begin{bmatrix} 7 & 6 \\ 6 & 5 \end{bmatrix}$ 3. $\begin{bmatrix} 5 & 2 \\ 3 & 1 \end{bmatrix}$

4. $\begin{bmatrix} 1 & 1 & 1 \\ 1 & 2 & 3 \\ 2 & 3 & 5 \end{bmatrix}$ 5. $\begin{bmatrix} 2 & 3 & 4 \\ 1 & 1 & 1 \\ 5 & 8 & 11 \end{bmatrix}$

6. $\begin{bmatrix} 1 & 1 & 1 \\ 1 & 2 & 4 \\ 1 & 3 & 9 \end{bmatrix}$
7. $\begin{bmatrix} 1 & 2 & 0 & 3 \\ 1 & 1 & 1 & -1 \\ 0 & 1 & 0 & 0 \\ 0 & 0 & 1 & 1 \end{bmatrix}$

8. $\begin{bmatrix} 2 & 1 & 1 & 1 \\ 1 & 2 & 1 & 1 \\ 1 & 1 & 2 & 1 \\ 1 & 1 & 1 & 2 \end{bmatrix}$
9. $\begin{bmatrix} -3 & 1 & 1 & 1 \\ 1 & -3 & 1 & 1 \\ 1 & 1 & -3 & 1 \\ 1 & 1 & 1 & -3 \end{bmatrix}$

10. $\begin{bmatrix} 1 & 1 & 1 & 1 \\ 0 & 2 & 1 & -1 \\ 0 & 0 & 3 & 1 \\ 0 & 0 & 0 & 2 \end{bmatrix}$

In problems 11-13, use the inverses you found in the preceding problems to solve the equations $AX = B$ for the following choices of A and B. In each case check by multiplying your answer by A.

11. $A =$ the matrix in problem 1, and $B = \begin{bmatrix} 5 \\ -3 \end{bmatrix}$.

12. $A =$ the matrix in problem 4, and $B = \begin{bmatrix} 5 \\ -2 \\ 5 \end{bmatrix}$.

13. $A =$ the matrix in problem 6 and $B = \begin{bmatrix} 1 \\ 0 \\ 1 \end{bmatrix}$.

14. If $A =$ the matrix in problem 1 and $B =$ the matrix in problem 2, solve the matrix equations $AX = B$ for X and $YA = B$ for Y. Does $X = Y$?

15. Same as number 14, except use $B =$ the matrix in problem 3.

16. Same as number 14 for $A =$ the matrix in problem 4 and $B =$ the matrix in problem 5.

1.3.2 Matlab

Matlab will compute A^{-1} for a square matrix A if A is invertible. You can find RREF($[A\ I]$) or you can use the command **inv(A)**.

At the EDU» prompt type

$$\boxed{\text{inv(A)}}$$

Matlab will return the inverse of A if A is invertible, or give a warning message.

$$\boxed{\text{I=eye(n)}}$$

returns an $n \times n$ identity matrix and names it I. Although Matlab uses i for the complex number $\sqrt{-1}$, it will allow you to redefine it: as, for example, you can give input $i = eye\,(n)$, naming the $n \times n$ identity matrix i.

$$\boxed{\text{B=A(:,4:6)}}$$

captures columns 4 through 6 of the matrix A and names the resulting matrix B.

Example 1.16 *We use Matlab to find the inverse of a matrix directly with the **inv** command.*

```
EDU» A=[1 2 2;2 1 3;-3 -2 5]
A=
        1     2     2
        2     1     3
       -3    -2    -5
EDU» inv(A)
ans =
    1.0000    6.0000    4.0000
    1.0000    1.0000    1.0000
   -1.0000   -4.0000   -3.0000
```

Example 1.17 *We show a Matlab session finding the inverse of the matrix A by the method of the preceding section.*

EDU» A=[1 2 2;2 1 3;-3 -2 -5]

A =

       1   2   2
       2   1   3
      −3   −2   −5

Comment: *We enter the 3x3 identity using the command* **I=eye(3)**.

EDU» I=eye(3)

I =

       1 0 0
       0 1 0
       0 0 1

EDU» C=[A I]

C =

       1   2   2   1 0 0
       2   1   3   0 1 0
      −3   −2   −5   0 0 1

EDU» D=rref(C)

D =

       1 0 0   1   6   4
       0 1 0   1   1   1
       0 0 1   −1   −4   −3

Comment: *We capture the last three columns of D (columns 4 through 6) with the command* **E=D(:,4:6)**

EDU» E=D(:,4:6):

E =

       1   6   4
       1   1   1
      −1   −4   −3

Comment: *We check to see if* E *is* A^{-1} *by multiplying* A *times* E :

EDU» A*E

ans =

       1 0 0
       0 1 0
       0 0 1

It checks.

Example 1.18 *If you enter a matrix that is not invertible, such as*

$$C = \begin{bmatrix} 1 & 1 & 1 \\ 2 & 2 & 2 \\ 1 & 3 & 1 \end{bmatrix},$$

Matlab produces the following results (note that the input is preceded by the EDU» prompt; the other lines are actual Matlab output):

```
EDU» C=[1 1 1;2 2 2;1 3 1]
C =
     1   1   1
     2   2   2
     1   3   1
EDU» D=inv(C)
Warning: Matrix is singular to working precision.
D =
     Inf Inf Inf
     Inf Inf Inf
     Inf Inf Inf
```

We have seen that we can solve equations of the form $AX = B$ by row reducing the augmented matrix [A B]. If A is invertible, we can also solve $AX = B$ using the command **X=inv(A)*B** or the left division command **X=A\B**.

$$\boxed{X=A\backslash B}$$

Matlab returns the solution of AX=B when A is invertible.

1.3.3 Matlab Problems

The following worksheets contain input for a Matlab session. Go to your computer or computer lab and start up the Matlab program. Type in the commands exactly as they appear below and observe the output.

Worksheet I

```
EDU» e=[1 3 5;2 6 4;3 6 4]
EDU» f=inv(e)
EDU» e*f
EDU» f*e
EDU» rats(f)
EDU» i=eye(3)
EDU» g=[e i]
EDU» t=rref(g)
EDU» rats(t)
EDU» a=[2 3 3;4 1 -2;2 -1 0]
EDU» b=[1;4;2]
EDU» x= inv(a)*b
EDU» a*x
EDU» x=a\b
EDU» c=[a b]
```

EDU» rref(c)
EDU» a=[1 3 1;2 6 2;3 3 3]
EDU» b=[2;4;3]
EDU» x=inv(a)*b
EDU».x=a\b
EDU» c=[a b]
EDU» rref(c)
EDU» quit

Worksheet II

EDU» a=[2 1 2;1 3 2;0 1 -1]
EDU» b=[-2 7;5 7;3 0]
EDU» x=inv(a)*b
EDU» a*x
EDU» x=a\b
EDU» c=rref([a b])
EDU» a=[3 2 1;1 -1 2;0 4 -4]
EDU» b=[4 3 -5;3 1 -5;-4 0 8]
EDU» c=rref([a b])
EDU» x=c(:,4:6)
EDU» a*x
EDU»quit

In the following problems, attempt to find a solution of the matrix equation $AX = B$ for the given matrices A and B, using Matlab commands $X = inv\,(A) * B$, $X = A \backslash B$, or $C = rref\,([A\ B])$. Use Matlab to check your answers.

1. $A = \begin{bmatrix} 1 & 2 & -1 \\ 3 & 1 & 4 \\ 5 & 6 & 1 \end{bmatrix}$, $\qquad B = \begin{bmatrix} 3 \\ -1 \\ 2 \end{bmatrix}$.

2. $A = \begin{bmatrix} 2.5 & 3.5 & 0.5 \\ 1.5 & -4.5 & 0.6 \\ 2.0 & 1.0 & -0.5 \end{bmatrix}$, $\qquad B = \begin{bmatrix} 0.3 \\ -0.1 \\ 1.5 \end{bmatrix}$.

3. $A = \begin{bmatrix} 1 & 1 & -1 & 3 & 4 \\ 2 & -5 & 6 & 0 & 1 \\ 1 & 0 & 3 & 2 & -1 \\ -4 & 1 & 1 & 2 & 1 \\ 3 & 0 & 0 & 1 & 5 \end{bmatrix}$, $B = \begin{bmatrix} 1 \\ -3 \\ 2 \\ 0 \\ 6 \end{bmatrix}$.

4. $A = \begin{bmatrix} 2 & 1 & 2 \\ 1 & 3 & 2 \\ 0 & 1 & -1 \end{bmatrix}$, $\qquad B = \begin{bmatrix} 4 & 3 & 1 \\ 2 & 2 & 2 \\ 1 & 1 & 4 \end{bmatrix}$.

5. $A = \begin{bmatrix} 1 & 3 & -2 \\ 1 & -1 & 2 \\ 2 & 2 & 0 \end{bmatrix}$, $\qquad B = \begin{bmatrix} 1 & 3 & 1 \\ 2 & 0 & 1 \\ -1 & 1 & 2 \end{bmatrix}$.

6. $A = \begin{bmatrix} 1 & 3 & -2 \\ 1 & -1 & 2 \\ 2 & 2 & 0 \end{bmatrix}$, $\qquad B = \begin{bmatrix} 4 & 1 & -1 \\ 0 & 1 & 3 \\ 4 & 2 & 2 \end{bmatrix}$.

1.4 Determinants

To every **square** matrix A there is associated a unique number called the determinant of A, $\det(A)$, or indicated by $|A|$.

Fact *A is invertible if and only if $\det(A) \neq 0$. In this case we also know that $RREF(A) = I$ and $AX = B$ has a unique solution for every B (with the same number of rows as A).*

For 2×2 matrices A, we have the following formula for computing $|A| = \det(A)$:

$$\begin{vmatrix} a & b \\ c & d \end{vmatrix} = ad - bc.$$

To compute larger determinants we use the following facts:

Fact *The determinant of an **upper triangular matrix** (all zeros below the main diagonal) is the product of the diagonal elements.*

Example 1.19

$$\begin{vmatrix} 2 & 1 & 5 \\ 0 & -3 & 4 \\ 0 & 0 & 4 \end{vmatrix} = (2)(-3)(4) = -24.$$

The effect that elementary row operations on A has on $\det(A)$ is easy to describe.

1. Exchanging two rows of A multiplies $|A|$ by -1.

2. Multiplying a row of A by a number c multiplies $|A|$ by c.

3. Adding a multiple of one row of A to another row of A **doesn't change** $|A|$.

Now RREF(A) is always upper triangular, so we know that every matrix can be changed into an upper triangular matrix using only elementary row operations. Thus if we change A to upper triangular using elementary row operations and keeping track of all the operations we did that changed $|A|$, we can calculate $|A|$.

Example 1.20 *We find the determinant of a 4×4 matrix by using elementary row operations to change it into an upper triangular matrix. Adding multiples of row 1 to rows 2 and 3, we get*

$$
\begin{vmatrix} 1 & 1 & 2 & -1 \\ 3 & 2 & 1 & 0 \\ 0 & 2 & 1 & 0 \\ 1 & 0 & 0 & 2 \end{vmatrix} = \begin{vmatrix} 1 & 1 & 2 & -1 \\ 0 & -1 & -5 & 3 \\ 0 & 2 & 1 & 0 \\ 0 & -1 & -2 & 3 \end{vmatrix}.
$$

Then adding multiples of row 2 to rows 3 and 4, we get

$$
\begin{vmatrix} 1 & 1 & 2 & -1 \\ 0 & -1 & -5 & 3 \\ 0 & 2 & 1 & 0 \\ 0 & -1 & -2 & 3 \end{vmatrix} = \begin{vmatrix} 1 & 1 & 2 & -1 \\ 0 & -1 & -5 & 3 \\ 0 & 0 & -9 & 6 \\ 0 & 0 & 3 & 0 \end{vmatrix}.
$$

Finally, adding $\frac{1}{3}$ times row 3 to row 4 gives

$$
\begin{vmatrix} 1 & 1 & 2 & -1 \\ 0 & -1 & -5 & 3 \\ 0 & 0 & -9 & 6 \\ 0 & 0 & 3 & 0 \end{vmatrix} = \begin{vmatrix} 1 & 1 & 2 & -1 \\ 0 & -1 & -5 & 3 \\ 0 & 0 & -9 & 6 \\ 0 & 0 & 0 & 2 \end{vmatrix} = 18.
$$

In the example above we did not have to use any row operations other than adding a multiple of one row to another. Sometimes it is convenient to use the other row operations as well.

Example 1.21 *Find the determinant of the matrix*

$$
\begin{vmatrix} 2 & 2 & 4 & -2 \\ 3 & 2 & 1 & 0 \\ 0 & 2 & 1 & 0 \\ 1 & 0 & 0 & 2 \end{vmatrix}.
$$

As a first step, we would like to get a 1 in the 1,1 position. If we multiply row 1 by $\frac{1}{2}$, the new determinant is multiplied by $\frac{1}{2}$, so we have

$$\begin{vmatrix} 2 & 2 & 4 & -2 \\ 3 & 2 & 1 & 0 \\ 0 & 2 & 1 & 0 \\ 1 & 0 & 0 & 2 \end{vmatrix} = 2 \begin{vmatrix} 1 & 1 & 2 & -1 \\ 3 & 2 & 1 & 0 \\ 0 & 2 & 1 & 0 \\ 1 & 0 & 0 & 2 \end{vmatrix}.$$

We recognize this as the determinant from the preceding example, so

$$\begin{vmatrix} 2 & 2 & 4 & -2 \\ 3 & 2 & 1 & 0 \\ 0 & 2 & 1 & 0 \\ 1 & 0 & 0 & 2 \end{vmatrix} = 2 \begin{vmatrix} 1 & 1 & 2 & -1 \\ 3 & 2 & 1 & 0 \\ 0 & 2 & 1 & 0 \\ 1 & 0 & 0 & 2 \end{vmatrix} = 2\,(18) = 36.$$

The first step above is important enough to state as a general principle. **A common factor in a row (or column) of a matrix can be "factored out" of the determinant.**

$$\begin{vmatrix} 3c & -2c & 4c \\ 1 & -3 & 5 \\ 2 & 6 & 1 \end{vmatrix} = c \begin{vmatrix} 3 & -2 & 4 \\ 1 & -3 & 5 \\ 2 & 6 & 1 \end{vmatrix}$$

$$\begin{vmatrix} 3 & -2 & 4c \\ 1 & -3 & 5c \\ 2 & 6 & 1c \end{vmatrix} = c \begin{vmatrix} 3 & -2 & 4 \\ 1 & -3 & 5 \\ 2 & 6 & 1 \end{vmatrix}.$$

It is also worth emphasizing that **when evaluating determinants, one may use elementary column operations as well as elementary row operations.** The effect of an elementary column operation on $|A|$ is the same as the effect of the corresponding type of row operation. This is because $|A'| = |A|$, where A' is the transpose of A.

Example 1.22 *As an example, we evaluate the determinant of the matrix in the previous example again, this time using column operations where convenient. First we factor a 2 out of column 4 and another 2 out of column 2 to get*

$$\begin{vmatrix} 2 & 2 & 4 & -2 \\ 3 & 2 & 1 & 0 \\ 0 & 2 & 1 & 0 \\ 1 & 0 & 0 & 2 \end{vmatrix} = 2 \begin{vmatrix} 2 & 2 & 4 & -1 \\ 3 & 2 & 1 & 0 \\ 0 & 2 & 1 & 0 \\ 1 & 0 & 0 & 1 \end{vmatrix} = 4 \begin{vmatrix} 2 & 1 & 4 & -1 \\ 3 & 1 & 1 & 0 \\ 0 & 1 & 1 & 0 \\ 1 & 0 & 0 & 1 \end{vmatrix}.$$

Now subtracting column 4 from column 1 gives

$$4 \begin{vmatrix} 3 & 1 & 4 & -1 \\ 3 & 1 & 1 & 0 \\ 0 & 1 & 1 & 0 \\ 0 & 0 & 0 & 1 \end{vmatrix}.$$

Next subtract column 3 from column 2 to get

$$4 \begin{vmatrix} 3 & -3 & 4 & -1 \\ 3 & 0 & 1 & 0 \\ 0 & 0 & 1 & 0 \\ 0 & 0 & 0 & 1 \end{vmatrix},$$

and finally subtract row 1 from row 2, giving

$$4 \begin{vmatrix} 3 & -3 & 4 & -1 \\ 0 & 3 & -3 & 1 \\ 0 & 0 & 1 & 0 \\ 0 & 0 & 0 & 1 \end{vmatrix} = 4 \times 9 = 36.$$

Another way of finding $|A|$ is **expanding by minors**. A minor M_{ij} of a matrix A is the submatrix of A obtained by omitting row i and column j.

Example 1.23 *If* $A = \begin{bmatrix} 3 & 5 & 2 \\ -1 & 4 & 2 \\ 2 & 0 & 1 \end{bmatrix}$, *then there are nine minors; for example,*

$$M_{11} = \begin{bmatrix} 4 & 2 \\ 0 & 1 \end{bmatrix}$$

$$M_{21} = \begin{bmatrix} 5 & 2 \\ 0 & 1 \end{bmatrix}$$

$$M_{33} = \begin{bmatrix} 3 & 5 \\ -1 & 4 \end{bmatrix}$$

etc.

Now expanding by minors around a given row involves taking each element of the row, multiplying it by $\pm$ the determinant of its minor, and adding up these terms. The term gets "+" if the sum of the row and column index is even, "-" otherwise.

Example 1.24 *Evaluate* $\begin{vmatrix} 3 & 5 & 2 \\ -1 & 4 & 2 \\ 2 & 0 & 1 \end{vmatrix}$. *We expand by minors around row 1.*

$$\begin{vmatrix} 3 & 5 & 2 \\ -1 & 4 & 2 \\ 2 & 0 & 1 \end{vmatrix} = 3 \begin{vmatrix} 4 & 2 \\ 0 & 1 \end{vmatrix} - 5 \begin{vmatrix} -1 & 2 \\ 2 & 1 \end{vmatrix} + 2 \begin{vmatrix} -1 & 4 \\ 2 & 0 \end{vmatrix}$$

$$= 3(4-0) - 5(-1-4) + 2(0-8)$$

$$= 12 + 25 - 16 = 21.$$

We could expand around row 2. It looks like this:

$$\begin{vmatrix} 3 & 5 & 2 \\ -1 & 4 & 2 \\ 2 & 0 & 1 \end{vmatrix} = (1) \begin{vmatrix} 5 & 2 \\ 0 & 1 \end{vmatrix} + 4 \begin{vmatrix} 3 & 2 \\ 2 & 1 \end{vmatrix} - 2 \begin{vmatrix} 3 & 5 \\ 2 & 0 \end{vmatrix}$$

$$= 1(5-0) + 4(3-4) - 2(0-10)$$

$$= 5 - 4 + 20 = 21.$$

We can also expand around any column: for example, around column 3:

$$\begin{vmatrix} 3 & 5 & 2 \\ -1 & 4 & 2 \\ 2 & 0 & 1 \end{vmatrix} = 2 \begin{vmatrix} -1 & 4 \\ 2 & 0 \end{vmatrix} - 2 \begin{vmatrix} 3 & 5 \\ 2 & 0 \end{vmatrix} + 1 \begin{vmatrix} 3 & 5 \\ -1 & 4 \end{vmatrix}$$

$$= 2(0-8) - 2(0-10) + 1(12+5)$$

$$= -16 + 20 + 17 = 21.$$

You can use any row or column. Multiply each entry times the determinant of its minor times $(-1)^{i+j}$, and add them up. Note that $(-1)^{i+j}$ is positive if the sum of the row and column indices is even, and negative if this sum is odd.

Remark *Often, a combination of the two methods, row reduction and expansion by minors, is best. First, do some row operations to produce lots of zeros in a certain row or column, and then expand around that row or column. We illustrate this in the next example.*

Example 1.25 *Evaluate* $\begin{vmatrix} 2 & 1 & 3 & 0 \\ 1 & 2 & -1 & 0 \\ 0 & 0 & 4 & 1 \\ 1 & 2 & 0 & 3 \end{vmatrix}$.

First, subtract 3 times row 3 from row 4 to get

$$\begin{vmatrix} 2 & 1 & 3 & 0 \\ 1 & 2 & -1 & 0 \\ 0 & 0 & 4 & 1 \\ 1 & 2 & 0 & 3 \end{vmatrix} = \begin{vmatrix} 2 & 1 & 3 & 0 \\ 1 & 2 & -1 & 0 \\ 0 & 0 & 4 & 1 \\ 1 & 2 & -12 & 0 \end{vmatrix}.$$

Now expand by minors around the last column.   Only one term survives.

$$\begin{vmatrix} 2 & 1 & 3 & 0 \\ 1 & 2 & -1 & 0 \\ 0 & 0 & 4 & 1 \\ 1 & 2 & -12 & 0 \end{vmatrix} = -1 \begin{vmatrix} 2 & 1 & 3 \\ 1 & 2 & -1 \\ 1 & 2 & -12 \end{vmatrix}.$$

Now subtract row 2 from row 3 in the 3×3 matrix,

$$-1 \begin{vmatrix} 2 & 1 & 3 \\ 1 & 2 & -1 \\ 1 & 2 & -12 \end{vmatrix} = -1 \begin{vmatrix} 2 & 1 & 3 \\ 1 & 2 & -1 \\ 0 & 0 & -11 \end{vmatrix},$$

and expand by minors around row 3:

$$-1 \begin{vmatrix} 2 & 1 & 3 \\ 1 & 2 & -1 \\ 0 & 0 & -11 \end{vmatrix} = -1(-11) \begin{vmatrix} 2 & 1 \\ 1 & 2 \end{vmatrix}$$

$$= 11(4-1) = 33.$$

Try evaluating the determinant of the original 4×4 matrix another way. You should get the same answer.   For example, subtract 4 times column 4 from column 3 and then expand around row 3.   Note that in evaluating determinants we may do column operations as well as row operations.   The effects are the same as the effects of the corresponding row operations.   In solving equations and finding inverses, however, we must stick strictly to row operations.

If a matrix can be divided into square blocks such that all the blocks above (or below) the main diagonal are zero, the matrix is called **block diagonal**.   For such matrices the determinant of the whole matrix is the product of the determinants of the diagonal blocks.   The following example will illustrate this.

Example 1.26 $\begin{vmatrix} 3 & 1 & 0 & 0 \\ 1 & -2 & 0 & 0 \\ -2 & 7 & 4 & 6 \\ 3 & 10 & -1 & 1 \end{vmatrix} = \begin{vmatrix} 3 & 1 \\ 1 & -2 \end{vmatrix} \begin{vmatrix} 4 & 6 \\ -1 & 1 \end{vmatrix} = (-7)(10) =$

$-70.$

Fact $|AB| = |A||B|.$

Fact *If a matrix A has a zero row or a zero column (a row or column of all zeros), then $|A| = 0$.*

Fact *If a row of A is a multiple of another row of A, then $|A| = 0$.*

Fact *If a column of A is a multiple of another column of A, then $|A| = 0$.*

Cramer's Rule. If A is square and $|A| \neq 0$, determinants can be used to solve the system $AX = B$. Cramer's rule says that

$$x_i = \frac{|A_i|}{|A|},$$

where A_i is the matrix obtained from A by replacing column i of A with the column vector B.

Example 1.27 *Solve the system*

$$\begin{bmatrix} 2 & 1 & -1 \\ 3 & 2 & 4 \\ -3 & 1 & 2 \end{bmatrix} \begin{bmatrix} x \\ y \\ z \end{bmatrix} = \begin{bmatrix} 4 \\ -3 \\ 2 \end{bmatrix}.$$

Using Cramer's rule, we have

$$x = \frac{\begin{vmatrix} 4 & 1 & -1 \\ -3 & 2 & 4 \\ 2 & 1 & 2 \end{vmatrix}}{\begin{vmatrix} 2 & 1 & -1 \\ 3 & 2 & 4 \\ -3 & 1 & 2 \end{vmatrix}} = \frac{21}{-27} = -\frac{7}{9}$$

$$y = \frac{\begin{vmatrix} 2 & 4 & -1 \\ 3 & -3 & 4 \\ -3 & 2 & 2 \end{vmatrix}}{-27} = \frac{-97}{-27} = \frac{97}{27}$$

$$z = \frac{\begin{vmatrix} 2 & 1 & 4 \\ 3 & 2 & -3 \\ -3 & 1 & 2 \end{vmatrix}}{-27} = \frac{53}{-27} = -\frac{53}{27}$$

1.4.1 Exercises

Find the determinants of the following matrices:

1. $\begin{bmatrix} 1 & 2 & -3 \\ 3 & 8 & -9 \\ -2 & 9 & 6 \end{bmatrix}$
2. $\begin{bmatrix} 1 & 3 & 9 \\ 2 & -4 & 8 \\ 3 & -3 & 3 \end{bmatrix}$
3. $\begin{bmatrix} 2 & 3 & 4 \\ 3 & 4 & 5 \\ 4 & 5 & 6 \end{bmatrix}$

4. $\begin{bmatrix} 1 & 4 & -6 & 8 \\ 3 & 1 & 0 & -1 \\ 4 & 2 & 1 & 0 \\ 2 & 0 & 0 & 1 \end{bmatrix}$ 5. $\begin{bmatrix} 1 & 2 & 3 \\ 2 & 3 & 4 \\ -3 & -4 & -5 \end{bmatrix}$

6. $\begin{bmatrix} 4 & 1 & 6 \\ 1 & 4 & 6 \\ 1 & 1 & 6 \end{bmatrix}$ 7. $\begin{bmatrix} -2 & 1 & 1 \\ 1 & -2 & 1 \\ 1 & 1 & -2 \end{bmatrix}$ 8. $\begin{bmatrix} 1 & 0 & 1 \\ 3 & 1 & 0 \\ 5 & -1 & -1 \end{bmatrix}$

9. $\begin{bmatrix} 1 & 0 & 2 \\ 3 & 0 & 4 \\ 2 & 0 & 6 \end{bmatrix}$ 10. $\begin{bmatrix} 2 & 3 & 4 \\ 3 & 4 & 5 \\ 4 & 5 & 6 \end{bmatrix}$ 11. $\begin{bmatrix} 2 & 2 & 2 \\ 3 & -3 & 3 \\ 4 & 8 & 12 \end{bmatrix}$

12. $\begin{bmatrix} 1 & 1 & 1 \\ 1 & 2 & 4 \\ 1 & 3 & 9 \end{bmatrix}$ 13. $\begin{bmatrix} 1 & 2 & 0 & 3 \\ 1 & 1 & 1 & -1 \\ 0 & 1 & 0 & 0 \\ 0 & 0 & 1 & 1 \end{bmatrix}$

14. $\begin{bmatrix} 2 & 1 & 1 & 1 \\ 1 & 2 & 1 & 1 \\ 1 & 1 & 2 & 1 \\ 1 & 1 & 1 & 2 \end{bmatrix}$ 15. $\begin{bmatrix} -3 & 1 & 1 & 1 \\ 1 & -3 & 1 & 1 \\ 1 & 1 & -3 & 1 \\ 1 & 1 & 1 & -3 \end{bmatrix}$

16. $\begin{bmatrix} 1 & 1 & 1 & 1 \\ -4 & 2 & 1 & -1 \\ 0 & 0 & 3 & 1 \\ 0 & 0 & -4 & 2 \end{bmatrix}$ 17. $\begin{bmatrix} a & 1 & 1 & 1 \\ 1 & a & 0 & 0 \\ 1 & 0 & a & 0 \\ 1 & 0 & 0 & a \end{bmatrix}$

18. $\begin{bmatrix} -2-k & 1 & 1 \\ 1 & -2-k & 1 \\ 1 & 1 & -2-k \end{bmatrix}$ 19. $\begin{bmatrix} 5-k & 1 & 1 & 1 \\ 1 & 5-k & 1 & 1 \\ 1 & 1 & 5-k & 1 \\ 1 & 1 & 1 & 5-k \end{bmatrix}$

20. $\begin{bmatrix} 4-k & 1 & 6 \\ 1 & 4-k & 6 \\ 1 & 1 & 6-k \end{bmatrix}$

21. Which of the matrices in problems 1-16 are not invertible?

22. In problems 17-20, for what value or values of a or k do the corresponding matrices fail to be invertible?

23. Solve the following system of equations for y using Cramer's Rule.

$$
\begin{array}{rrrrrrrr}
w & - & x & + & y & - & z & = & 2 \\
w & + & x & + & y & - & 5z & = & 2 \\
  &   & x & + & y & + & z & = & 9 \\
  &   &   &   & y & - & z & = & 1
\end{array}
$$

24. Solve the following system for x using Cramer's Rule.

$$
\begin{array}{rrrrrrr}
2x & + & y & + & z & = & 7 \\
x & + & 2y & + & z & = & 8 \\
x & + & y & + & 2z & = & 9
\end{array}
$$

1.4.2 Matlab

To find $|A|$ with Matlab use the **det** command. Enter the matrix A as before and at the EDU» prompt, type

$$\boxed{\text{d=det(A)}}.$$

Matlab will find the determinant of A and name it d.

Matlab will find the determinant of any square matrix with numbers in it. The problems above with letters in the entries of A generally cannot be done on Matlab, but could be done by Maple, Mathematica, or other computer algebra systems. To do them with Matlab, one needs to have the symbolic toolbox. However, numbers 18, 19, and 20 above are of the form $A - kI$. Their determinant is the characteristic polynomial of the matrix A, and Matlab is programmed to find characteristic polynomials. The command is poly(A), but more about this in Chapter 3.

A word about Matlab notation. When you see $-1.2454e+003$, it means $-1,245.5$. The e stands for exponent (not the base of natural logarithms e), so e+003 means exponent 3, and the base used is 10, so we multiply by 10^3. If you see $3.5564e$-013, it means 3.5564×10^{-13}, which is a very small number! Usually, this means that the number is really 0, and this is just roundoff error. If you are computing determinants and your answer comes out like this with a large negative exponent, it means the determinant is probably zero, and your matrix is probably not invertible.

1.4.3 Matlab Exercises

The following worksheet contains input for a Matlab session. Go to your computer or computer lab, call up the Matlab program, type in the inputs as shown, and observe the output.

Worksheet

EDU» a=[4 2 1;5 -3 2;-2 1 4]
EDU» det(a)
EDU» det(a')
EDU» b=[1 2 -1;3 1 2;1 1 1]
EDU» det(b)
EDU» det(a*b)
EDU» c=inv(a)
EDU» det(c)
EDU» 1/det(a)
EDU» rats(c)
EDU» quit

In problems 1-4, use the Matlab program to find the determinants of the following matrices.

1.
$$\begin{bmatrix} 3 & 1 & -1 & 3 & 2 \\ 4 & 1 & 1 & 5 & 3 \\ 5 & 3 & 1 & 5 & 3 \\ 2 & 2 & 2 & 2 & -1 \\ 3 & 0 & -3 & 0 & 1 \end{bmatrix}$$

2.
$$\begin{bmatrix} 3.5 & 1 & -2.7 & 0 & 1.1 \\ 2.3 & 0 & 5.1 & 1 & 2.3 \\ -4.5 & 6.3 & 2.4 & .5 & .5 \\ 1 & 1.5 & 4 & 3 & -6.4 \\ 2 & 1.5 & 3.2 & 2 & 1 \end{bmatrix}$$

3.
$$\begin{bmatrix} 2 & 1 & 5 & 10 \\ 20 & 20 & 30 & 5 \\ 2 & 4 & -10 & 6 \\ 4 & -40 & 6 & 8 \end{bmatrix}$$

4.
$$\begin{bmatrix} 1.3 & -4.2 & 3.2 & 4 \\ -8.5 & 3.6 & -7.8 & 1.6 \\ -5.9 & -4.8 & -1.4 & 9.6 \\ 1.2 & 5 & 3.7 & 2.5 \end{bmatrix}$$

5.   Which one of the four matrices above would you suspect is not invertible, and which would you be confident are invertible?

6. Using Cramer's rule, solve for y in the system $\begin{bmatrix} 4 & 6 & -3 \\ 3 & 5 & -2 \\ 2 & 1 & 5 \end{bmatrix} \begin{bmatrix} x \\ y \\ z \end{bmatrix} =$

$\begin{bmatrix} 5 \\ 3 \\ 5 \end{bmatrix}$.

7. Using Cramer's rule, solve for z in the system of equations

$$\begin{array}{rcrcrcrcr} 4w & + & 3x & + & 2y & + & z & = & 10 \\ -3w & + & 8x & - & 3y & & & = & 2 \\ w & + & x & + & y & + & z & = & 4 \\ w & - & x & - & y & + & 2z & = & 1. \end{array}$$

8. Using Cramer's rule, solve for w in the system of equations

$$
\begin{array}{rcrcrcrcl}
3w &+& x &+& y &+& z &=& 9 \\
w &+& 3x &+& y &+& z &=& 7 \\
w &+& x &+& 3y &+& z &=& 7 \\
2w &+& x &+& y &+& 3z &=& 9.
\end{array}
$$

Chapter 2

Subspaces and Basis

2.1 Dependence Relations and the Column Space

A dependence relation on a set of vectors is a linear combination of these vectors that equals the zero vector with at least one of the the coefficients being nonzero.

Example 2.1 *The following is an example of a dependence relation:*

$$2 \begin{bmatrix} 2 \\ 1 \\ 2 \end{bmatrix} + 3 \begin{bmatrix} 1 \\ 3 \\ 4 \end{bmatrix} + (-1) \begin{bmatrix} 7 \\ 11 \\ 16 \end{bmatrix} = \begin{bmatrix} 0 \\ 0 \\ 0 \end{bmatrix}.$$

When such a dependence relation exists, the vectors are called **linearly dependent**; otherwise, they are **linearly independent**.

Fact *A set of vectors is linearly dependent if and only if one of them is a linear combination of some of the others.*

Example 2.2 *The dependence relation above could be rewritten as*

$$\begin{bmatrix} 7 \\ 11 \\ 16 \end{bmatrix} = 2 \begin{bmatrix} 2 \\ 1 \\ 2 \end{bmatrix} + 3 \begin{bmatrix} 1 \\ 3 \\ 4 \end{bmatrix}$$

or

$$\begin{bmatrix} 2 \\ 1 \\ 2 \end{bmatrix} = \frac{1}{2} \begin{bmatrix} 7 \\ 11 \\ 16 \end{bmatrix} - \frac{3}{2} \begin{bmatrix} 1 \\ 3 \\ 4 \end{bmatrix}.$$

Fact *Elementary row operations on the matrix A do not change dependence relations on the column vectors of A.*

This is because elementary row operations on A do not change the solutions of the system of linear equations $AX = 0$, and any nonzero solution of $AX = 0$ gives a dependence relation on the columns of A, and vice versa.

Example 2.3 $\begin{bmatrix} 2 & 1 & 7 \\ 1 & 3 & 11 \\ 2 & 4 & 16 \end{bmatrix} \begin{bmatrix} 2 \\ 3 \\ -1 \end{bmatrix} = \begin{bmatrix} 0 \\ 0 \\ 0 \end{bmatrix}$ *is another way to write the dependence relation in previous examples.*

Now dependence relations on the column vectors of a matrix that is in RREF are easy to see. We start with a simple example.

Example 2.4 *Consider the matrix* $\begin{bmatrix} 2 & 6 & 1 \\ -1 & -3 & 4 \\ 2 & 6 & 3 \end{bmatrix}$. *Its RREF is* $\begin{bmatrix} 1 & 3 & 0 \\ 0 & 0 & 1 \\ 0 & 0 & 0 \end{bmatrix}$.
We notice that the second column is 3 times the first column in both matrices. The third column is not a linear combination of the previous columns. This is obvious in the RREF, since

$$a \begin{bmatrix} 1 \\ 0 \\ 0 \end{bmatrix} + b \begin{bmatrix} 3 \\ 0 \\ 0 \end{bmatrix} = \begin{bmatrix} a + 3b \\ 0 \\ 0 \end{bmatrix} \neq \begin{bmatrix} 0 \\ 1 \\ 0 \end{bmatrix}.$$

Example 2.5 *Consider the matrix* $\begin{bmatrix} 3 & 5 & 8 \\ 1 & 2 & 3 \\ -2 & 4 & 2 \end{bmatrix}$. *Its RREF is* $\begin{bmatrix} 1 & 0 & 1 \\ 0 & 1 & 1 \\ 0 & 0 & 0 \end{bmatrix}$.
We see that the last column is the sum of the first two columns in both matrices. We can also see that the second column is not a multiple of the first column in either matrix. The first two columns form a linearly independent set, but the three columns of this matrix form a linearly dependent set.

Problem *Express the vector $(3, 4, 2)$ as a linear combination of the vectors $(1, -1, 3)$ and $(4, 2, 2)$, if possible.*

Solution ***Always put the vector you are trying to express in the last column for this method.*** *We form the matrix* $\begin{bmatrix} 1 & 4 & 3 \\ -1 & 2 & 4 \\ 3 & 2 & 2 \end{bmatrix}$ *and find that the RREF is* $\begin{bmatrix} 1 & 0 & 0 \\ 0 & 1 & 0 \\ 0 & 0 & 1 \end{bmatrix}$. *Since the last column of the RREF is not a linear combination of the first two columns, we conclude that this is also true of the original matrix. Thus we conclude that it is not possible to express $(3, 4, 2)$ as a linear combination of $(1, -1, 3)$ and $(4, 2, 2)$.*

Problem *Express the vector* $(5, 7, -5)$ *as a linear combination of the vectors* $(1, -1, 3)$ *and* $(4, 2, 2)$, *if possible.*

Solution *Form the matrix* $\begin{bmatrix} 1 & 4 & 5 \\ -1 & 2 & 7 \\ 3 & 2 & -5 \end{bmatrix}$; *the RREF is* $\begin{bmatrix} 1 & 0 & -3 \\ 0 & 1 & 2 \\ 0 & 0 & 0 \end{bmatrix}$.

We see that in the RREF the last column is -3 *times the first column plus* *2 times the second column. This must be true in both matrices, so we have*

$$\begin{bmatrix} 5 \\ 7 \\ -5 \end{bmatrix} = -3 \begin{bmatrix} 1 \\ -1 \\ 3 \end{bmatrix} + 2 \begin{bmatrix} 4 \\ 2 \\ 2 \end{bmatrix},$$

which can also be written as $(5, 7, -5) = -3 \, (1, -1, 3) + 2 \, (4, 2, 2)$.

Example 2.6 *Consider the matrix* $A = \begin{bmatrix} 3 & 2 & 4 & 1 & 3 & 4 \\ 0 & -1 & 1 & 4 & 3 & 1 \\ 5 & 4 & 6 & 3 & 7 & 5 \\ 7 & 6 & 8 & -2 & 4 & 0 \end{bmatrix}$.

The relations between the columns of A *are not obvious. The RREF of* A *is*

$$B = \mathrm{RREF}(A) = \begin{bmatrix} 1 & 0 & 2 & 0 & 0 & 0 \\ 0 & 1 & -1 & 0 & 1 & 0 \\ 0 & 0 & 0 & 1 & 1 & 0 \\ 0 & 0 & 0 & 0 & 0 & 1 \end{bmatrix}.$$

One can see immediately that in B *the two first columns are linearly independent, and that the third column equals twice the first minus the second:*

$$\begin{bmatrix} 2 \\ -1 \\ 0 \\ 0 \end{bmatrix} = 2 \begin{bmatrix} 1 \\ 0 \\ 0 \\ 0 \end{bmatrix} - \begin{bmatrix} 0 \\ 1 \\ 0 \\ 0 \end{bmatrix}.$$

The fourth column of B *cannot be written as a linear combination of of preceding columns, but the fifth column is the sum of the second and the fourth:*

$$\begin{bmatrix} 0 \\ 1 \\ 1 \\ 0 \end{bmatrix} = \begin{bmatrix} 0 \\ 1 \\ 0 \\ 0 \end{bmatrix} + \begin{bmatrix} 0 \\ 0 \\ 1 \\ 0 \end{bmatrix}.$$

The sixth column of B cannot be written as a linear combination of preceding columns.   Thus we see that columns 1, 2, 4, and 6 form a linearly independent set, and columns 3 and 5 can be written in terms of these as above. Since the matrix B comes from the matrix A by a sequence of elementary row operations, the same relationships must hold between the columns of the matrix A. So we can conclude that columns 1, 2, 4, 6 of A are linearly independent, and columns 3 and 5 of A are linear combinations of columns 1, 2, 4, and 6 of A, as $(col\,3) = 2\,(col1) - (col2)$, *while* $(col5) = (col2) + (col4)$. *We can check this by noting that*

$$\begin{bmatrix} 4 \\ 1 \\ 6 \\ 8 \end{bmatrix} = 2 \begin{bmatrix} 3 \\ 0 \\ 5 \\ 7 \end{bmatrix} - \begin{bmatrix} 2 \\ -1 \\ 4 \\ 6 \end{bmatrix}$$

and

$$\begin{bmatrix} 3 \\ 3 \\ 7 \\ 4 \end{bmatrix} = \begin{bmatrix} 2 \\ -1 \\ 4 \\ 6 \end{bmatrix} + \begin{bmatrix} 1 \\ 4 \\ 3 \\ -2 \end{bmatrix}.$$

The relations between the columns of A were not obvious, but the relations between the columns of $B = \mathrm{RREF}\,(A)$ *were obvious.*

The **span** of a set of vectors is the set of all linear combinations of these vectors. This set is always a subspace of whatever space the vectors come from. The **column space** of A is the span of the column vectors of A. The **row space** of A is the span of the row vectors of A.

A **basis** of a subspace is a linearly independent spanning set.

Fact   *Once a basis is chosen, every vector in the subspace can be expressed uniquely as a linear combination of those basis vectors.*

From $\mathrm{RREF}\,(A)$ we can see how to select a basis for the column space of A, and also how to express the remaining columns as linear combinations of these basis columns. In the preceding example, columns 1, 2, 4, and 6 form a basis of the column space of A.

Fact   *The columns of A corresponding to columns of* $\mathrm{RREF}(A)$ *that contain a leading 1 (of some row) form a basis for the column space of A.*

Problem   *Find a basis for the column space of the matrix*

$$A = \begin{bmatrix} 3 & 6 & 5 & 2 \\ 5 & 10 & 3 & -2 \\ -2 & -4 & 6 & 8 \end{bmatrix}.$$

Solution *The RREF of this matrix is* $\begin{bmatrix} 1 & 2 & 0 & -1 \\ 0 & 0 & 1 & 1 \\ 0 & 0 & 0 & 0 \end{bmatrix}$, *so the first and third columns of A form a basis for the column space of A. Thus the set of triples* $\{(3, 5, -2), (5, 3, 6)\}$ *is a basis for the column space of A.*

Fact *The columns of a matrix* (A) *are linearly independent if and only if every column of* RREF (A) *has a leading 1.*

This gives a quick way to check for linear independence.

Problem *Determine whether or not the following vectors are linearly independent:* $(1, 1, 3, 2, 5), (2, 3, 1, 5, 4), (3, 3, -1, 2, 2).$

Solution *Use the three vectors as the columns of a matrix A, and find* RREF (A).

$$A = \begin{bmatrix} 1 & 2 & 3 \\ 1 & 3 & 3 \\ 3 & 1 & -1 \\ 2 & 5 & 2 \\ 5 & 4 & 2 \end{bmatrix}.$$

Now

$$\mathrm{RREF}(A) = \begin{bmatrix} 1 & 0 & 0 \\ 0 & 1 & 0 \\ 0 & 0 & 1 \\ 0 & 0 & 0 \\ 0 & 0 & 0 \end{bmatrix}.$$

Therefore, the original vectors are linearly independent (and are a basis for the column space).

Problem *Determine if the following vectors are linearly independent, and if they are not, find a dependence relation on the vectors.*
$(2, 1, 3, -1, 2), (1, 3, -1, 2, 2), (1, 1, 2, -1, 1), (6, 6, 7, -1, 7).$

Solution *Use the vectors as columns of a matrix* (A).

$$A = \begin{bmatrix} 2 & 1 & 1 & 6 \\ 1 & 3 & 1 & 6 \\ 3 & -1 & 2 & 7 \\ -1 & 2 & -1 & -1 \\ 2 & 2 & 1 & 7 \end{bmatrix}.$$

Find RREF (A).

$$\text{RREF}\,(A) = \begin{bmatrix} 1 & 0 & 0 & 2 \\ 0 & 1 & 0 & 1 \\ 0 & 0 & 1 & 1 \\ 0 & 0 & 0 & 0 \\ 0 & 0 & 0 & 0 \end{bmatrix},$$

so we see that the vectors are not linearly independent, but in fact the last one is a linear combination of the first three. You can check that $(6, 6, 7, -1, 7) = 2(2, 1, 3, -1, 2) + (1, 3, -1, 2, 2) + (1, 1, 2, -1, 1)$.

Problem *Let* $W = sp\{(3, 2, 1, 1), (-1, 2, 2, 1), (6, 4, 2, 2), (2, 4, 3, 2)\}$. *Select a basis for W from among the given vectors, and express the remaining vectors in terms of this basis.*

Solution *Use the vectors as the columns of a matrix*

$$A = \begin{bmatrix} 3 & -1 & 6 & 2 \\ 2 & 2 & 4 & 4 \\ 1 & 2 & 2 & 3 \\ 1 & 1 & 2 & 2 \end{bmatrix}.$$

Then $W = $ column space A. The RREF of A is

$$\begin{bmatrix} 1 & 0 & 2 & 1 \\ 0 & 1 & 0 & 1 \\ 0 & 0 & 0 & 0 \\ 0 & 0 & 0 & 0 \end{bmatrix},$$

so the first two vectors are a basis for W :

$$\text{basis of } W = \{(3, 2, 1, 1), (-1, 2, 2, 1)\}$$

and $(6, 4, 2, 2) = 2(3, 2, 1, 1)$, *while* $(2, 4, 3, 2) = (3, 2, 1, 1) + (-1, 2, 2, 1)$.

Fact *A subspace W of R^n may have many different bases, but the number of elements in any basis of W is always the same.*

The **dimension** of a vector space W is the number of vectors in a basis of W. In the preceding problem, the dimension of W was 2.

The dimension of R^n is n. The n vectors $(1, 0, 0, \ldots, 0), (0, 1, 0, \ldots, 0), \ldots (0, 0, \ldots, 0, 1)$ are a basis for R^n, called the natural or standard basis, but any n linearly independent vectors in R^n form a basis for R^n.

Fact *More than n vectors in R^n cannot be linearly independent.*

Fact *Fewer than n vectors in R^n cannot span R^n.*

Fact *A basis of R^n must have exactly n vectors.*

Given n vectors in R^n, we can test to see if they are a basis of R^n. Put the vectors as columns of a matrix B. Then B is square, and the vectors are a basis of R^n if and only if $\text{RREF}(B) = I$ or equivalently if and only if $\det(B) \neq 0$. If the columns of (B) are a basis for R^n then B is invertible, and we can express every vector v in R^n uniquely as a linear combination of the columns of B by solving $BX = v$.

Problem *Are the vectors $(1, 3, 1), (2, 2, -1), (1, -1, 2)$ a basis of R^3?*

Solution *Let $B = \begin{bmatrix} 1 & 2 & 1 \\ 3 & 2 & -1 \\ 1 & -1 & 2 \end{bmatrix}$. $\text{RREF}(B) = \begin{bmatrix} 1 & 0 & 0 \\ 0 & 1 & 0 \\ 0 & 0 & 1 \end{bmatrix}$, so the given vectors are a basis of R^3. [Note that we also know at this point that $\det(B) \neq 0$ and that B is invertible.]*

Problem *Express the vector $(5, -2, 6)$ as a linear combination of the basis vectors of the preceding problem.*

Solution *We want to solve*

$$x \begin{bmatrix} 1 \\ 3 \\ 1 \end{bmatrix} + y \begin{bmatrix} 2 \\ 2 \\ -1 \end{bmatrix} + z \begin{bmatrix} 1 \\ -1 \\ 2 \end{bmatrix} = \begin{bmatrix} 5 \\ -2 \\ 6 \end{bmatrix}$$

or, equivalently,

$$\begin{bmatrix} 1 & 2 & 1 \\ 3 & 2 & -1 \\ 1 & -1 & 2 \end{bmatrix} \begin{bmatrix} x \\ y \\ z \end{bmatrix} = \begin{bmatrix} 5 \\ -2 \\ 6 \end{bmatrix}.$$

We can solve this either by row reduction or by inverting the coefficient matrix. The augmented matrix is

$$\begin{bmatrix} 1 & 2 & 1 & 5 \\ 3 & 2 & -1 & -2 \\ 1 & -1 & 2 & 6 \end{bmatrix}.$$

The RREF is

$$\begin{bmatrix} 1 & 0 & 0 & -\frac{1}{16} \\ 0 & 1 & 0 & \frac{13}{16} \\ 0 & 0 & 1 & \frac{55}{16} \end{bmatrix}.$$

Thus we have

$$\begin{bmatrix} 5 \\ -2 \\ 6 \end{bmatrix} = -\frac{1}{16}\begin{bmatrix} 1 \\ 3 \\ 1 \end{bmatrix} + \frac{13}{16}\begin{bmatrix} 2 \\ 2 \\ -1 \end{bmatrix} + \frac{55}{16}\begin{bmatrix} 1 \\ -1 \\ 2 \end{bmatrix}.$$

The coefficients $-\frac{1}{16}, \frac{13}{16}, \frac{55}{16}$ are called the **coordinates** of the vector $(5, -2, 6)$ with respect to the given basis.

If we use the notation $[v]_B$ to stand for the coordinates (written as a column) of the vector v with respect to the basis B, then we have the relation

$$v = B\,[v]_B\,.$$

We can solve for the coordinates

$$[v]_B = B^{-1}v.$$

In the example above,

$$v = \begin{bmatrix} 5 \\ -2 \\ 6 \end{bmatrix} \text{ and } [v]_B = \begin{bmatrix} -\frac{1}{16} \\ \frac{13}{16} \\ \frac{55}{16} \end{bmatrix},$$

and they are related by

$$\begin{bmatrix} 5 \\ -2 \\ 6 \end{bmatrix} = \begin{bmatrix} 1 & 2 & 1 \\ 3 & 2 & -1 \\ 1 & -1 & 2 \end{bmatrix}\begin{bmatrix} -\frac{1}{16} \\ \frac{13}{16} \\ \frac{55}{16} \end{bmatrix}.$$

2.1.1   Matlab

All the problems in this section are solved just by finding the RREF of some matrix, so no new Matlab commands are needed for this section. The following exercises may be done by hand or using the Matlab **rref** command.

2.1.2 Exercises

1. Express $(3, 4)$ as a linear combination of $(1, 2)$ and $(2, 3)$ if possible.

2. Express $(1, 1, 2)$ as a linear combination of $(1, 1, 1), (1, -1, 1)$, and $(1, 3, 9)$ if possible.

3. Express $(1, 0, 4, 5)$ as a linear combination of $(2, 0, 8, 1), (3, 0, 12, 7)$, and $(4, 0, 16, 3)$ if possible.

4. Express $(1, 2, 3, 4)$ as a linear combination of $(1, 3, 2, 5), (2, 1, 4, 6), (-3, 0, -6, 1)$, and $(4, 6, 8, 1)$ if possible.

5. Express $(4, 3, 2, 1)$ as a linear combination of $(1, 1, 1, 1), (1, -1, 1, -1), (1, 2, 4, 8)$, and $(1, 3, 9, 27)$ if possible.

In problems 6-20, determine whether the given sets of vectors are linearly dependent or linearly independent. For the sets that are linearly dependent, write one of the vectors as a linear combination of the others.

6. $(1, 4), (2, 8)$

7. $(2, 3), (7, 9)$

8. $(1, 2, 3), (3, 5, 9), (2, -1, 6)$

9. $(1, 1, 1), (2, 3, 4), (3, 4, 5)$

10. $(1, -1, 1), (1, 2, 4), (1, 3, 9)$

11. $(1, 1, 1), (1, -1, 1), (1, 2, 4), (1, 3, 9)$

12. $(1, -1, 1, -1), (1, 1, 1, 1), (0, 2, 0, 3)$

13. $(1, 2, 3), (2, 1, 3), (4, -1, 1), (2, 2, 2)$

14. $(2, 1, 2, 3), (6, 3, 5, 0), (4, 2, 4, 6)$

15. $(-3, 1, 1, 1), (1, -3, 1, 1), (1, 1, -3, 1), (1, 1, 1, -3)$

16. $(2, 1, -1, 1), (5, 3, 6, 0), (-3, -2, -1, 1), (4, 2, 4, 2)$

17. $(0, 6, -7, 3, 1), (1, 1, 2, 0, 7), (1, 3, 5, 7, 9), (0, 0, 1, 1, 1)$

18. $(0, 1, 0, 1, 0), (1, 0, 1, 0, 1), (1, 2, 3, -1, -3)$

19. $(2, 1, -1, 3), (1, -1, 2, -1), (1, 8, -13, 14), (3, 0, 1, 1)$

20. $(0,1,0,0,1),(1,0,1,0,1),(-3,2,-3,0,-1),(2,-3,2,0,-1)$

In problems 21-35, find a basis of the column space of the given matrix.

21. $\begin{bmatrix} 1 & 2 & -3 \\ 3 & 8 & -9 \\ -2 & 9 & 6 \end{bmatrix}$ 22. $\begin{bmatrix} 1 & 3 & 9 \\ 2 & -4 & 8 \\ 3 & -3 & 3 \end{bmatrix}$ 23. $\begin{bmatrix} 2 & 3 & 4 & 9 \\ 3 & 4 & 5 & 12 \\ 4 & 5 & 6 & 15 \end{bmatrix}$

24. $\begin{bmatrix} 1 & 2 & 4 & -6 & 8 \\ 3 & 6 & 1 & 0 & -1 \\ 4 & 8 & 2 & 1 & 0 \\ 2 & 4 & 0 & 0 & 1 \end{bmatrix}$ 25. $\begin{bmatrix} 1 & 2 & 3 & 6 \\ 2 & 3 & 4 & 9 \\ -3 & -4 & -5 & 0 \end{bmatrix}$

26. $\begin{bmatrix} 4 & 1 & 1 & 6 \\ 1 & 4 & 1 & 6 \\ 1 & 1 & 4 & 6 \end{bmatrix}$ 27. $\begin{bmatrix} -2 & 1 & 1 \\ 1 & -2 & 1 \\ 1 & 1 & -2 \end{bmatrix}$

28. $\begin{bmatrix} 1 & 2 & 4 & 0 & 1 \\ 3 & 6 & 12 & 1 & 0 \\ 5 & 10 & 20 & -1 & -1 \end{bmatrix}$ 29. $\begin{bmatrix} 1 & 0 & 2 & 3 & 4 \\ 3 & 0 & 4 & 5 & 12 \\ 2 & 0 & 6 & 8 & 8 \end{bmatrix}$

30. $\begin{bmatrix} 2 & 3 & 4 & 5 \\ 3 & 4 & 5 & 6 \\ 4 & 5 & 6 & 7 \end{bmatrix}$ 31. $\begin{bmatrix} 2 & 2 & 2 \\ 3 & -3 & 3 \\ 4 & 8 & 12 \end{bmatrix}$

32. $\begin{bmatrix} \frac{1}{2} & \frac{1}{2} & \frac{1}{2} & 1 & 0 \\ \frac{1}{3} & -\frac{1}{3} & \frac{1}{3} & 0 & 1 \\ \frac{1}{4} & \frac{1}{2} & 1 & 0 & 0 \end{bmatrix}$ 33. $\begin{bmatrix} 0 & 5 & 4 & 3 & 0 \\ 0 & 1 & -1 & 1 & -1 \\ 0 & 8 & 6 & 4 & 2 \end{bmatrix}$

34. $\begin{bmatrix} 8 & 7 & 6 & 0 & 4 \\ 7 & 0 & 5 & 4 & 0 \\ 6 & 5 & 0 & 3 & 2 \end{bmatrix}$ 35. $\begin{bmatrix} 2 & 5 & 4 \\ 3 & 4 & 1 \\ 5 & 9 & 5 \end{bmatrix}$

In problems 36-45, for each given subspace, select a basis of the subspace from the given spanning set, give the dimension of the subspace, and express the other given vectors as linear combinations of your chosen basis.

36. $sp\{(1,0,2),(2,3,4),(3,4,6)\}$
37. $sp\{(1,1,1),(1,-1,1),(2,3,2)\}$
38. $sp\{(1,1,1),(1,-1,1),(1,2,4),(2,3,5)\}$
39. $sp\{(1,0,3,4),(0,2,3,4),(1,2,0,4),(1,2,3,0)\}$
40. $sp\{(2,3,4,5),(3,4,5,6),(4,5,6,7),(5,6,7,8)\}$

41. $sp\{(1,0,0,2),(1,0,5,6),(0,0,1,-1),(1,0,1,2),(2,-1,-2,3)\}$
42. $sp\{(1,2,4,0,1),(3,6,12,1,0),(5,10,20,-1,-1),(1,3,2,5,6)\}$
43. $sp\{(1,2,1,2,1),(1,0,1,0,2),(0,1,1,5,0),(0,0,1,2,3),(0,1,2,0,3)\}$
44. $sp\{(1,2,0,3,4),(1,1,1,1,1),(0,1,0,1,2),(0,0,1,2,3),(2,4,2,7,10)\}$
45. $sp\{(1,2,1,0,-1),(1,3,1,-1,1),(2,1,0,-1,-2),(0,0,0,1,2)\}$

In problems 46-50, in each case decide if the given vectors form a basis of R^n.

46. Is $\{(1,3,-2),(2,2,4),(1,1,-1)\}$ a basis of R^3?
47. Is $\{(1,3,1),(2,-1,2),(4,3,4)\}$ a basis of R^3?
48. Is $\{(1,2,1),(3,1,1),(-1,1,1)\}$ a basis of R^3?
49. Is $\{(1,1,2,2),(2,1,2,2),(1,3,1,2),(1,4,2,2)\}$ a basis of R^4?
50. Is $\{(1,1,2,2),(2,1,2,2),(1,3,1,2),(4,5,5,6)\}$ a basis of R^4?

In problems 51-55, find the coordinates of the v with respect to the given basis B.

51. $v=(5,2,-4)$ and basis $B=\{(1,1,-2),(2,1,3),(2,1,1)\}$.
52. $v=(6,3,6)$ and basis $B=\{(1,0,1),(0,1,0),(1,1,0)\}$.
53. $v=(-3,1,4)$ and basis $B=\{(2,3,-1),(1,3,-2),(1,1,1)\}$.
54. $v=(1,1,2,2)$ and basis
    $B=\{(1,1,1,1),(1,1,1,0),(1,1,0,0),(1,0,0,0)\}$.
55. $v=(3,1,2,-1)$ and basis
    $B=\{(2,1,2,-1),(1,3,3,1),(1,3,1,0),(1,2,1,1)\}$.

2.2 The Row Space

As mentioned in the preceding section, the **row space** of a matrix A is the set of all linear combinations of the rows of A, which is called the **span** of the rows of A.

Fact *Elementary row operations do not change the row space of a matrix A.*

This is because elementary row operations produce new rows that are linear combinations of the original rows, and each elementary row operation can be undone by an elementary row operation of the same kind, so the old rows are also linear combinations of the new ones.

Fact *The nonzero rows of* RREF (A) *are a basis of the row space of* (A).

Example 2.7 *Find a basis of the row space of* $A = \begin{bmatrix} 1 & 3 & 2 & -2 & 4 \\ 2 & 6 & 4 & -4 & 8 \\ 3 & 5 & 1 & 3 & 5 \\ 4 & 8 & 3 & 1 & 9 \end{bmatrix}.$

$$\text{RREF}(A) = \begin{bmatrix} 1 & 0 & -\frac{7}{4} & \frac{19}{4} & -\frac{5}{4} \\ 0 & 1 & \frac{5}{4} & -\frac{9}{4} & \frac{7}{4} \\ 0 & 0 & 0 & 0 & 0 \\ 0 & 0 & 0 & 0 & 0 \end{bmatrix},$$

so a basis of the row space is the set $\{(1, 0, -\frac{7}{4}, \frac{19}{4}, -\frac{5}{4}), (0, 1, \frac{5}{4}, -\frac{9}{4}, \frac{7}{4})\}.$

Remark   *Notice that the first two rows of A are not a basis of row space A because the second row of A is twice the first row.   However, the first two columns of A are a basis for column space A. For the basis of the row space, we use rows from the RREF.   For the basis of the column space, we use columns from the original matrix.   You get a basis of the row space and a basis of the column space with just one row reduction.*

Fact   *The row space of (A) and the column space of (A) have the same dimension.*

This is because in both cases the dimension (number of vectors in a basis) is equal to the number of leading 1's in the RREF(A). This number is called the **rank** of A.

Problem   *Given the matrix* $\begin{bmatrix} 2 & 2 & -3 & 4 & 1 \\ 5 & 3 & 2 & 2 & -1 \\ 3 & 1 & 5 & -2 & -2 \\ 3 & 6 & 3 & 0 & 2 \end{bmatrix}$, *find its rank.*

Solution   *The RREF is* $\begin{bmatrix} 1 & 0 & 0 & \frac{20}{29} & -\frac{47}{87} \\ 0 & 1 & 0 & \frac{2}{29} & \frac{62}{87} \\ 0 & 0 & 1 & -\frac{24}{29} & -\frac{19}{87} \\ 0 & 0 & 0 & 0 & 0 \end{bmatrix}$, *so the rank is 3.*

Problem   *Do the vectors* $(1, 2), (3, 5), (2, 2)$ *span* R^2?

Solution   *You can use the vectors as either rows or columns.   They will span R^2 if and only if the rank of the matrix is 2.   Let* $A = \begin{bmatrix} 1 & 3 & 2 \\ 2 & 5 & 2 \end{bmatrix},$

RREF is $\begin{bmatrix} 1 & 0 & -4 \\ 0 & 1 & 2 \end{bmatrix}$, *so the answer is yes.*

Remark   *In R^2 any two linearly independent vectors will span, and two vectors are linearly independent if one is not a multiple of the other. Since it is easy to see that $(3,5)$ is not a multiple of $(1,2)$, these two alone span R^2, and so the given set spans R^2. We didn't really need to use the RREF.*

Problem   *Do the vectors $(1,1,3),(3,2,2),(4,3,5),(2,1,-1)$ span R^3?*

Solution   *Put these vectors either as rows or columns. They span R^3 if and only if the rank is 3. Let $A = \begin{bmatrix} 1 & 3 & 4 & 2 \\ 1 & 2 & 3 & 1 \\ 3 & 2 & 5 & -1 \end{bmatrix}$; RREF is $\begin{bmatrix} 1 & 0 & 1 & -1 \\ 0 & 1 & 1 & 1 \\ 0 & 0 & 0 & 0 \end{bmatrix}$, so the rank is 2, and the given vectors do not span R^3. (They span a two dimensional subspace of R^3; in other words, they all lie in the same plane.)*

Problem   *Do the vectors $(3,1,2),(2,1,5),(4,4,-2),(2,1,2)$ span R^3?*

Solution   *Put these vectors as columns, obtaining $\begin{bmatrix} 3 & 2 & 4 & 2 \\ 1 & 1 & 4 & 1 \\ 2 & 5 & -2 & 2 \end{bmatrix}$. The RREF is $\begin{bmatrix} 1 & 0 & 0 & \frac{6}{17} \\ 0 & 1 & 0 & \frac{5}{17} \\ 0 & 0 & 1 & \frac{3}{34} \end{bmatrix}$, so the rank is 3. They do span R^3.*

Fact   *Two matrices of the same size have the same row space if and only if they have the same $\mathrm{RREF}(A)$.*

Using this fact, we can solve problems.

Problem   *Determine whether or not the subspaces S and W are the same subspace of R^4, where $S = sp\{(4,4,8,0),(2,5,7,3)\}$ and $W = sp\{(1,3,4,2),(1,2,3,1),(3,2,5,-1)\}$.*

Solution   *If we let $A = \begin{bmatrix} 4 & 4 & 8 & 0 \\ 2 & 5 & 7 & 3 \\ 0 & 0 & 0 & 0 \end{bmatrix}$ and $B = \begin{bmatrix} 1 & 3 & 4 & 2 \\ 1 & 2 & 3 & 1 \\ 3 & 2 & 5 & -1 \end{bmatrix}$, then $S =$ row space of A, and $W =$ row space of B, and the two matrices are the same size. Now $\mathrm{RREF}(A) = \begin{bmatrix} 1 & 0 & 1 & -1 \\ 0 & 1 & 1 & 1 \\ 0 & 0 & 0 & 0 \end{bmatrix}$ and $\mathrm{RREF}(B) = \begin{bmatrix} 1 & 0 & 1 & -1 \\ 0 & 1 & 1 & 1 \\ 0 & 0 & 0 & 0 \end{bmatrix}$; therefore, $S = W$.*

Problem   *Determine whether or not the subspaces S and W are the same subspace of R^4, where $S = sp\{(3,4,8,0),(2,1,7,3),(1,1,0,1)\}$ and $W = sp\{(3,3,4,2),(2,4,3,1),(3,3,5,-1)\}$.*

Solution   *Let $A = \begin{bmatrix} 3 & 4 & 8 & 0 \\ 2 & 1 & 7 & 3 \\ 1 & 1 & 0 & 1 \end{bmatrix}$ and $B = \begin{bmatrix} 3 & 3 & 4 & 2 \\ 2 & 4 & 3 & 1 \\ 3 & 3 & 5 & -1 \end{bmatrix}$.   Then $S =$ row space of A, and $W =$ row space of B. Now*

$$\text{RREF}(A) = \begin{bmatrix} 1 & 0 & 0 & \frac{44}{15} \\ 0 & 1 & 0 & -\frac{29}{15} \\ 0 & 0 & 1 & -\frac{2}{15} \end{bmatrix}$$

and

$$\text{RREF}(B) = \begin{bmatrix} 1 & 0 & 0 & \frac{13}{3} \\ 0 & 1 & 0 & \frac{1}{3} \\ 0 & 0 & 1 & -3 \end{bmatrix},$$

so $S \neq W$, although the two subspaces do have the same dimension, namely 3; they are not the same subspace of R^4.

Remark   *The row space of A is the column space of A' (transpose of A), and vice versa; however, it is not necessary to transpose.   You can find a basis of the row space and a basis of the column space at the same time with just one row reduction using the methods of this section and the preceding section.*

2.2.1   Matlab

As in the preceding section, all the problems in this section can be solved using only the **rref** command. Matlab also has a command that will return the rank of a matrix A.

$$\boxed{\text{rank(A)}}$$

will return the **rank** of A.

   The following exercises can be done by hand or with the help of the Matlab commands **rref** and **rank**.

2.2.2 Exercises

In problems 1-12, find a basis of the row space and a basis for the column space for each of the following matrices.

1. $\begin{bmatrix} 1 & -1 & -2 \\ 2 & -2 & 9 \\ 3 & -3 & 7 \end{bmatrix}$ 2. $\begin{bmatrix} 1 & 2 & 4 \\ 2 & 4 & 8 \\ 3 & 3 & -1 \end{bmatrix}$ 3. $\begin{bmatrix} 1 & 3 & -1 \\ 5 & 3 & 7 \\ 9 & 2 & 16 \end{bmatrix}$

4. $\begin{bmatrix} 1 & 0 & 1 & 5 \\ 2 & 0 & 3 & 4 \\ 4 & 0 & -1 & -8 \\ 5 & 0 & 1 & 1 \end{bmatrix}$ 5. $\begin{bmatrix} 2 & 3 & 4 & 5 \\ 3 & 4 & 5 & 6 \\ 4 & 5 & 6 & 7 \\ 5 & 6 & 7 & 8 \end{bmatrix}$

6. $\begin{bmatrix} 1 & -3 & 2 & 4 \\ 5 & -15 & 3 & 6 \\ 4 & -12 & 4 & 8 \\ 0 & 0 & 5 & 10 \end{bmatrix}$ 7. $\begin{bmatrix} 1 & 4 & 1 & 2 & 8 \\ 2 & 8 & 2 & 3 & 12 \\ 3 & 12 & 3 & -1 & -4 \\ 4 & 16 & -1 & -4 & -16 \end{bmatrix}$

8. $\begin{bmatrix} 1 & 5 & 6 & 1 & 3 \\ 2 & 10 & 12 & 5 & 9 \\ 3 & 15 & 18 & 6 & 12 \\ 0 & 0 & 0 & 4 & 7 \end{bmatrix}$ 9. $\begin{bmatrix} 1 & 3 & 2 & 0 & 2 & 4 \\ 5 & 15 & 12 & 0 & -1 & -2 \\ 8 & 17 & 3 & 0 & 3 & 6 \end{bmatrix}$

10. $\begin{bmatrix} 1 & 2 & 0 & 4 & 5 & 6 \\ 2 & 3 & 4 & 0 & 6 & 7 \\ 4 & 0 & 6 & 7 & 8 & 9 \end{bmatrix}$ 11. $\begin{bmatrix} -4 & 1 & 1 & 1 & 1 \\ 1 & -4 & 1 & 1 & 1 \\ 1 & 1 & -4 & 1 & 1 \\ 1 & 1 & 1 & -4 & 1 \\ 1 & 1 & 1 & 1 & -4 \end{bmatrix}$

12. $\begin{bmatrix} 1 & 1 & 1 & 1 & 1 & 1 \\ 1 & -1 & 1 & -1 & 1 & -1 \\ 1 & 3 & 4 & 8 & 16 & 32 \\ 4 & 1 & 7 & 7 & 19 & 31 \end{bmatrix}$

For each of the following sets of vectors, determine whether or not they span R^n, where n is the number of components in the given vectors.

13. $\{(1,-1,-2),(2,-2,9),(3,-3,7)\}$

14. $\{(1,2,4),(2,4,8),(3,3,-1)\}$

15. $\{(1,2,3),(-1,-3,-2),(-2,9,7)\}$

16. $\{(1,2,3),(2,4,3),(4,8,-1)\}$

17. $\{(1,2,3,4),(2,3,4,5),(3,4,5,6),(4,5,6,7),(5,6,7,8)\}$

18. $\{(1,2,3,4),(2,3,6,5),(3,4,5,6),(4,-5,6,7)\}$

19. $\{(1,2,3,4),(5,6,7,8),(8,9,0,1),(-1,0,2,1)\}$

20. $\{(-3,1,1,1),(1,-3,1,1),(1,1,-3,1),(1,1,1,-3)\}$

21. $\{(0,1,1,1,1),(1,0,1,1,1),(1,1,0,1,1),(1,1,1,0,1),(1,1,1,1,0)\}$

22. $\{(1,1,1,1,1),(1,-1,1,-1,1),(1,2,4,8,16),(1,-2,4,-8,16),(1,3,9,27,81)\}$

In problems 23-25, determine if the given subspaces are identical.

23. $S = sp\{(1,3,2),(2,2,1),(0,4,3)\}, T = sp\{(-1,1,1),(3,1,-1),(1,1,0)\}$

24. $S = sp\{(1,-1,1),(2,1,5),(3,2,8)\}, T = sp\{(4,4,12),(1,5,7)\}$

25. $S = sp\{(1,1,2),(2,1,1),(1,0,1)\}, T = sp\{(1,3,2),(2,4,2),(2,5,3)\}$

2.3   Null Space

The **null space** of a matrix A is the set of all solutions of $AX = 0$. We have a method for obtaining a basis for the null space. A basis for the null space cannot be read directly from RREF(A), but with a few modifications of the RREF, to what we call the **Hermite form** of A or $H(A)$, we can read off a basis of the null space.

Procedure   *To obtain the Hermite form of A:*

1. Find RREF(A).

2. Add or delete zero rows from RREF(A) until you obtain a square matrix. (Do **not** add or delete zero columns.)

3. Exchange rows until the leading 1's are all on the left-right (main) diagonal of A.

You now have the $H(A)$, the Hermite form of A.

If I is the identity matrix of the same size as $H(A)$, we have the following useful fact:

> **The nonzero columns of $H(A) - I$ are a basis for the null space of A.**

The reason this works is that it can be shown that a matrix in Hermite form is idempotent; that is, $H^2 = H$. Therefore, $H(H - I) = 0$, showing that the columns of $H - I$ are in the null space of H.

Example 2.8 Let $A = \begin{bmatrix} 2 & 1 & 4 \\ 5 & 4 & 13 \\ 3 & -2 & -1 \end{bmatrix}$, RREF$(A) = \begin{bmatrix} 1 & 0 & 1 \\ 0 & 1 & 2 \\ 0 & 0 & 0 \end{bmatrix}$. In this case the matrix is already square, and the leading 1's are already on the diagonal, so the matrix is already in Hermite form. So $H(A) - I = \begin{bmatrix} 0 & 0 & 1 \\ 0 & 0 & 2 \\ 0 & 0 & -1 \end{bmatrix}$. A basis for the null space of A is the vector $\begin{bmatrix} 1 \\ 2 \\ -1 \end{bmatrix}$, which could also be written $(1, 2, -1)$. All solutions of $AX = 0$ are multiples of this vector; in other words, all solutions are of the form $X = c\begin{bmatrix} 1 \\ 2 \\ -1 \end{bmatrix}$, or equivalently, $(x, y, z) = c(1, 2, -1) = (c, 2c, -c)$.

Example 2.9 Let $A = \begin{bmatrix} 2 & 3 & -1 & 1 & 4 \\ -3 & 1 & -4 & 4 & -6 \\ 2 & 2 & 0 & 1 & 4 \end{bmatrix}$.

$$\text{RREF}(A) = \begin{bmatrix} 1 & 0 & 1 & 0 & 2 \\ 0 & 1 & -1 & 0 & 0 \\ 0 & 0 & 0 & 1 & 0 \end{bmatrix}.$$

We add two zero rows to make it square, obtaining

$$\begin{bmatrix} 1 & 0 & 1 & 0 & 2 \\ 0 & 1 & -1 & 0 & 0 \\ 0 & 0 & 0 & 1 & 0 \\ 0 & 0 & 0 & 0 & 0 \\ 0 & 0 & 0 & 0 & 0 \end{bmatrix}$$

and exchange the third and fourth rows to put the last leading 1 on the diagonal, getting

$$H(A) = \begin{bmatrix} 1 & 0 & 1 & 0 & 2 \\ 0 & 1 & -1 & 0 & 0 \\ 0 & 0 & 0 & 0 & 0 \\ 0 & 0 & 0 & 1 & 0 \\ 0 & 0 & 0 & 0 & 0 \end{bmatrix}.$$

Now

$$H(A) - I = \begin{bmatrix} 0 & 0 & 1 & 0 & 2 \\ 0 & 0 & -1 & 0 & 0 \\ 0 & 0 & -1 & 0 & 0 \\ 0 & 0 & 0 & 0 & 0 \\ 0 & 0 & 0 & 0 & -1 \end{bmatrix},$$

Thus a basis for the null space of A is $\begin{bmatrix} 1 \\ -1 \\ -1 \\ 0 \\ 0 \end{bmatrix}$ *and* $\begin{bmatrix} 2 \\ 0 \\ 0 \\ 0 \\ -1 \end{bmatrix}$. *All solutions*

of $AX = 0$ *are of the form* $X = s \begin{bmatrix} 1 \\ -1 \\ -1 \\ 0 \\ 0 \end{bmatrix} + t \begin{bmatrix} 2 \\ 0 \\ 0 \\ 0 \\ -1 \end{bmatrix}$.

The **nullity** of a matrix is defined to be the dimension of its null space.

Fact *The rank plus the nullity of a matrix equals the number of columns of the matrix.*

Recall that the rank of a matrix A is the number of leading 1's in RREF (A).   The nullity of a matrix is the number of columns that do not have leading 1's in RREF (A).

2.3.1   Exercises

For each of the following matrices, find the Hermite form, a basis of the null space, and all solutions of the associated system of linear homogeneous equations.

1. $\begin{bmatrix} 1 & 2 \\ 2 & 4 \end{bmatrix}$ 2. $\begin{bmatrix} 1 & 0 & 3 \\ 0 & 2 & 0 \\ 3 & 0 & 1 \end{bmatrix}$ 3. $\begin{bmatrix} 2 & 1 & 5 \\ 1 & 3 & 10 \\ 2 & 3 & 11 \end{bmatrix}$

4. $\begin{bmatrix} 1 & 2 & 5 & 0 & 8 \\ 3 & 6 & 1 & 0 & 5 \\ 4 & 8 & 1 & 0 & 3 \end{bmatrix}$ 5. $\begin{bmatrix} 1 & -2 & 1 & 1 \\ 1 & 1 & -2 & 1 \\ -2 & 1 & 1 & -2 \end{bmatrix}$

6. $\begin{bmatrix} -4 & 1 & 1 & 1 \\ 1 & -4 & 1 & 1 \\ 1 & 1 & -4 & 1 \\ 1 & 1 & 1 & -4 \end{bmatrix}$ 7. $\begin{bmatrix} 1 & 2 & 4 & 1 & 1 \\ -2 & -4 & -8 & 1 & 1 \\ 3 & 6 & 12 & 0 & 0 \end{bmatrix}$

8. $\begin{bmatrix} 0 & 1 & 2 & 1 & 1 \\ 1 & 0 & 0 & 3 & 3 \\ 1 & 2 & 4 & 5 & 5 \end{bmatrix}$ 9. $\begin{bmatrix} 1 & 1 & 1 & 1 \\ 1 & 2 & 3 & 4 \\ 2 & 3 & 4 & 5 \\ 3 & 4 & 5 & 6 \\ 4 & 5 & 6 & 7 \end{bmatrix}$

10. $\begin{bmatrix} 1 & 2 & 3 & 4 & 5 \\ 5 & 4 & 3 & 2 & 1 \\ 1 & 1 & 1 & 1 & 1 \\ 0 & 0 & 0 & 0 & 0 \end{bmatrix}$

2.3.2 Matlab

To find a basis of the null space of a matrix A, we can use Matlab to find RREF (A), and then continue to find $H(A)$ and $H(A) - I$ by hand. Matlab also has a built-in command to find a basis of the null space of a matrix A.

$$\boxed{\text{N=null(A)}}$$

returns a matrix N whose columns are an orthonormal basis for the null space of A. An **orthonormal basis** consists of vectors of length 1 that are mutually orthogonal (dot product zero). For some uses we want an orthonormal basis, but for many we don't, and by forcing the vectors to be of length 1, irrational numbers are often introduced. Using the **rats** command on N doesn't usually improve things much. But there is another command that returns an answer closer to the one we get by hand:

$$\boxed{\text{N=null(A,'r')}}$$

returns a matrix N whose columns are a basis for the null space of A. [The vectors are -1 times the vectors we get by hand. The difference is because we use the columns of $H(A) - I$ rather than $I - H(A)$. We do this because you are less likely to make an error when doing it by hand if you just subtract I.] The output of this command appears as decimals (or decimal approximations). Applying the **rats** command to this output will usually produce an exact basis as we would get them by hand (except for the minus).

Remark *The command just introduced uses the apostrophe key on your keyboard. It,s A comma apostrophe r apostrophe.*

A couple of examples will illustrate how these commands work.

Example 2.10 *The following is a Matlab session, showing input, output, and comments.*

EDU» A=[1 2 3;3 4 5;5 6 7]

A =

       1   2   3
       3   4   5
       5   6   7

EDU» rref(A)

ans =

       1   0   −1
       0   1   2
       0   0   0

Comment: Using our method we get $(-1, 2, -1)$ as a basis for the null space, which is one-dimensional.

EDU» d=null(A)

d =

        0.4082
       −0.8165
        0.4082

Comment: This is just a decimal approximation of $(\frac{1}{\sqrt{6}}, \frac{-2}{\sqrt{6}}, \frac{1}{\sqrt{6}})$, our basis vector multiplied by -1 and divided by $\sqrt{6}$, its length.

EDU» n=null(A,'r')

n =

       1
      −2
       1

Comment: This is just the negative of the answer we would obtain by hand. When the null space is one-dimensional, any answer you get for the basis vector will just be a multiple of any of the other answers. However, if the null space is two-dimensional or higher, then different bases may look entirely different. We see this in the following example.

Example 2.11 *EDU» A=[1 2 3 1;4 5 6 1;7 8 9 1]*

A =

       1   2   3   1
       4   5   6   1
       7   8   9   1

EDU» rref(A)

ans =

       1   0   −1   −1
       0   1   2   1
       0   0   0   0

Comment: So a basis of the null space would consist of the vectors $(-1, 2, -1, 0)$ and $(-1, 1, 0, -1)$.

EDU» d=null(A)

d =

$$\begin{matrix} 0.2345 & -0.5276 \\ 0.2930 & 0.7621 \\ -0.5276 & -0.2345 \\ 0.7621 & -0.2930 \end{matrix}$$

Comment: This is an orthonormal basis of the same two-dimensional subspace of R^4. We can check that the columns of d form an orthonormal set by computing d'*d. The i,j entry in d'*d contains the dot product of column i with column j, so if the columns are orthonormal, d'*d will be the identity.

EDU» d'*d

ans =

$$\begin{matrix} 1.0000 & 0.0000 \\ 0.0000 & 1.0000 \end{matrix}$$

Comment: We can check that the columns of d are in the null space of a by computing a*d. It should give a 2×3 matrix of all zeros.

EDU» a*d

ans =

1.0e-014 *

$$\begin{matrix} 0.0222 & 0.0888 \\ 0 & -0.0222 \\ 0 & -0.1776 \end{matrix}$$

Comment: Every entry is multiplied by 10^{-14}, so is effectively zero. Now we use the null(A,'r') command.

EDU» n=null(A,'r')

n =

$$\begin{matrix} 1 & 1 \\ -2 & -1 \\ 1 & 0 \\ 0 & 1 \end{matrix}$$

Comment: This is just the negative of the vectors we got by hand. We check that we have null space vectors by multiplying a*n.

EDU» a*n

ans =

$$\begin{matrix} 0 & 0 \\ 0 & 0 \\ 0 & 0 \end{matrix}$$

Example 2.12 *We enter another matrix.*

EDU» A=[1 2 3;1 2 3;2 4 6]

A =

```
       1  2  3
       1  2  3
       2  4  6
EDU» rref(A)

ans =
       1  2  3
       0  0  0
       0  0  0
```

Comment: So a basis of null space is $(2, -1, 0)$ and $(3, 0, -1)$.

```
EDU» d=null(A)

d =
      -0.3586   -0.8944
      -0.7171    0.4472
       0.5976         0
EDU» n=null(A,'r')

n =
      -2  -3
       1   0
       0   1
```

Comment: The following matrix has the same null space as the one just done, but Matlab gives us a different orthonormal basis.

```
EDU» B=[1 2 3;1 2 3;1 2 3]

B =
       1  2  3
       1  2  3
       1  2  3
EDU»rref(B)

ans=
       1  2  3
       0  0  0
       0  0  0
EDU» d=null(A)

d =
      -0.1690   -0.9487
       0.8452         0
      -0.5071    0.3162
```

If the matrix A is invertible, so that the null space is the trivial subspace containing only the zero vector, Matlab returns the empty set as the basis of the null space.

```
a =[1 2 1;3 2 1;1 1 1]

a=
```

```
        1  2  1
        3  2  1
        1  1  1
EDU» det(a)
ans =
-2
EDU» d=null(a)
d =
Empty matrix: 3-by-0
EDU» n=null(a,'r')
n =
Empty matrix: 3-by-0
```

2.3.3   Matlab Exercises

The following worksheets give input for a Matlab session.   Go to your computer or lab, enter the commands, and observe the output.

Worksheet I

```
EDU» a=[1 1 2 3;1 0 1 1;2 1 3 4]
EDU» r=rref(a)
EDU» n=null(a,'r')
EDU» a*n
EDU» d=null(a)
EDU» a*d
EDU» d'*d
EDU» quit
```

Worksheet II

```
EDU» a=[3 3 1 1;2 2 4 4]
EDU» r=rref(a)
EDU» r1=r(1,:)
EDU» r2=r(2,:)
EDU» u=[0 0 0 0]
EDU» h=[r1;u;r2;u]
EDU» i=eye(4)
EDU» h-i
EDU» n=null(a,'r')
EDU» a*n
EDU» d=null(a)
EDU» a*d
EDU» d'*d
```

EDU» quit

Worksheet III

EDU» a=[4 1 5 -6;3 2 -1 4]
EDU» rref(a)
EDU» n=null(a,'r')
EDU» rats(n)
EDU» a*n
EDU» quit

For the following matrices, find the rank, nullity, and a basis of the null space using Matlab.

1. $\begin{bmatrix} 1 & 3 & 1 & 3 \\ 2 & 4 & -3 & 1 \\ 1 & 1 & -4 & 2 \end{bmatrix}$ 2. $\begin{bmatrix} 3 & 2 & 4 & 1 & 3 & 4 \\ 0 & -1 & 1 & 4 & 3 & 1 \\ 5 & 4 & 6 & 3 & 7 & 5 \\ 7 & 6 & 8 & -2 & 4 & 0 \end{bmatrix}$

3. $\begin{bmatrix} 2 & -3 & 1 & 2 \\ -1 & 2 & 4 & 3 \end{bmatrix}$ 4. $\begin{bmatrix} 1 & 2 & 0 & 3 \\ 3 & 3 & 2 & 0 \end{bmatrix}$

5. $\begin{bmatrix} 1 & \frac{1}{2} & 3 & \frac{5}{2} \\ 2 & \frac{3}{2} & \frac{1}{2} & 3 \end{bmatrix}$. 6. $\begin{bmatrix} \frac{1}{2} & \frac{1}{3} & \frac{1}{2} \\ \frac{2}{3} & \frac{1}{2} & \frac{1}{2} \end{bmatrix}$

2.4 Solving Equations Revisited

We can use the basis of the null space of A to describe all solutions of $AX = B$ because of the following fact:

Fact *If you have one solution of $AX = B$, call it X_1, then the complete solution set of $AX = B$ is obtained by adding X_1 to every vector in the null space of A.*

In other words, if N is the null space of A, the solution set of $AX = B$ is $X_1 + N$. When A is invertible, $N = \{0\}$ and X_1 is the unique solution.

Procedure *To find the complete solution set of $AX = B$, row reduce the augmented matrix $[A\,B]$ to RREF, and then fix it up so that the A part is in Hermite form, carrying the last column along. Then the last column is X_1, your particular solution, and you can get a basis of the null space by subtracting I from the Hermite form of A.*

Example 2.13 *Find all solutions to $AX = B$, where*

$$A = \begin{bmatrix} 1 & 2 & 3 & 4 \\ 2 & 2 & 4 & 6 \\ 1 & -1 & 0 & 1 \end{bmatrix} \text{ and } B = \begin{bmatrix} -1 \\ 2 \\ 5 \end{bmatrix}.$$

We form the augmented matrix

$$[A\,B] = \begin{bmatrix} 1 & 2 & 3 & 4 & -1 \\ 2 & 2 & 4 & 6 & 2 \\ 1 & -1 & 0 & 1 & 5 \end{bmatrix}.$$

Now we row reduce:

$$\text{RREF}\,([A\,B]) = \begin{bmatrix} 1 & 0 & 1 & 2 & 3 \\ 0 & 1 & 1 & 1 & -2 \\ 0 & 0 & 0 & 0 & 0 \end{bmatrix}.$$

Add a zero row to put the A part in Hermite form:

$$\begin{bmatrix} 1 & 0 & 1 & 2 & 3 \\ 0 & 1 & 1 & 1 & -2 \\ 0 & 0 & 0 & 0 & 0 \\ 0 & 0 & 0 & 0 & 0 \end{bmatrix}.$$

One solution is

$$X_1 = \begin{bmatrix} 3 \\ -2 \\ 0 \\ 0 \end{bmatrix}$$

and a basis of the null space is

$$\begin{bmatrix} 1 \\ 1 \\ -1 \\ 0 \end{bmatrix} \text{ and } \begin{bmatrix} 2 \\ 1 \\ 0 \\ -1 \end{bmatrix},$$

so the complete solution set of $AX = B$ is

$$X = \begin{bmatrix} 3 \\ -2 \\ 0 \\ 0 \end{bmatrix} + s\begin{bmatrix} 1 \\ 1 \\ -1 \\ 0 \end{bmatrix} + t\begin{bmatrix} 2 \\ 1 \\ 0 \\ -1 \end{bmatrix}.$$

Example 2.14 *Find all solutions to $AX = B$, where*

$$A = \begin{bmatrix} 1 & 2 & 1 \\ 2 & 4 & -1 \\ 1 & 2 & 2 \end{bmatrix} \text{ and } B = \begin{bmatrix} 1 \\ 8 \\ -1 \end{bmatrix}.$$

We form the augmented matrix

$$[A\,B] = \begin{bmatrix} 1 & 2 & 1 & 1 \\ 2 & 4 & -1 & 8 \\ 1 & 2 & 2 & -1 \end{bmatrix}.$$

Now we row reduce:

$$\text{RREF}\,([A\,B]) = \begin{bmatrix} 1 & 2 & 0 & 3 \\ 0 & 0 & 1 & -2 \\ 0 & 0 & 0 & 0 \end{bmatrix}.$$

To put the A part in Hermite form, we exchange the last two rows, getting

$$\begin{bmatrix} 1 & 2 & 0 & 3 \\ 0 & 0 & 0 & 0 \\ 0 & 0 & 1 & -2 \end{bmatrix}.$$

From this we see that one solution is $X_1 = \begin{bmatrix} 3 \\ 0 \\ -2 \end{bmatrix}$, *and a basis of the null space is* $\begin{bmatrix} 2 \\ -1 \\ 0 \end{bmatrix}$. *Thus all solutions of $AX = B$ are of the form*

$$X = \begin{bmatrix} 3 \\ 0 \\ -2 \end{bmatrix} + s \begin{bmatrix} 2 \\ -1 \\ 0 \end{bmatrix}.$$

Example 2.15 *Find all solutions to $AX = B$, where*

$$A = \begin{bmatrix} 1 & 3 & 0 & 2 \\ 2 & 6 & 1 & 1 \\ 3 & 9 & 1 & 3 \end{bmatrix} \text{ and } B = \begin{bmatrix} 4 \\ 7 \\ 11 \end{bmatrix}.$$

We form the augmented matrix

$$[A\,B] = \begin{bmatrix} 1 & 3 & 0 & 2 & 4 \\ 2 & 6 & 1 & 1 & 7 \\ 3 & 9 & 1 & 3 & 11 \end{bmatrix}.$$

Now we row reduce:

$$\text{RREF}\,([A\,B]) = \begin{bmatrix} 1 & 3 & 0 & 2 & 4 \\ 0 & 0 & 1 & -3 & -1 \\ 0 & 0 & 0 & 0 & 0 \end{bmatrix}.$$

Add a zero row to put the A part in Hermite form.

$$\begin{bmatrix} 1 & 3 & 0 & 2 & 4 \\ 0 & 0 & 0 & 0 & 0 \\ 0 & 0 & 1 & -3 & -1 \\ 0 & 0 & 0 & 0 & 0 \end{bmatrix}.$$

The last column is now our particular solution, $X_1 = \begin{bmatrix} 4 \\ 0 \\ -1 \\ 0 \end{bmatrix}$, *and a basis*

of the null space is $\begin{bmatrix} 3 \\ -1 \\ 0 \\ 0 \end{bmatrix}$ *and* $\begin{bmatrix} 2 \\ 0 \\ -3 \\ -1 \end{bmatrix}$, *so all solutions are given by*

$$X = \begin{bmatrix} 4 \\ 0 \\ -1 \\ 0 \end{bmatrix} + s \begin{bmatrix} 3 \\ -1 \\ 0 \\ 0 \end{bmatrix} + t \begin{bmatrix} 2 \\ 0 \\ -3 \\ -1 \end{bmatrix}.$$

Example 2.16 *Find all solutions to* $AX = B$, *where*

$$A = \begin{bmatrix} 1 & 2 & -1 \\ 2 & 5 & 1 \\ 1 & 4 & 5 \\ 1 & 3 & 2 \end{bmatrix} \text{ and } B = \begin{bmatrix} 2 \\ 8 \\ 10 \\ 6 \end{bmatrix}.$$

We form the augmented matrix

$$[A\,B] = \begin{bmatrix} 1 & 2 & -1 & 2 \\ 2 & 5 & 1 & 8 \\ 1 & 4 & 5 & 10 \\ 1 & 3 & 2 & 6 \end{bmatrix},$$

and find

$$\text{RREF}([A\,B]) = \begin{bmatrix} 1 & 0 & -7 & -6 \\ 0 & 1 & 3 & 4 \\ 0 & 0 & 0 & 0 \\ 0 & 0 & 0 & 0 \end{bmatrix}.$$

We delete a zero row to put the A part in Hermite form, getting

$$\begin{bmatrix} 1 & 0 & -7 & -6 \\ 0 & 1 & 3 & 4 \\ 0 & 0 & 0 & 0 \end{bmatrix}.$$

The last column gives our particular solution, $X_1 = \begin{bmatrix} -6 \\ 4 \\ 0 \end{bmatrix}$, *and a basis of*

the null space is $\begin{bmatrix} -7 \\ 3 \\ -1 \end{bmatrix}$, *so all solutions are given by*

$$X = \begin{bmatrix} -6 \\ 4 \\ 0 \end{bmatrix} + s \begin{bmatrix} -7 \\ 3 \\ -1 \end{bmatrix}.$$

2.4.1   Matlab

No new Matlab commands are needed for this section. The following exercises can be worked by hand or with the aid of Matlab to find the RREFs when they are not given.

2.4.2   Exercises

In the following problems, find a particular solution to $AX = B$, a basis of the null space of A, and use these to express all solutions of $AX = B$. In problems 1-8, the RREF of the augmented matrix of the system is given. (We use the symbol $\sim$ between two matrices to indicate that one matrix can be transformed into the other by a sequence of elementary row operations.) In problems 9 and 10, the matrix A and the column vector B are given.

1. $[A\,B] \sim \begin{bmatrix} 1 & 0 & -2 & 1 \\ 0 & 1 & 4 & 3 \end{bmatrix}.$

2. $[A\,B] \sim \begin{bmatrix} 1 & 2 & 0 & -1 & 5 \\ 0 & 0 & 1 & 3 & 7 \\ 0 & 0 & 0 & 0 & 0 \end{bmatrix}.$

3. $[A\,B] \sim \begin{bmatrix} 1 & 0 & 2 & 3 & 0 & 2 \\ 0 & 1 & -1 & -4 & 0 & 5 \\ 0 & 0 & 0 & 0 & 1 & 4 \end{bmatrix}$

4. $[A\,B] \sim \begin{bmatrix} 1 & -2 & 3 & 6 \\ 0 & 0 & 0 & 0 \\ 0 & 0 & 0 & 0 \end{bmatrix}$

5. $[A\,B] \sim \begin{bmatrix} 1 & 0 & 2 & 3 & 2 \\ 0 & 1 & -1 & -4 & 5 \\ 0 & 0 & 0 & 0 & 0 \end{bmatrix}$

6. $[A\,B] \sim \begin{bmatrix} 1 & 0 & 3 & 0 \\ 0 & 1 & 2 & 0 \\ 0 & 0 & 0 & 1 \\ 0 & 0 & 0 & 0 \end{bmatrix}$

7. $[A\,B] \sim \begin{bmatrix} 1 & 2 & 0 & 4 \\ 0 & 0 & 1 & 5 \end{bmatrix}$

8. $[A\,B] \sim \begin{bmatrix} 1 & 0 & 3 \\ 0 & 1 & 2 \\ 0 & 0 & 0 \\ 0 & 0 & 0 \end{bmatrix}$

9. $A = \begin{bmatrix} 1 & 0 & 2 & 0 \\ 1 & 2 & -4 & 0 \\ 1 & 2 & -4 & 1 \end{bmatrix} \qquad B = \begin{bmatrix} 4 \\ 3 \\ 5 \end{bmatrix}$

10. $A = \begin{bmatrix} 1 & 0 & 2 & -\frac{1}{5} \\ 5 & 1 & 13 & 3 \\ 5 & 2 & 16 & 7 \\ 5 & 1 & 13 & 3 \end{bmatrix} \qquad B = \begin{bmatrix} \frac{1}{2} \\ \frac{9}{2} \\ \frac{13}{2} \\ \frac{9}{2} \end{bmatrix}$

Chapter 3

Eigenvalues and Diagonalization

3.1 Eigenvalues and Eigenvectors

In this section we will be working with square matrices.

If A is a square matrix and X a nonzero column vector such that

$$AX = cX$$

for some real number c, then c is an eigenvalue of A and X is an eigenvector of A for the eigenvalue c.

Example 3.1 *Let* $A = \begin{bmatrix} 3 & 1 & 1 \\ 1 & 3 & 1 \\ 1 & 1 & 3 \end{bmatrix}$.

$$\begin{bmatrix} 3 & 1 & 1 \\ 1 & 3 & 1 \\ 1 & 1 & 3 \end{bmatrix} \begin{bmatrix} 1 \\ 1 \\ 1 \end{bmatrix} = \begin{bmatrix} 5 \\ 5 \\ 5 \end{bmatrix} = 5 \begin{bmatrix} 1 \\ 1 \\ 1 \end{bmatrix}.$$

This shows that 5 is an eigenvalue of A, and $\begin{bmatrix} 1 \\ 1 \\ 1 \end{bmatrix}$ *is an eigenvector of A for the eigenvalue 5.*

Remark *We must require the eigenvector X in the definition to be nonzero. Otherwise, since $A0 = c0$ for every matrix A and every real number c, every number c would be an eigenvalue for every matrix A, and the concept would be useless. Also, since we are working with R^n and matrices with real entries, we restrict ourselves to real numbers for the eigenvalues.*

Fact *The equation*

$$\mathbf{AX} = \mathbf{cX}$$

is equivalent to the equation

$$(\mathbf{A} - \mathbf{cI})\,\mathbf{X} = \mathbf{0}.$$

So in looking for eigenvalues, we are looking for values of c for which the null space of $(A - cI)$ is not just the zero space. This will happen if and only if $|(A - cI)| = 0$. Thus an eigenvalue of A is a number which when subtracted from each entry on the main diagonal of A will produce a matrix with determinant zero. (From this it follows that 0 is an eigenvalue of A if and only if $|A| = 0$.)

It is fairly easy to test a given number and see if it is an eigenvalue of A. It is also easy to test a vector and see if it is an eigenvector of A.

Example 3.2 *Is 1 an eigenvalue of the matrix $A = \begin{bmatrix} 3 & 2 & 2 \\ -2 & -1 & -2 \\ 2 & 2 & 3 \end{bmatrix}$? To test if 1 is an eigenvalue of this matrix, we subtract 1 from each entry of the main diagonal of A, getting*

$$A - I = \begin{bmatrix} 2 & 2 & 2 \\ -2 & -2 & -2 \\ 2 & 2 & 2 \end{bmatrix}.$$

Since this matrix clearly has determinant 0, we see that 1 is an eigenvalue of A. Is 2 an eigenvalue of A? Subtracting 2 from the main diagonal entries of A gives

$$A - 2I = \begin{bmatrix} 1 & 2 & 2 \\ -2 & -3 & -2 \\ 2 & 2 & 1 \end{bmatrix}.$$

The determinant of this matrix is 1, so 2 is not an eigenvalue.

Example 3.3 Is $\begin{bmatrix} 0 \\ 0 \\ 1 \\ 2 \end{bmatrix}$ an eigenvector for $A = \begin{bmatrix} 2 & 1 & 0 & 0 \\ 0 & 2 & 0 & 0 \\ 1 & 3 & 1 & 1 \\ 2 & -2 & -2 & 4 \end{bmatrix}$? We compute

$$\begin{bmatrix} 2 & 1 & 0 & 0 \\ 0 & 2 & 0 & 0 \\ 1 & 3 & 1 & 1 \\ 2 & -2 & -2 & 4 \end{bmatrix} \begin{bmatrix} 0 \\ 0 \\ 1 \\ 2 \end{bmatrix} = \begin{bmatrix} 0 \\ 0 \\ 3 \\ 6 \end{bmatrix} = 3 \begin{bmatrix} 0 \\ 0 \\ 1 \\ 2 \end{bmatrix}.$$

Thus $\begin{bmatrix} 0 \\ 0 \\ 1 \\ 2 \end{bmatrix}$ is an eigenvector of A for the eigenvalue 3.

We can easily check a specific number or vector to see if it is an eigenvalue or eigenvector of A. However, we can't expect to find all eigenvalues of a matrix A just by testing various numbers. We need a general method to find the eigenvalues and eigenvectors of a matrix A.

Fact If A is an $n \times n$ matrix, then $p(k) = |A - kI|$ is a polynomial of degree n in k. This is called the **characteristic polynomial** of A. The roots of $p(k)$ are the eigenvalues of A. The equation $p(k) = 0$ is called the **characteristic equation** of A.

Definition The algebraic multiplicity of an eigenvalue is its multiplicity as a root of the characteristic polynomial.

For polynomials of degree higher than 2 it is often difficult to find the roots. Characteristic polynomials have some special properties that may help.

Fact For a polynomial $p(k)$ with integer coefficients and leading coefficient ± 1, the only possible rational roots are ± 1 and $\pm$ factors of the constant term.

Procedure One can test for rational roots by plugging the factors of the constant term into the polynomial $p(k)$. If none of them produces 0, there are no rational roots; however, there could be roots that are real but irrational. When you have found a root r of the characteristic equation, that is one eigenvalue of A. Since $p(r) = 0$, we must have $(k - r)$ a factor of $p(k)$, so we divide out that factor and now we have a lower-degree polynomial to work with to find the rest of the eigenvalues of A.

Fact   *The constant term of the polynomial $p(k) = |A - kI|$ equals $|A|$ and also equals the product of all the eigenvalues of A.*

Fact   *The sum of the eigenvalues is the trace of the matrix A. (The **trace** of a matrix is defined as the sum of the entries on the main diagonal.)*

Remark   *Some books use $|kI - A|$ as the characteristic polynomial. Since this differs from $|A - kI|$ by a factor of $(-1)^n$ the two polynomials have the same roots.*

Fact   ***The eigenvectors of A for an eigenvalue r are the nonzero vectors in the null space of $(\mathbf{A} - \mathbf{rI})$.***

Definition   *For a matrix A the **eigenspace** of an eigenvalue r consists of the eigenvectors for r and the zero vector; thus the **eigenspace of r is the null space of $(\mathbf{A} - \mathbf{rI})$.** The geometric multiplicity of r is the dimension of this space.*

Fact   *The geometric multiplicity is always $\leq$ the algebraic multiplicity.*

Fact   *An eigenvalue of algebraic multiplicity 1 always has geometric multiplicity 1 also.*

Example 3.4 *Find all eigenvalues and eigenvectors of the matrix $A = \begin{bmatrix} 2 & 3 \\ 1 & 4 \end{bmatrix}$. The characteristic polynomial is*

$$p(k) = |A - kI| = \begin{vmatrix} 2 - k & 3 \\ 1 & 4 - k \end{vmatrix}.$$

Expanding the determinant, we get

$$\begin{aligned} p(k) &= (2 - k)(4 - k) - 3 \\ &= 8 - 6k + k^2 - 3 \\ &= k^2 - 6k + 5 \\ &= (k - 5)(k - 1), \end{aligned}$$

so the eigenvalues of this matrix are 5 and 1. Now we find the eigenvectors for each eigenvalue. First we consider the eigenvalue 5. Eigenvectors going with 5 are in the null space of $(A - 5I)$. We know this matrix has a nonzero *null space, because its determinant is zero. We use the techniques of Section 2.3 to find the null space.*

$$(A - 5I) = \begin{bmatrix} -3 & 3 \\ 1 & -1 \end{bmatrix}.$$

The RREF of this matrix is

$$\text{RREF}\,(A - 5I) = \begin{bmatrix} 1 & -1 \\ 0 & 0 \end{bmatrix} = H.$$

This is also the Hermite form, H. Then

$$H - I = \begin{bmatrix} 0 & -1 \\ 0 & -1 \end{bmatrix}$$

and a basis for the null space of $(A - 5I)$ is $\begin{bmatrix} -1 \\ -1 \end{bmatrix}$, or we can use $\begin{bmatrix} 1 \\ 1 \end{bmatrix}$.

Thus the eigenvectors of A for $k = 5$ are all vectors of the form $\begin{bmatrix} s \\ s \end{bmatrix}$ for $s \neq 0$. Now to find the eigenvectors for $k = 1$, we look for the null space of $(A - 1I) = (A - I)$.

$$A - I = \begin{bmatrix} 1 & 3 \\ 1 & 3 \end{bmatrix}.$$

The RREF is

$$\text{RREF}(A - I) = \begin{bmatrix} 1 & 3 \\ 0 & 0 \end{bmatrix},$$

so the null space basis is $\begin{bmatrix} 3 \\ -1 \end{bmatrix}$, and the eigenvectors of A for $k = 1$ are all vectors of the form $\begin{bmatrix} 3s \\ -s \end{bmatrix}$ for $s \neq 0$. As a check we perform the following multiplications:

$$\begin{bmatrix} 2 & 3 \\ 1 & 4 \end{bmatrix} \begin{bmatrix} s \\ s \end{bmatrix} = \begin{bmatrix} 5s \\ 5s \end{bmatrix} = 5 \begin{bmatrix} s \\ s \end{bmatrix}$$

and

$$\begin{bmatrix} 2 & 3 \\ 1 & 4 \end{bmatrix} \begin{bmatrix} 3s \\ -s \end{bmatrix} = \begin{bmatrix} 3s \\ -s \end{bmatrix}.$$

Example 3.5 *Find all eigenvalues and eigenvectors of the matrix*

$$A = \begin{bmatrix} 4 & 1 & -2 \\ 2 & 5 & -4 \\ -2 & -2 & 7 \end{bmatrix}.$$

The characteristic polynomial is

$$p(k) = \begin{vmatrix} 4-k & 1 & -2 \\ 2 & 5-k & -4 \\ -2 & -2 & 7-k \end{vmatrix}.$$

Before expanding, we look for some way to get more zeros using row or column operations. Adding row 3 to row 2, we obtain

$$p(k) = \begin{vmatrix} 4-k & 1 & -2 \\ 0 & 3-k & 3-k \\ -2 & -2 & 7-k \end{vmatrix}.$$

We notice that we can factor out $(3-k)$ from row 2, so we have

$$p(k) = (3-k) \begin{vmatrix} 4-k & 1 & -2 \\ 0 & 1 & 1 \\ -2 & -2 & 7-k \end{vmatrix}.$$

At this point we can already see that $k = 3$ is an eigenvalue. *The rest of the determinant will be quadratic in k and easily solved by the quadratic formula if you aren't able to factor it. Now we continue to find the other eigenvalues. Subtracting column 2 from column 3 will give us another 0 in row 2; thus*

$$p(k) = (3-k) \begin{vmatrix} 4-k & 1 & -3 \\ 0 & 1 & 0 \\ -2 & -2 & 9-k \end{vmatrix}.$$

Now expanding by minors around row 2, we get

$$\begin{aligned} p(k) &= (3-k) \begin{vmatrix} 4-k & -3 \\ -2 & 9-k \end{vmatrix} \\ &= (3-k)\left((4-k)(9-k) - 6\right) \\ &= (3-k)(36 - 13k + k^2 - 6) \\ &= (3-k)(k^2 - 13k + 30) \\ &= (3-k)(k - 10)(k - 3). \end{aligned}$$

Thus **the eigenvalues are 3 and 10**, *with 3 being a repeated root. We note that* **3 has algebraic multiplicity 2.** *We now proceed to find the* *eigenvectors for each of these eigenvalues. First we seek the null space of* $(A - 3I)$:

$$(A - 3I) = \begin{bmatrix} 1 & 1 & -2 \\ 2 & 2 & -4 \\ -2 & -2 & 4 \end{bmatrix}.$$

The RREF is

$$\text{RREF}(A - 3I) = \begin{bmatrix} 1 & 1 & -2 \\ 0 & 0 & 0 \\ 0 & 0 & 0 \end{bmatrix},$$

which is also the Hermite form, so a basis for the null space is $\begin{bmatrix} 1 \\ -1 \\ 0 \end{bmatrix}$ *and*

$\begin{bmatrix} -2 \\ 0 \\ -1 \end{bmatrix}$. *The eigenvectors of A for k = 3 are all vectors of the form*

$s \begin{bmatrix} 1 \\ -1 \\ 0 \end{bmatrix} + t \begin{bmatrix} -2 \\ 0 \\ -1 \end{bmatrix}$, *where not both s and t are zero. You can check by multiplying A times vectors of this form. We note that the dimension of the eigenspace of A for the k = 3 is 2. Thus* **the geometric multiplicity of the eigenvalue 3 is 2.** *To find the eigenvectors for k = 10, we look for the null space of* $(A - 10I)$.

$$(A - 10I) = \begin{bmatrix} -6 & 1 & -2 \\ 2 & -5 & -4 \\ -2 & -2 & -3 \end{bmatrix}$$

$$\text{RREF}(A - 10I) = \begin{bmatrix} 1 & 0 & \frac{1}{2} \\ 0 & 1 & 1 \\ 0 & 0 & 0 \end{bmatrix},$$

This is also the Hermite form, so a basis of the null space is $\begin{bmatrix} \frac{1}{2} \\ 1 \\ -1 \end{bmatrix}$, *and*

the eigenvectors of A for k = 10 are all vectors of the form $\begin{bmatrix} \frac{1}{2}s \\ s \\ -s \end{bmatrix}$. *You can check by multiplying A times vectors of this form.*

Warning *Do not do row or column operations on A before subtracting k from the diagonal. Row and column operations on a matrix usually change the eigenvalues.*

Warning *One can't always factor out a nice factor as we did above. Sometimes the characteristic polynomial has no rational roots. Some or all of the roots may even be imaginary, as in the next example.*

Example 3.6 *Let* $A = \begin{bmatrix} 0 & -1 \\ 1 & 0 \end{bmatrix}$. *Then* $|A - kI| = \begin{vmatrix} -k & -1 \\ 1 & -k \end{vmatrix} = k^2 + 1$.
This polynomial has no real roots, so A has no real eigenvalues and no real eigenvectors.

Remark *Since polynomials of odd degree with real coefficients must have at least one real root, real matrices of size $n \times n$, where n is odd, must have at least one real eigenvalue.*

One special type of matrix whose eigenvalues are easy to find is a matrix with some fixed number on the main diagonal and $1's$ everywhere else.

Example 3.7 *Let* $A = \begin{bmatrix} 5 & 1 & 1 \\ 1 & 5 & 1 \\ 1 & 1 & 5 \end{bmatrix}$. *It is easy to see that if we subtract 4 from the main diagonal, we get*

$$A - 4I = \begin{bmatrix} 1 & 1 & 1 \\ 1 & 1 & 1 \\ 1 & 1 & 1 \end{bmatrix},$$

a matrix of determinant 0; thus 4 is an eigenvalue. In fact, this matrix has rank 1; thus the dimension of the null space of $(A - 4I)$ is 2. Thus 4 is an eigenvalue of geometric multiplicity 2, and hence of algebraic multiplicity at least 2. Now observe the rows of A add up to the row vector $(7, 7, 7)$. Therefore, if we subtract 7 from the diagonal, we get the matrix

$$A - 7I = \begin{bmatrix} -2 & 1 & 1 \\ 1 & -2 & 1 \\ 1 & 1 & -2 \end{bmatrix},$$

whose rows add up to the zero vector. Thus the rows of this matrix are linearly dependent, so its determinant is 0. Therefore, 7 is also an eigenvalue of this matrix. There are no other eigenvalues of this matrix. This is because 4 has algebraic multiplicity at least 2 and 7 is also a root, so the characteristic polynomial, which is of degree 3, factors as $p(k) = (4 - k)(4 - k)(7 - k)$ and can have no other roots.

Fact *For triangular matrices (upper or lower), which includes diagonal matrices, the eigenvalues are just the entries on the main diagonal.*

Example 3.8 *Find the eigenvalues of the matrix*

$$A = \begin{bmatrix} 3 & 6 & 10 \\ 0 & 3 & 8 \\ 0 & 0 & 5 \end{bmatrix}.$$

The charateristic polynomial is

$$
\begin{aligned}
p(k) &= |A = kI| = \begin{bmatrix} 3-k & 6 & 10 \\ 0 & 3-k & 8 \\ 0 & 0 & 5-k \end{bmatrix} \\
&= (3-k)(3-k)(5-k).
\end{aligned}
$$

Thus, the eigenvalues are 3 and 5, with algebraic multiplicity 2 and 1, respectively.

3.1.1   Exercises

For the following matrices: a) Find all real eigenvalues. b) For each real eigenvalue find a basis of the corresponding eigenspace. c) For each real eigenvalue state its algebraic multiplicity and its geometric multiplicity.

1. $\begin{bmatrix} -1 & 2 \\ 3 & 4 \end{bmatrix}$ 2. $\begin{bmatrix} -1 & 1 \\ 6 & -2 \end{bmatrix}$ 3. $\begin{bmatrix} 0 & 4 \\ -1 & 0 \end{bmatrix}$

4. $\begin{bmatrix} 7 & 1 \\ 6 & 6 \end{bmatrix}$ 5. $\begin{bmatrix} 3 & 1 \\ 0 & 3 \end{bmatrix}$ 6. $\begin{bmatrix} 3 & 1 \\ 1 & 3 \end{bmatrix}$

7. $\begin{bmatrix} 1 & 4 \\ -1 & 5 \end{bmatrix}$ 8. $\begin{bmatrix} 1 & -2 \\ 3 & 2 \end{bmatrix}$ 9. $\begin{bmatrix} 3 & 6 & 10 \\ 0 & 3 & 8 \\ 0 & 0 & 5 \end{bmatrix}$

10. $\begin{bmatrix} 5 & 2 & 2 \\ 2 & 5 & 2 \\ 2 & 2 & 5 \end{bmatrix}$ 11. $\begin{bmatrix} 5 & 2 & 2 \\ 2 & 2 & 5 \\ 2 & 5 & 2 \end{bmatrix}$ 12. $\begin{bmatrix} 2 & 5 & 2 \\ 2 & 2 & 5 \\ 5 & 2 & 2 \end{bmatrix}$

13. $\begin{bmatrix} 5 & -1 & 2 \\ 3 & 1 & 2 \\ 6 & -2 & 6 \end{bmatrix}$ 14. $\begin{bmatrix} 3 & 3 & -2 \\ 2 & 8 & -4 \\ -2 & -6 & 6 \end{bmatrix}$

15. $\begin{bmatrix} 4 & 3 & -2 \\ 3 & 4 & 2 \\ 9 & 11 & 1 \end{bmatrix}$ 16. $\begin{bmatrix} 2 & 2 & 1 & 0 \\ 2 & -1 & -2 & 0 \\ 1 & -2 & 2 & 0 \\ 0 & 0 & 0 & 3 \end{bmatrix}$

17. $\begin{bmatrix} 3 & 1 & -1 \\ 4 & 0 & 0 \\ 6 & -3 & 2 \end{bmatrix}$ 18. $\begin{bmatrix} 1 & -1 & 1 \\ -4 & 7 & -2 \\ -6 & 7 & -2 \end{bmatrix}$

19. $\begin{bmatrix} 1 & -1 & 1 \\ -4 & 7 & -2 \\ -6 & 9 & -2 \end{bmatrix}$ 20. $\begin{bmatrix} 5 & 2 & 2 \\ 6 & 6 & 4 \\ 9 & 6 & 8 \end{bmatrix}$

3.1.2   Matlab

Matlab has some useful commands for finding eigenvalues and eigenvectors.

$$\boxed{\text{p=poly(A)}}$$

returns a row vector whose components are the coefficients of the characteristic polynomial of A. Matlab uses $p(k) = |kI - A|$ instead of $|A - kI|$ as we do.   As discussed above, these polynomials have the same roots.

$$\boxed{\text{r=roots(p)}}$$

returns a column vector containing the roots of p, repeated according to algebraic multiplicity.

$$\boxed{\text{E=eig(A)}}$$

returns a column vector containing the eigenvalues of A, repeated according to algebraic multiplicity.

Example 3.9 *The following is an example of a Matlab session using these commands.*

```
EDU» A=[15 20 14;-20 -29 -22;14 22 18]
A =
        15     20     14
       -20    -29    -22
        14     22     18
```

EDU» p=poly(A)

p =

    1.0000   −4.0000   1.0000   6.0000

Comment: Thus $p(k) = k^3 - 4k^2 + k + 6$.

EDU» r=roots(p)

r =

    3.0000

    2.0000

  −1.0000

EDU» E=eig(A)

E =

  −1.0000

    2.0000

    3.0000

Comment: Matlab will compute the eigenvectors as follows:

EDU» I=eye(3)

I =

   1   0   0

   0   1   0

   0   0   1

EDU» C=A+I

C =

    16   20   14

  −20 −28 −22

    14   22   19

EDU» N1=null(C,'r')

N1 =

    1.0000

  −1.5000

    1.0000

Comment: $N1$ is a basis of the eigenspace for $k = -1$. To check that $N1$ is an eigenvalue for $k = -1$, we multiply.

EDU» A*N1

ans =

  −1.0000

    1.5000

  −1.0000

EDU» C=A-2*I

C =

    13   20   14

  −20 −31 −22

    14   22   16

EDU» N2=null(C,'r')

```
N2 =
      2
     -2
      1
```

Comment: $N2$ is a basis of the eigenspace for $k = 2$.

```
EDU» A*N2
ans =
      4
     -4
      2
EDU» C=A-3*I
C =
      12    20    14
     -20   -32   -22
      14    22    15
EDU» N3=null(C,'r')
```

Comment: $N3$ is a basis of the eigenspace for $k = 3$.

```
N3 =
      0.5000
     -1.0000
      1.0000
EDU» A*N3
ans =
      1.5000
     -3.0000
      3.0000
```

Example 3.10 *Another Matlab session finding eigenvalues and eigenvectors.*

```
EDU» A=[1 2 2;-2 -3 -2;2 2 1]
A =
      1    2    2
     -2   -3   -2
      2    2    1
EDU» E=eig(A)
E =
      1.0000
     -1.0000
     -1.0000
EDU» I=eye(3)
I =
      1   0   0
      0   1   0
      0   0   1
```

```
EDU» C=A+I
C =
        2    2    2
       -2   -2   -2
        2    2    2
EDU» N=null(C,'r')
N =
       -1   -1
        1    0
        0    1
```

Comment: Columns of N are a basis of the eigenspace for $k = -1$. We check that multiplication by A multiplies both columns of N by -1, confirming that both columns of N are eigenvectors for $k = -1$.

```
EDU» A*N
ans =
        1    1
       -1    0
        0   -1
EDU» C=A-I
C =
        0    2    2
       -2   -4   -2
        2    2    0
EDU» N1=null(C,'r')
N1 =
        1
       -1
        1
```

Comment: The column $N1$ is a basis of the eigenspace for $k = 1$. We check that A times $N1$ equals $N1$, confirming that $N1$ is an eigenvector for $k = 1$.

```
EDU» A*N1
ans =
        1
       -1
        1
```

Example 3.11 *We find eigenvalues and eigenvectors of an upper triangular matrix.*

```
EDU» A=[3 1 0;0 3 0;0 0 4]
A =
```

```
     3   1   0
     0   3   0
     0   0   4
```

Comment: The eigenvalues are 3 and 4.

EDU» I=eye(3)

I =
```
     1   0   0
     0   1   0
     0   0   1
```

EDU» C=A-3*I

C =
```
     0   1   0
     0   0   0
     0   0   1
```

Comment: C has rank 2, so the eigenspace of A for $k = 3$ has dimension 1. A basis for this eigenspace is $N3$.

EDU» N3=null(C,'r')

N3 =
```
     1
     0
     0
```

EDU» A*N3

ans =
```
     3
     0
     0
```

EDU» C=A-4*I

C =
```
    -1    1   0
     0   -1   0
     0    0   0
```

Comment: A basis of the eigenspace for $k = 4$ is $N4$.

EDU» N4=null(C,'r')

N4 =
```
     0
     0
     1
```

EDU» A*N4

ans =
```
     0
     0 .
     4
```

Example 3.12 *Here we use Matlab to find the eigenvalues and eigenvectors of a matrix whose eigenvalues are not all real.*

```
EDU» A=[2 2 5;5 2 2;2 5 2]
A =
        2   2   5
        5   2   2
        2   5   2
EDU» p=poly(A)
p =
        1.0000   −6.0000   −18.0000   −81.0000
EDU» x=roots(p)
x =
                        9.0000
           −1.50000 + 2.5981i
           −1.50000 − 2.5981i
EDU» eig(A)
ans =
                        9.0000
           −1.50000 + 2.5981i
           −1.50000 − 2.5981i
EDU» I=eye(3)
I =
        1   0   0
        0   1   0
        0   0   1
EDU» C=A-9*I
C =
       −7    2    5
        5   −7    2
        2    5   −7
EDU» N=null(C,'r')
N =
        1
        1
        1
```

Comment: We verify that N is an eigenvector of A by computing A*N.

```
EDU» A*N
ans =
        9
        9
        9
```

3.1.3   Matlab Exercises

The first two exercises are worksheets. Go to your computer or computer lab, enter the commands as shown, and observe the output.

Worksheet I

EDU» a=[6 1 2;2 7 4;-1 -1 3]
EDU» p=poly(a)
EDU» r=roots(p)
EDU» e=eig(a)
EDU» i=eye(3)
EDU» c=a-6*i
EDU» n6=null(c,'r')
EDU» a*n6
EDU» c=a-5*i
EDU» n5=null(c,'r')
EDU» a*n5
EDU» quit

Worksheet II

EDU» a=[5 2 2 2;2 5 2 2;2 2 5 2;2 2 2 5]
EDU» p=poly(a)
EDU» r=roots(p)
EDU» e=eig(a)
EDU» i=eye(4)
EDU» c=a-3*i
EDU» n1=null(c,'r')
EDU» a*n1
EDU» d=a-11*i
EDU» n2=null(d,'r')
EDU» a*n2
EDU» quit

For the following matrices use Matlab to find all real eigenvalues, and for each real eigenvalue, find a basis of the corresponding eigenspace. Give the algebraic and geometric multiplicity for each real eigenvalue. The matrices in these problems are the same as those of Exercises 3.1.1.

1. $\begin{bmatrix} -1 & 2 \\ 3 & 4 \end{bmatrix}$ 2. $\begin{bmatrix} -1 & 1 \\ 6 & -2 \end{bmatrix}$ 3. $\begin{bmatrix} 0 & 4 \\ -1 & 0 \end{bmatrix}$

4. $\begin{bmatrix} 7 & 1 \\ 6 & 6 \end{bmatrix}$ 5. $\begin{bmatrix} 3 & 1 \\ 0 & 3 \end{bmatrix}$ 6. $\begin{bmatrix} 3 & 1 \\ 1 & 3 \end{bmatrix}$

7. $\begin{bmatrix} 1 & 4 \\ -1 & 5 \end{bmatrix}$ 8. $\begin{bmatrix} 1 & -2 \\ 3 & 2 \end{bmatrix}$ 9. $\begin{bmatrix} 3 & 6 & 10 \\ 0 & 3 & 8 \\ 0 & 0 & 5 \end{bmatrix}$

10. $\begin{bmatrix} 5 & 2 & 2 \\ 2 & 5 & 2 \\ 2 & 2 & 5 \end{bmatrix}$ 11. $\begin{bmatrix} 5 & 2 & 2 \\ 2 & 2 & 5 \\ 2 & 5 & 2 \end{bmatrix}$ 12. $\begin{bmatrix} 2 & 5 & 2 \\ 2 & 2 & 5 \\ 5 & 2 & 2 \end{bmatrix}$

13. $\begin{bmatrix} 5 & -1 & 2 \\ 3 & 1 & 2 \\ 6 & -2 & 6 \end{bmatrix}$ 14. $\begin{bmatrix} 3 & 3 & -2 \\ 2 & 8 & -4 \\ -2 & -6 & 6 \end{bmatrix}$ 15. $\begin{bmatrix} 4 & 3 & -2 \\ 3 & 4 & 2 \\ 9 & 11 & 1 \end{bmatrix}$

16. $\begin{bmatrix} 2 & 2 & 1 & 0 \\ 2 & -1 & -2 & 0 \\ 1 & -2 & 2 & 0 \\ 0 & 0 & 0 & 3 \end{bmatrix}$ 17. $\begin{bmatrix} 3 & 1 & -1 \\ 4 & 0 & 0 \\ 6 & -3 & 2 \end{bmatrix}$

18. $\begin{bmatrix} 1 & -1 & 1 \\ -4 & 7 & -2 \\ -6 & 7 & -2 \end{bmatrix}$ 19. $\begin{bmatrix} 1 & -1 & 1 \\ -4 & 7 & -2 \\ -6 & 9 & -2 \end{bmatrix}$ 20. $\begin{bmatrix} 5 & 2 & 2 \\ 6 & 6 & 4 \\ 9 & 6 & 8 \end{bmatrix}$

3.1.4   Optional Matlab: Searching for Rational Roots with the Polyval Command

A Matlab command that is useful when searching for rational roots of a polynomial is

$$\boxed{\text{polyval(p,x)}}$$

This command evaluates p at each component of the vector x and returns the result as a vector. The vector x can be either a row or a column vector; the returned vector will then be the same. As usual, the polynomial p is entered as a vector of the coefficients of p, starting with the leading coefficient. The polynomial may be entered either as a row or a column, and this has no influence on the output vector.

The rational roots of a polynomial with integer coefficients and leading coeficient ± 1 must be integers and must be divisors of the constant term. For example, if $p(k) = k^3 - 4k^2 - 5k + 6$, the only possible rational roots of p are $\pm 1, \pm 2, \pm 3, \pm 6$. In Matlab we enter p=[1 -4 -5 6] and x=[1 -1 2 -2 3 -3 6 -6], and then the command polyval(p,x), which returns a vector whose entries are p(1), p(-1), p(2), p(-2), p(3), p(-3), p(6), p(-6). If none of these are zero, we know that p has no rational roots. It may still be the case that the roots of p are all real, just not rational. [If the constant term of $p(k)$ is zero, then of course 0 is a root and we can factor out some power of k. Factor out the highest power of k possible, and then apply the rational root search to the remaining factor, which will now have nonzero constant term.]

Example 3.13 *Find all rational roots of* $p(k) = k^3 - 4k^2 - 5k + 6$.

EDU» % We enter a polynomial named p.
EDU» p=[1 -4 -5 6]
p =
$\qquad$ 1   −4   −5   6
EDU» % We enter a row vector named x of possible rational roots of p.
EDU» x=[1 -1 2 -2 3 -3 6 -6]
x =
$\qquad$ 1   −1   2   −2   3   −3   6   −6
EDU» polyval(p,x)
ans =
$\qquad$ −2   6   −12   −8   −18   −42   48   −324
EDU» % p has no rational roots.
EDU» roots(p)
ans =
$\qquad$ 4.7831
$\qquad$ −1.5780
$\qquad$ 0.7949
EDU» % We enter a new polynomial named np, with $np(k) = k^3 - 2k^2 - 5k + 6$.
EDU» np=[1 -2 -5 6]
np =
$\qquad$ 1   −2   −5   6
EDU» % We see that np has the same possible rational roots as p.
EDU» x
x =
$\qquad$ 1   −1   2   −2   3   −3   6   −6
EDU» polyval(np,x)
ans =
$\qquad$ 0   8   −4   0   0   −24   120   −252
EDU» % We see that 1, -2, and 3 are roots.
EDU» roots(np)
ans =
$\qquad$ 3.0000
$\qquad$ −2.0000
$\qquad$ 1.0000

EDU» % We enter another new poly named h, with $h(k) = k^3 - 3k^2 - 2k + 6$.

EDU» h=[1 -3 -2 6]

h =

    1 −3 −2 6

EDU» % We see that h has the same possible rational roots as p and np

EDU» x

x =

    1 −1 2 −2 3 −3 6 −6

EDU» polyval(h,x)

ans =

    2 4 −2 −10 0 −42 102 −306

EDU» % We see that 3 is the only rational root of h.

EDU» roots(h)

ans =

    3.0000

    1.4142

   −1.4142

Comment: Dividing by $k - 3$, we see that $h(k) = k^3 - 3k^2 - 2k + 6 = (k - 3)\left(k^2 - 2\right)$. The roots are 3, $\sqrt{2}$, and $-\sqrt{2}$.

3.1.5 Optional Matlab Exercises

Worksheet

EDU» p=[1 -5 12 -12]

EDU» x=[1 2 3 4 6 12]

EDU» polyval(p,x)

EDU» y=-x

EDU» polyval(p,y)

EDU» p=[1 -3 2 -10]

EDU» x=[1 2 5 10]

EDU» polyval(p,x)

EDU» polyval(p,-x)

EDU» p=[1 3 -10 -12]

EDU» x=[1 2 3 4 6 12]

EDU» polyval(p,x)

EDU» polyval(p,-x)

EDU» quit

Test the following polynomials for rational roots.

1. $p(k) = k^3 + 4k^2 - 3k - 12$

2. $p(k) = k^4 + 2k^3 - 11k^2 - 6k + 24$

3. $p(k) = k^2 - 3k - 6$

4. $p(k) = k^3 - 3k^2 + 8k - 5$

5. $p(k) = k^3 + 3k^2 - 13k - 15$

6. $p(k) = k^3 + k^2 - 2k + 7$

7. $p(k) = k^3 + 2k^2 - 7k + 40$

8. $p(k) = k^3 - 6k^2 + 15k - 18$

9. $p(k) = k^3 - 2k^2 + 3k - 10$

10. $p(k) = k^3 + 8k^2 + 10k - 25$

3.2 Diagonalization

The columns of P are eigenvectors of A if and only if

$$\boxed{AP = PD}$$

where D is a matrix with eigenvalues of A on the diagonal and zeros elsewhere.

Example 3.14

$$AP = \begin{bmatrix} 2 & 1 \\ 1 & 2 \end{bmatrix} \begin{bmatrix} 1 & -1 \\ 1 & 1 \end{bmatrix} = \begin{bmatrix} 3 & -1 \\ 3 & 1 \end{bmatrix}.$$

The first column of P is an eigenvector of A for $k = 3$. The second column of P is an eigenvector of A for $k = 1$.

$$PD = \begin{bmatrix} 1 & -1 \\ 1 & 1 \end{bmatrix} \begin{bmatrix} 3 & 0 \\ 0 & 1 \end{bmatrix} = \begin{bmatrix} 3 & -1 \\ 3 & 1 \end{bmatrix}$$

Example 3.15

$$AP = \begin{bmatrix} 6 & 1 & 2 \\ 2 & 7 & 4 \\ -1 & -1 & 3 \end{bmatrix} \begin{bmatrix} -1 & -1 & -2 \\ -2 & 1 & 0 \\ 1 & 0 & 1 \end{bmatrix} = \begin{bmatrix} -6 & -5 & -10 \\ -12 & 5 & 0 \\ 6 & 0 & 5 \end{bmatrix}.$$

The columns of P are eigenvalues of A for 6, 5, and 5, respectively.

$$PD = \begin{bmatrix} -1 & -1 & -2 \\ -2 & 1 & 0 \\ 1 & 0 & 1 \end{bmatrix} \begin{bmatrix} 6 & 0 & 0 \\ 0 & 5 & 0 \\ 0 & 0 & 5 \end{bmatrix} = \begin{bmatrix} -6 & -5 & -10 \\ -12 & 5 & 0 \\ 6 & 0 & 5 \end{bmatrix}.$$

The examples above illustrate the following facts.

Fact *If v is a column of P, the corresponding column of AP is Av.*

Fact *Right multiplication by a diagonal matrix multiplies each column by the corresponding diagonal entry.*

An $n \times n$ matrix A is said to be **diagonalizable** (over the real numbers) if there exists an invertible (real) matrix P such that

$$\boxed{P^{-1}AP = D}$$

where D is a diagonal matrix. For an invertible matrix P, this is equivalent to

$$\boxed{AP = PD}$$

Thus if we can find an invertible $n \times n$ matrix P whose columns are all eigenvectors of A, then A is diagonalizable.

Procedure *To find a matrix P that diagonalizes A, first find all eigenvalues of A. If A has any complex eigenvalues, you can stop; A is not diagonalizable (over the real numbers). If the eigenvalues of A are all real, find a basis for each eigenspace of A and use these vectors as the columns of P. If the dimensions of the eigenspaces add up to less than n, then A is not diagonalizable.*

Fact *A is diagonalizable if and only if the eigenvalues are all real and the geometric multiplicity equals the algebraic multiplicity for each eigenvalue of A.*

Fact *If an $n \times n$ matrix A has n distinct real eigenvalues, then A is diagonalizable.*

Example 3.16 *Find a matrix P such that $P^{-1}AP$ is diagonal or show that this is impossible for the matrix*

$$A = \begin{bmatrix} 6 & 1 & 1 \\ 1 & 6 & 1 \\ 1 & 1 & 6 \end{bmatrix}.$$

The characteristic polynomial is $p(k) = -(k-5)^2(k-8)$. The eigenvalues of A are 5 and 8. A will be diagonalizable if and only if the eigenspace for $k = 5$ has dimension 2. We get a basis for the eigenspace going with $k = 5$ by finding a basis for the null space of

$$[A - 5I] = \begin{bmatrix} 1 & 1 & 1 \\ 1 & 1 & 1 \\ 1 & 1 & 1 \end{bmatrix}.$$

This matrix has rank 1, so the null space has dimension 2. Thus we know that A is diagonalizable. To find the matrix P that does the job, we need a basis of the null space of this matrix.

$$\text{RREF}\,([A-5I]) = \begin{bmatrix} 1 & 1 & 1 \\ 0 & 0 & 0 \\ 0 & 0 & 0 \end{bmatrix}.$$

A basis for the null space is thus $\begin{bmatrix} 1 \\ -1 \\ 0 \end{bmatrix}$ *and* $\begin{bmatrix} 1 \\ 0 \\ -1 \end{bmatrix}$. *Next we need a basis of the eigenspace for $k = 8$, which is the null space of*

$$[A - 8I] = \begin{bmatrix} -2 & 1 & 1 \\ 1 & -2 & 1 \\ 1 & 1 & -2 \end{bmatrix}$$

and

$$\text{RREF}\,([A-8I]) = \begin{bmatrix} 1 & 0 & -1 \\ 0 & 1 & -1 \\ 0 & 0 & 0 \end{bmatrix}.$$

A basis of the null space is $\begin{bmatrix} -1 \\ -1 \\ -1 \end{bmatrix}$, *or* $\begin{bmatrix} 1 \\ 1 \\ 1 \end{bmatrix}$. *Combining this with the basis of the eigenspace for $k = 5$, we find that*

$$P = \begin{bmatrix} 1 & 1 & 1 \\ -1 & 0 & 1 \\ 0 & -1 & 1 \end{bmatrix}.$$

You can check that $AP = PD$, and that P is invertible.

Remark *The diagonalizing matrix P is not unique. As we saw in Chapter 2 when discussing null space, there are infinitely many bases for a given nonzero subspace. Also, the order of the columns in P may be changed. Then $P^{-1}AP$ will still be diagonal, but the order of the eigenvalues on the diagonal will be changed to correspond with the columns of P.*

Example 3.17 *In the preceding example, we found a matrix P whose columns are eigenvectors of A for the eigenvalues $5, 5,$ and 8, respectively. For this P we have*

$$P^{-1}AP = \begin{bmatrix} 5 & 0 & 0 \\ 0 & 5 & 0 \\ 0 & 0 & 8 \end{bmatrix}.$$

If we permute the columns of P, putting the eigenvector for $k = 8$ first, for example, as in

$$Q = \begin{bmatrix} 1 & 1 & 1 \\ 1 & -1 & 0 \\ 1 & 0 & -1 \end{bmatrix},$$

this will also diagonalize A, but we will have

$$Q^{-1}AQ = \begin{bmatrix} 8 & 0 & 0 \\ 0 & 5 & 0 \\ 0 & 0 & 5 \end{bmatrix}.$$

We could also get a matrix that looks completely different by choosing a different basis for the eigenspace going with $k = 5$. For example, if

$$S = \begin{bmatrix} 1 & 2 & 4 \\ 1 & -1 & -3 \\ 1 & -1 & -1 \end{bmatrix},$$

you can check that

$$S^{-1}AS = \begin{bmatrix} 8 & 0 & 0 \\ 0 & 5 & 0 \\ 0 & 0 & 5 \end{bmatrix}.$$

Example 3.18 *We now consider a matrix that cannot be diagonalized.*

$$A = \begin{bmatrix} 4 & 1 & 0 \\ 0 & 4 & 1 \\ 0 & 0 & 7 \end{bmatrix}.$$

The characteristic polynomial of A is $p(k) = -(k-4)^2(k-7)$. The eigenvalues are 4 and 7. The eigenvalue 4 has algebraic multiplicity 2, so the matrix will be diagonalizable if and only if the geometric multiplicity of 4 is also equal to 2. The eigenspace for $k = 4$ is the null space of the matrix $A - 4I$:

$$A - 4I = \begin{bmatrix} 0 & 1 & 0 \\ 0 & 0 & 1 \\ 0 & 0 & 3 \end{bmatrix}$$

and

$$\mathrm{RREF}\,(A - 4I) = \begin{bmatrix} 0 & 1 & 0 \\ 0 & 0 & 1 \\ 0 & 0 & 0 \end{bmatrix}.$$

This matrix has rank 2, so its null space is of dimension 1. Therefore, A is not diagonalizable.

Example 3.19 *Let $A = \begin{bmatrix} 4 & 0 & -3 \\ -1 & 3 & -2 \\ 1 & 0 & 1 \end{bmatrix}$. To find the eigenvalues of A, we compute*

$$|A - kI| = \begin{vmatrix} 4-k & 0 & -3 \\ -1 & 3-k & -2 \\ 1 & 0 & 1-k \end{vmatrix}.$$

Expanding by minors around the second column gives

$$\begin{vmatrix} 4-k & 0 & -3 \\ -1 & 3-k & -2 \\ 1 & 0 & 1-k \end{vmatrix} = (3-k)\begin{vmatrix} 4-k & -3 \\ 1 & 1-k \end{vmatrix}$$
$$= (3-k)\{(4-k)(1-k)+3\}$$
$$= (3-k)(k^2 - 5k + 7).$$

You can check using the quadratic formula that the roots of $(k^2 - 5k + 7)$ are complex numbers. Thus the matrix A is not diagonalizable (over the real numbers).

Remark *If we were allowed to use complex numbers in P and D, the matrix A in the preceding example does satisfy $P^{-1}AP = D$ for some invertible matrix P and diagonal matrix D. (This is because it has three distinct complex eigenvalues.) However, matrices with a repeated root whose eigenspace dimension is too small can't be diagonalized even if we allow complex numbers.*

Fact *$P^{-1}AP$ and A have the same eigenvalues but not the same eigenvectors.*

Fact *If $P^{-1}AP = D$, for some diagonal matrix D, the numbers on the main diagonal of D must be the eigenvalues of A.*

3.2.1 Exercises

For each of the following matrices, determine whether or not it can be diagonalized, and if it can be, find a matrix P that diagonalizes it. The first 20 matrices are the same matrices as those of problems 1-20 in Exercises 3.1.1 and 3.1.3. If you have done those exercises, you can use the results of those computations here.

1. $\begin{bmatrix} -1 & 2 \\ 3 & 4 \end{bmatrix}$
2. $\begin{bmatrix} -1 & 1 \\ 6 & -2 \end{bmatrix}$
3. $\begin{bmatrix} 0 & 4 \\ -1 & 0 \end{bmatrix}$

4. $\begin{bmatrix} 7 & 1 \\ 6 & 6 \end{bmatrix}$
5. $\begin{bmatrix} 3 & 1 \\ 0 & 3 \end{bmatrix}$
6. $\begin{bmatrix} 3 & 1 \\ 1 & 3 \end{bmatrix}$

7. $\begin{bmatrix} 1 & 4 \\ -1 & 5 \end{bmatrix}$
8. $\begin{bmatrix} 1 & -2 \\ 3 & 2 \end{bmatrix}$
9. $\begin{bmatrix} 3 & 6 & 10 \\ 0 & 3 & 8 \\ 0 & 0 & 5 \end{bmatrix}$

10. $\begin{bmatrix} 5 & 2 & 2 \\ 2 & 5 & 2 \\ 2 & 2 & 5 \end{bmatrix}$
11. $\begin{bmatrix} 5 & 2 & 2 \\ 2 & 2 & 5 \\ 2 & 5 & 2 \end{bmatrix}$
12. $\begin{bmatrix} 2 & 5 & 2 \\ 2 & 2 & 5 \\ 5 & 2 & 2 \end{bmatrix}$

13. $\begin{bmatrix} 5 & -1 & 2 \\ 3 & 1 & 2 \\ 6 & -2 & 6 \end{bmatrix}$
14. $\begin{bmatrix} 3 & 3 & -2 \\ 2 & 8 & -4 \\ -2 & -6 & 6 \end{bmatrix}$
15. $\begin{bmatrix} 4 & 3 & -2 \\ 3 & 4 & 2 \\ 9 & 11 & 1 \end{bmatrix}$

16. $\begin{bmatrix} 2 & 2 & 1 & 0 \\ 2 & -1 & -2 & 0 \\ 1 & -2 & 2 & 0 \\ 0 & 0 & 0 & 3 \end{bmatrix}$
17. $\begin{bmatrix} 3 & 1 & -1 \\ 4 & 0 & 0 \\ 6 & -3 & 2 \end{bmatrix}$

18. $\begin{bmatrix} 1 & -1 & 1 \\ -4 & 7 & -2 \\ -6 & 7 & -2 \end{bmatrix}$
19. $\begin{bmatrix} 1 & -1 & 1 \\ -4 & 7 & -2 \\ -6 & 9 & -2 \end{bmatrix}$
20. $\begin{bmatrix} 5 & 2 & 2 \\ 6 & 6 & 4 \\ 9 & 6 & 8 \end{bmatrix}$

For the matrices in problems 21-30, determine whether or not the matrix is diagonalizable

21. $\begin{bmatrix} 4 & 1 & 5 \\ 1 & 4 & 5 \\ 1 & 1 & 2 \end{bmatrix}$
22. $\begin{bmatrix} 2 & 1 & 0 \\ -1 & 4 & 0 \\ 0 & 1 & 2 \end{bmatrix}$
23. $\begin{bmatrix} 2 & 1 & -1 \\ 3 & -1 & 2 \\ 1 & -1 & 2 \end{bmatrix}$

24. $\begin{bmatrix} 2 & 0 & 0 & 0 \\ 3 & 2 & 0 & 0 \\ 0 & 1 & 3 & 1 \\ 1 & 0 & 1 & 3 \end{bmatrix}$
25. $\begin{bmatrix} 4 & 0 & 2 \\ -1 & 3 & -2 \\ 1 & 2 & 1 \end{bmatrix}$
26. $\begin{bmatrix} 4 & 0 & -2 \\ -1 & 3 & 2 \\ 1 & 1 & -1 \end{bmatrix}$

27. $\begin{bmatrix} 4 & 0 & -3 \\ -1 & 3 & -2 \\ 1 & 0 & 1 \end{bmatrix}$
28. $\begin{bmatrix} 4 & 1 & 0 \\ 0 & 4 & 1 \\ 0 & 0 & 4 \end{bmatrix}$
29. $\begin{bmatrix} 3 & 2 & 1 \\ 0 & 7 & 2 \\ 0 & -2 & 2 \end{bmatrix}$

30. $\begin{bmatrix} 3 & 1 \\ -1 & 5 \end{bmatrix}$.

3.2.2 Matlab

For matrices with rational (integer or fraction) eigenvalues, we can diagonalize by finding the eigenvalues and eigenvectors with Matlab as in the preceding section, but there is also the following command

$$[P,D]=\text{eig}(A)$$

returns matrices P and D such that $AP = PD$. P consists of eigenvectors of A and D is a diagonal matrix with the eigenvalues of A on the main diagonal repeated according to algebraic multiplicity. The first column of P is an eigenvector for the 1,1 entry in D. The second column of P is an eigenvector for the eigenvalue in the 2,2 position of D, etc. We can check in Matlab by computing $AP - PD$. This should be the zero matrix, but due to roundoff error, you sometimes get very small numbers instead.

Warning *Even though Matlab always returns a P and a diagonal D, we know that not all matrices are diagonalizable!*

In order for A to be diagonalizable, we need D to have only real number entries and P to be invertible. Once you have P and D with $AP = PD$, check to see if P is invertible by computing $\det(P)$. If $\det(P) \neq 0$ and the entries of D are real, then $P^{-1}AP = D$ and A is diagonalizable.

Warning *The columns of P are normalized (length 1) and thus are usually not exact eigenvectors, only decimal approximations.*

Warning *The Matlab outputs of the [P,D]=eig(A) command may contain complex numbers even when the eigenvalues of A are real and complex numbers are not needed for diagonalization.*

Despite the pitfalls noted above, the command [P,D]=eig(A) is useful in cases where the eigenvalues of A are irrational.

Example 3.20 *The following shows Matlab input and output plus comments.*

EDU» A=[15 20 14;-20 -29 -22;14 22 18]
A =
$$\begin{array}{rrr} 15 & 20 & 14 \\ -20 & -29 & -22 \\ 14 & 22 & 18 \end{array}$$
EDU» E=eig(A)
E =
$$\begin{array}{r} -1.0000 \\ 2.0000 \\ 3.0000 \end{array}$$

Comment: We know that A is diagonalizable because its eigenvalues are all real and distinct.

Comment: We can find a matrix P that diagonalizes A by finding a basis for each eigenspace using the command null(A-k*I,'r') as follows:

EDU» I=eye(3)
I =
$$\begin{array}{rrr} 1 & 0 & 0 \\ 0 & 1 & 0 \\ 0 & 0 & 1 \end{array}$$
EDU» N1=null(A+I,'r')
N1 =
$$\begin{array}{r} 1.0000 \\ -1.5000 \\ 1.0000 \end{array}$$
EDU» N2=null(A-2*I,'r')
N2 =
$$\begin{array}{r} 2 \\ -2 \\ 1 \end{array}$$
EDU» N3=null(A-3*I,'r')
N3 =
$$\begin{array}{r} .5000 \\ -1.0000 \\ 1.0000 \end{array}$$
EDU» P=[N1 N2 N3]
P =

```
     1.0000     2.0000     0.5000
    -1.5000    -2.0000    -1.0000
     1.0000     1.0000     1.0000
```

EDU» inv(P)*A*P

ans =

```
    -1.0000          0   -0.0000
    -0.0000     2.0000   -0.0000
     0.0000     0.0000     3.0000
```

Comment: Now we use the [P,D]=eig(A) command.

EDU [P,D]=eig(A)

P =

```
    -0.4851    -0.6667    -0.3333
     0.7276     0.6667     0.6667
    -0.4851    -0.3333    -0.6667
```

D =

```
    -1.0000          0          0
          0     2.0000          0
          0          0     3.0000
```

Comment: Matlab has normalized the eigenvectors in P, making each column a vector of length 1, but now the columns of the new P are not exact eigenvectors, only decimal approximations.   In the first P we got exact eigenvectors.

EDU» A*P-P*D

ans =

1.0e-014 *

```
     0.1166     0.1110     0.1221
    -0.8660    -0.7105    -0.9548
     0.5496     0.3331     0.3109
```

Comment: The entries of this matrix are all multiplied by 10^{-14}, so $AP - PD$ is zero to an accuracy of 14 decimal places.   This confirms that $AP = PD$, so the columns of P are eigenvectors of A.

EDU» det(P)

ans =

-0.0269

Comment: Since $\det(P) \neq 0$, P is invertible.   Checking, we get

EDU» inv(P)*A*P

ans =

```
    -1.0000    -0.0000    -0.0000
     0.0000     2.0000     0.0000
     0.0000     0.0000     3.0000
```

We now do some examples of matrices with eigenvalues of algebraic multiplicity > 1. Matlab puts bases of the eigenspaces as columns of P. Matlab uses vectors of length 1, but not necessarily orthonormal bases. If the geometric multiplicity is less than the algebraic multiplicity for some eigenvalue, Matlab repeats one or more of the eigenvectors to bring P up to size $n \times n$.

Example 3.21 *We enter another matrix.*

```
EDU» A=[1 2 2;-2 -3 -2;2 2 1]
A =
        1    2    2
       -2   -3   -2
        2    2    1
EDU» E=eig(A)
E =
        1.0000
       -1.0000
       -1.0000
EDU» I=eye(3)
I =
        1   0   0
        0   1   0
        0   0   1
EDU» N1=null(A-I,'r')
N1 =
        1
       -1
        1
EDU» N2=null(A+I,'r')
N2 =
       -1   -1
        1    0
        0    1
```

Comment: We see that the eigenspace for -1 has dimension 2; thus A is diagonalizable.

```
EDU» P=[N1 N2]
P =
        1   -1   -1
       -1    1    0
        1    0    1
EDU» inv(P)*A*P
ans =
        1    0    0
        0   -1    0
        0    0   -1
```

Comment: Now we use the [P,D]=eig(A) command, which finds a different diagonalizing matrix P, with eigenvectors normalized but no longer exact.

EDU [P,D]=eig(A)

P =

0.5774	−0.0000	−0.1555
−0.5774	−0.7071	0.7719
0.5774	0.7071	−0.6164

D =

1.0000	0	0
0	−1.0000	0
0	0	−1.0000

EDU» det(P)

ans =

-0.0635

Comment: Since $\det(P) \neq 0$, P is invertible.

EDU» inv(P)*A*P

ans

1.0000	0	0
0	−1.0000	0
0	0	−1.0000

Example 3.22 *Now we look at a matrix that is not diagonalizable.*

EDU» A=[3 1 0;0 3 0;0 0 4]

A =

3	1	0
0	3	0
0	0	4

EDU» E=eig(A)

E =

3

3

4

EDU» I=eye(3)

I =

1	0	0
0	1	0
0	0	1

EDU» C=A-3*I

C =

0	1	0
0	0	0
0	0	1

Comment: C has rank 2, so the eigenspace of A for $k = 3$ has dimension 1. Thus the geometric multiplicity of 3 is 1, not equal to the algebraic multiplicity. **Therefore, A is not diagonalizable.** A basis of the eigenspace for $k = 3$ is

EDU» null(C,'r')

ans =
       1
       0
       0

Comment: Notice in the following output that the first two columns of P are eigenvectors of A for 3 but are not linearly independent!

EDU [P,D]=eig(A)

P =
       1.0000   −1.0000   0
            0   0   0
            0   0   1.0000

D =
       3   0   0
       0   3   0
       0   0   4

EDU» A*P-P*D

ans =
       0   0   0
       0   0   0
       0   0   0

Comment: $A * P - P * D = 0$, but P is not invertible.

Comment: If we hadn't already noticed that P is not invertible, we could check using either the **det** or the **rank** command.

EDU» det(P)

ans =
       7.0000e-018

Comment: This warns us that $\det(P)$ is probably 0.

EDU» rank(P)

ans =
       2

Comment: This confirms that (P) is not invertible.

Example 3.23 *In this example we consider a matrix that is associated with the Fibonacci numbers. The matrix is*

$$A = \begin{bmatrix} 0 & 1 \\ 1 & 1 \end{bmatrix}.$$

The characteristic polynomial of A is $k^2 - k - 1$, which has roots

$$r_1 = \frac{1 + \sqrt{5}}{2} \ \text{and} \ r_2 = \frac{1 - \sqrt{5}}{2}.$$

The matrix A is diagonalizable because it has two distinct real roots. It is not too difficult to show that a basis for the eigenspace for r_1 is $\begin{bmatrix} r_2 \\ -1 \end{bmatrix}$, and a basis for the eigenspace for r_2 is $\begin{bmatrix} r_1 \\ -1 \end{bmatrix}$. Now we investigate how Matlab handles this matrix.

```
EDU» A=[0 1;1 1]
A =
      0  1
      1  1
EDU» p=poly(A)
p =
      1.0000  −1.0000  −1.0000
EDU» roots(p)
ans =
        1.6180
       −0.6180
EDU» eig(A)
ans =
        1.6180
       −0.6180
EDU» I=eye(2)
I =
      1  0
      0  1
EDU» null(A+.6180*I,'r')
ans =
Empty matrix: 2-by-0
```

Comment: Because -0.6180 is only an approximation of the eigenvalue, this method of finding the eigenspace basis fails.

```
EDU» null(A-1.6180*I,'r')
ans =
Empty matrix: 2-by-0
```

Comment: We try the [P,D]=eig(A) command.

```
EDU [P,D]=eig(A)
P =
       0.8507  0.5257
      −0.5257  0.8507
```

D =
       −0.6180   0
           0   1.6180
EDU» det(P)

ans =
     1
EDU» inv(P)*A*P

ans =
       −0.6180   0.0000
        0.0000   1.6180

Comment: Computer algebra systems such as Maple would do exact calculations in the preceding problem and give output using $\sqrt{5}$. The exact outputs are quite easy to interpret when dealing with roots of quadratics. However in the following example, the characteristic polynomial of A has three roots, all real but irrational. The characteristic polynomial is a cubic and does not factor using rational numbers only. These roots are not easy to express exactly. In these cases the decimal approximation is easier to deal with.

Example 3.24 *Consider the following matrix, which has no rational eigenvalues.*

$$A = \begin{bmatrix} 3 & 2 & 2 \\ 5 & 1 & 2 \\ 4 & 1 & 1 \end{bmatrix}.$$

Matlab can give us approximate eigenvalues and eigenvectors as follows:

EDU» A=[3 2 2;5 1 2;4 1 1]
A =
     3   2   2
     5   1   2
     4   1   1
EDU» p=poly(A)
p =
     1.0000   −5.0000   −13.0000   −5.0000
EDU» roots(p)
ans =
      6.9685
     −1.4855
     −0.4830
EDU» eig(A)
ans =

```
         6.9685
        −1.4855
        −0.4830
EDU [P,D]=eig(A)
P =
      0.5769     0.5328    −0.1782
      0.6493    −0.5647    −0.5230
      0.4955    −0.6303     0.8335
D =
      6.9685          0          0
          0    −1.4855          0
          0          0    −0.4830
EDU» det(P)
ans =
-0.8651
EDU» inv(P)*A*P
ans =
      6.9685     0.0000    −0.0000
      0.0000    −1.4855    −0.0000
     −0.0000    −0.0000    −0.4830
```

3.2.3   Matlab Exercises

Worksheet I

```
EDU» a=[6 1 2;2 7 4;-1 -1 3])
EDU» e=eig(a)
EDU» i=eye(3)
EDU» n1=null(a-6*i,'r')
EDU» n2=null(a-5*i,'r')
EDU» p=[n1 n2]
EDU» a*p
EDU» inv(p)*a*p
EDU» [p,d]=eig(a)
EDU» a*p-p*d
EDU» det(p)
EDU» inv(p)*a*p
EDU» quit
```

Worksheet II

```
EDU» a=[5 2 2 2;2 5 2 2;2 2 5 2;2 2 2 5]
EDU» p=poly(a)
EDU» roots(p)
```

```
EDU» e=eig(A)
EDU» i=eye(4)
EDU» n1=null(a-11*i,'r')
EDU» n2=null(a-3*i,'r')
EDU» p=[n1 n2]
EDU» a*p
EDU» inv(p)*a*p
EDU [p,d]=eig(a)
EDU» a*p-p*d
EDU» det(p)
EDU» inv(p)*a*p
EDU» quit
```

Use Matlab to find the eigenvalues of the following matrices. Determine which of the following matrices are diagonalizable, and for those that are, find a P that does it. (Problems 7-12 have some irrational eigenvalues.)

1. $\begin{bmatrix} 5 & 1 \\ 3 & 3 \end{bmatrix}$ 2. $\begin{bmatrix} 7 & 0 & -8 \\ 8 & -1 & -8 \\ 4 & 0 & -5 \end{bmatrix}$ 3. $\begin{bmatrix} 1 & 1 & 1 \\ -4 & 5 & 2 \\ 4 & 0 & 3 \end{bmatrix}$

4. $\begin{bmatrix} 4 & 0 & -2 \\ -1 & 3 & -2 \\ 1 & 0 & 1 \end{bmatrix}$ 5. $\begin{bmatrix} 7 & 4 & -1 \\ 4 & 7 & -1 \\ -4 & -4 & 4 \end{bmatrix}$ 6. $\begin{bmatrix} -5 & 1 & 0 \\ 0 & 2 & 1 \\ 0 & 0 & 2 \end{bmatrix}$

7. $\begin{bmatrix} 0 & 2 \\ 1 & 0 \end{bmatrix}$ 8. $\begin{bmatrix} 4 & 1 & -3 \\ 2 & 2 & 0 \\ 1 & 1 & -2 \end{bmatrix}$ 9. $\begin{bmatrix} 7 & 0 & 3 \\ 8 & -1 & -8 \\ 4 & 0 & -5 \end{bmatrix}$

10. $\begin{bmatrix} -2 & 3 & -1 \\ 4 & 0 & 1 \\ 5 & 2 & 1 \end{bmatrix}$ 11. $\begin{bmatrix} 1 & 2 & 1 \\ 3 & 1 & 1 \\ 4 & -1 & 1 \end{bmatrix}$ 12. $\begin{bmatrix} 5 & 2 & 2 \\ 3 & 4 & 1 \\ 2 & 2 & 0 \end{bmatrix}$.

Here are a couple of matrices that Matlab's [P,D]=eig(A) command doesn't handle well; however, you can find the eigenvalues and determine whether or not they are diagonalizable using other Matlab commands, as in the examples above:

13. $\begin{bmatrix} 8 & -9 & 5 \\ 12 & -21 & 13 \\ 17 & -35 & 22 \end{bmatrix}$ 14. $\begin{bmatrix} 1 & 2 & 3 & 1 \\ 4 & 5 & 6 & 1 \\ 7 & 8 & 9 & 1 \\ 10 & 11 & 12 & 1 \end{bmatrix}$

3.3   Orthonormal Basis

A basis of a subspace W is an **orthonormal basis** if its vectors are of length 1 and mutually orthogonal. We have noted in previous sections that the columns of an $m \times n$ matrix Q are orthonormal if and only if $Q'Q = I_{n \times n}$. Every nonzero subspace of R^n has an orthonormal basis (in fact, infinitely many of them if the dimension of W is > 1). Any basis of W can be transformed into an orthonormal basis of W. For a subspace W of dimension 1, just divide the one basis vector by its length and you have an orthonormal basis.

Example 3.25 *Let W be the subspace spanned by the vectors $(1, 3, 1)$ and $(2, 6, 2)$. A basis for this space is $(1, 3, 1)$. The length of this vector is $\sqrt{11}$, so an orthonormal basis is $\left(\frac{1}{\sqrt{11}}, \frac{3}{\sqrt{11}}, \frac{1}{\sqrt{11}} \right)$. The negative of this vector is also an orthonormal basis for W. In this case these are the only possibilites, since we must have a multiple of this vector that also has length 1.*

For higher dimensions, it is best to find an orthogonal basis first and then divide each vector by its length (normalize). For dimension 2, suppose that u_1 and u_2 form a basis for a subspace W. We can get an orthogonal basis as follows:

$$\text{Let } v_1 = u_1$$
$$\text{and let } v_2 = u_2 - \left(\frac{u_2 \cdot v_1}{v_1 \cdot v_1} \right) v_1.$$

Then divide both v_1 and v_2 by their respective lengths. Geometrically, what we have done is subtract from u_2 its projection on u_1, giving a vector v_2 that is orthogonal to u_1 but still in the subspace W.

Example 3.26 *Find an orthonormal basis for $W = sp\{(1, 1, 2), (1, 3, 2)\}$. We let $v_1 = (1, 1, 2)$ (this choice is arbitrary; we could have chosen the other vector) and*

$$
\begin{aligned}
v_2 &= (1, 3, 2) - \left(\frac{(1, 3, 2) \cdot (1, 1, 2)}{(1, 1, 2) \cdot (1, 1, 2)} \right) (1, 1, 2) \\
&= (1, 3, 2) - \frac{8}{6} (1, 1, 2) \\
&= (1, 3, 2) - \left(\frac{4}{3}, \frac{4}{3}, \frac{8}{3} \right) \\
&= \left(-\frac{1}{3}, \frac{5}{3}, -\frac{2}{3} \right).
\end{aligned}
$$

Any multiple of $\left(-\frac{1}{3}, \frac{5}{3}, -\frac{2}{3} \right)$ will also be orthogonal to $(1, 1, 2)$, so we prefer to use $(-1, 5, -2)$ as the second vector. You can check that these are orthogonal by computing their dot product, $-1 + 5 - 4 = 0$. To check that they still span the same space W (they must unless we have made an arithmetic *mistake), we can use the fact that two matrices have the same row space if and only if they have the same RREF. We form*

$$A = \begin{bmatrix} 1 & 1 & 2 \\ 1 & 3 & 2 \end{bmatrix}, \quad \text{RREF}(A) = \begin{bmatrix} 1 & 0 & 2 \\ 0 & 1 & 0 \end{bmatrix},$$

and

$$B = \begin{bmatrix} 1 & 1 & 2 \\ -1 & 5 & -2 \end{bmatrix}, \quad \text{RREF}(B) = \begin{bmatrix} 1 & 0 & 2 \\ 0 & 1 & 0 \end{bmatrix}.$$

All that remains is to divide each of the new basis vectors by its length. Thus we find that an orthonormal basis for W is

$$\left(\frac{1}{\sqrt{6}}, \frac{1}{\sqrt{6}}, \frac{2}{\sqrt{6}} \right) \ and \ \left(-\frac{1}{\sqrt{30}}, \frac{5}{\sqrt{30}}, -\frac{2}{\sqrt{30}} \right).$$

This orthonormal basis is not unique. We could have started with $v_1 = (1,3,2)$. This would have produced a different orthonormal basis. In fact, there are infinitely many orthonormal bases for W. (W is a plane through the origin in R^3. Rigid rotation of W through any angle around its normal will map any orthonormal basis of W onto another orthonormal basis of W.)

One can use the same process for dimension 3 or higher, but it becomes more difficult because you must subtract from u_3 its projection on both v_1 and v_2, as indicated below.

(Gram-Schmidt) To find an orthogonal basis of a subspace W given a basis $\mathbf{u}_1, \mathbf{u}_2, \ldots, \mathbf{u}_n$ of W:

1. Let

$$\mathbf{v}_1 = \mathbf{u}_1.$$

2. Let

$$\mathbf{v}_2 = \mathbf{u}_2 - \left(\frac{\mathbf{u}_2 \cdot \mathbf{v}_1}{\mathbf{v}_1 \cdot \mathbf{v}_1} \right) \mathbf{v}_1.$$

3. Let

$$\mathbf{v}_3 = \mathbf{u}_3 - \left(\frac{\mathbf{u}_3 \cdot \mathbf{v}_1}{\mathbf{v}_1 \cdot \mathbf{v}_1} \right) \mathbf{v}_1 - \left(\frac{\mathbf{u}_3 \cdot \mathbf{v}_2}{\mathbf{v}_2 \cdot \mathbf{v}_2} \right) \mathbf{v}_2.$$

4. Let

$$\mathbf{v}_4 = \mathbf{u}_4 - \left(\frac{\mathbf{u}_4 \cdot \mathbf{v}_1}{\mathbf{v}_1 \cdot \mathbf{v}_1} \right) \mathbf{v}_1 - \left(\frac{\mathbf{u}_4 \cdot \mathbf{v}_2}{\mathbf{v}_2 \cdot \mathbf{v}_2} \right) \mathbf{v}_2 - \left(\frac{\mathbf{u}_4 \cdot \mathbf{v}_3}{\mathbf{v}_3 \cdot \mathbf{v}_3} \right) \mathbf{v}_3.$$

5. Continue to

$$\mathbf{v}_n = \mathbf{u}_n - \left(\frac{\mathbf{u}_n \cdot \mathbf{v}_1}{\mathbf{v}_1 \cdot \mathbf{v}_1}\right)\mathbf{v}_1 - \left(\frac{\mathbf{u}_n \cdot \mathbf{v}_2}{\mathbf{v}_2 \cdot \mathbf{v}_2}\right)\mathbf{v}_2 \cdots - \left(\frac{\mathbf{u}_n \cdot \mathbf{v}_{n-1}}{\mathbf{v}_{n-1} \cdot \mathbf{v}_{n-1}}\right)\mathbf{v}_{n-1}.$$

6. Now $\{\mathbf{v}_1, \mathbf{v}_2, \ldots, \mathbf{v}_n\}$ is an orthogonal basis of S.

The process given above amounts to subtracting from each $\mathbf{u}_i$ its projection on the preceding $\mathbf{v}_i$, starting with $\mathbf{v}_1 = \mathbf{u}_1$. If you want an orthonormal basis, just divide each $\mathbf{v}_i$ by its length.

If your subspace W is defined as the null space of a matrix, there are two ways that you could get an orthonormal basis for W. We will give an example of each way.

The **first method** is to get a regular basis of the null space, using the Hermite form as we have been doing, and then use the Gram-Schmidt procedure to get an orthonormal basis.

Example 3.27 *Find an orthonormal basis for the null space of*

$$A = \begin{bmatrix} 1 & 2 & 1 \end{bmatrix}.$$

In this case we have

$$H(A) = \begin{bmatrix} 1 & 2 & 1 \\ 0 & 0 & 0 \\ 0 & 0 & 0 \end{bmatrix},$$

so a basis for the null space is $\begin{bmatrix} 2 \\ -1 \\ 0 \end{bmatrix}$ *and* $\begin{bmatrix} 1 \\ 0 \\ -1 \end{bmatrix}$. *Let*

$$v_1 = \begin{bmatrix} 1 \\ 0 \\ -1 \end{bmatrix}$$

and

$$\begin{aligned}
v_2 &= \begin{bmatrix} 2 \\ -1 \\ 0 \end{bmatrix} - \left(\frac{(2,-1,0) \cdot (1,0,-1)}{(1,0,-1) \cdot (1,0,-1)}\right) \begin{bmatrix} 1 \\ 0 \\ -1 \end{bmatrix} \\
&= \begin{bmatrix} 2 \\ -1 \\ 0 \end{bmatrix} - \left(\frac{2}{2}\right) \begin{bmatrix} 1 \\ 0 \\ -1 \end{bmatrix} \\
&= \begin{bmatrix} 1 \\ -1 \\ 1 \end{bmatrix}.
\end{aligned}$$

Dividing v_1 and v_2 by their respective lengths, we get an orthonormal basis for the null space of A:

$$\begin{bmatrix} \frac{1}{\sqrt{2}} \\ 0 \\ -\frac{1}{\sqrt{2}} \end{bmatrix} \quad and \quad \begin{bmatrix} \frac{1}{\sqrt{3}} \\ -\frac{1}{\sqrt{3}} \\ \frac{1}{\sqrt{3}} \end{bmatrix}.$$

A **second method** we could have used to find an orthogonal basis for the null space of A takes advantage of the following fact.

Fact *A vector is in the null space of a matrix A if and only if it is orthogonal to all the rows of A.*

Example 3.28 *Find an orthogonal basis of the null space of*

$$A = \begin{bmatrix} 1 & 2 & 1 \end{bmatrix}.$$

We see that $(2, -1, 0)$ and $(1, 0, -1)$ are in the null space of A. These vectors are not orthogonal, but we can keep one of them, say $(1, 0, -1)$, and search for another that is in the null space or A and is also orthogonal to $(1, 0, -1)$. Any vector in the null space of

$$B = \begin{bmatrix} 1 & 2 & 1 \\ 1 & 0 & -1 \end{bmatrix}$$

would satisfy these conditions. We find that $\mathrm{RREF}(B) = \begin{bmatrix} 1 & 0 & -1 \\ 0 & 1 & 1 \end{bmatrix}$;

thus $H(B) = \begin{bmatrix} 1 & 0 & -1 \\ 0 & 1 & 1 \\ 0 & 0 & 0 \end{bmatrix}$, $H(B) - I = \begin{bmatrix} 0 & 0 & -1 \\ 0 & 0 & 1 \\ 0 & 0 & -1 \end{bmatrix}$, *so $(-1, 1, -1)$ is*

in the null space of B. Thus $(-1, 1, -1)$ is in the null space of A and also orthogonal to $(1, 0, -1)$. It follows that $(-1, 1, -1)$ and $(1, 0, -1)$ form an orthogonal basis for the null space of A. It remains only to divide each of these vectors by its length and we have an orthonormal basis.

This second method will work for higher dimensions as well; in fact, it is often easier in these cases. We will illustrate this in another example, which we will do both ways.

Example 3.29 *Let $A = \begin{bmatrix} 1 & 3 & 1 & 1 \end{bmatrix}$. Find an orthogonal basis for the null space of A. $\mathrm{RREF}(A)$ is $\begin{bmatrix} 1 & 3 & 1 & 1 \end{bmatrix}$, and the Hermite form of A is*

$$H(A) = \begin{bmatrix} 1 & 3 & 1 & 1 \\ 0 & 0 & 0 & 0 \\ 0 & 0 & 0 & 0 \\ 0 & 0 & 0 & 0 \end{bmatrix}.$$

Thus

$$H\left(A\right) - I = \begin{bmatrix} 0 & 3 & 1 & 1 \\ 0 & -1 & 0 & 0 \\ 0 & 0 & -1 & 0 \\ 0 & 0 & 0 & -1 \end{bmatrix}.$$

A basis for the null space of A is $\{(3, -1, 0, 0), (1, 0, -1, 0), (1, 0, 0, -1)\}$. *However, these vectors are not orthogonal. We use the Gram-Schmidt process to transform this basis to an orthogonal basis. First, we reorder the basis, because in the Gram-Schmidt process it is an advantage to have vectors with lots of 0's and 1's come first. So we have the basis* $\{(1, 0, 0, -1), (1, 0, -1, 0), (3, -1, 0, 0)\}$ *We let*

$$v_1 = (1, 0, 0, -1).$$

Then

$$\begin{aligned} v_2 &= (1, 0, -1, 0) - \left(\frac{(1, 0, -1, 0) \cdot (1, 0, 0, -1)}{(1, 0, 0, -1) \cdot (1, 0, 0, -1)}\right) (1, 0, 0, -1) \\ &= (1, 0, -1, 0) - \frac{1}{2}(1, 0, 0, -1) \\ &= \left(\frac{1}{2}, 0, -1, \frac{1}{2}\right), \end{aligned}$$

but since any multiple of this vector is also orthogonal to v_1, we prefer to use

$$v_2 = (1, 0, -2, 1).$$

Now

$$\begin{aligned} v_3 &= (3, -1, 0, 0) - \left(\frac{(3, -1, 0, 0) \cdot (1, 0, 0, -1)}{(1, 0, 0, -1) \cdot (1, 0, 0, -1)}\right) (1, 0, 0, -1) \\ &\quad - \left(\frac{(3, -1, 0, 0) \cdot (1, 0, -2, 1)}{(1, 0, -2, 1) \cdot (1, 0, -2, 1)}\right) (1, 0, -2, 1) \\ &= (3, -1, 0, 0) - \frac{3}{2}(1, 0, 0, -1) - \frac{3}{6}(1, 0, -2, 1) \\ &= (3, -1, 0, 0) - \frac{3}{2}(1, 0, 0, -1) - \frac{1}{2}(1, 0, -2, 1) \\ &= (1, -1, 1, 1). \end{aligned}$$

So an orthogonal basis of the null space of A is

$$\{(1, 0, 0, -1), (1, 0, -2, 1), (1, -1, 1, 1)\}.$$

Normalizing gives

$$\left\{ \frac{1}{\sqrt{2}} (1,0,0,-1), \frac{1}{\sqrt{6}} (1,0,-2,1), \frac{1}{2} (1,-1,1,1) \right\}.$$

Example 3.30 *Now let us try another method of obtaining an orthogonal basis for the null space of $A = \begin{bmatrix} 1 & 3 & 1 & 1 \end{bmatrix}$. We observe that the dimension of the null space is 3, and just by inspection we can easily pick two vectors $(3,-1,0,0)$ and $(0,0,1,-1)$ that are in the null space of A and are mutually orthogonal. To find a third vector that is in null space of A and also orthogonal to these two, we find the null space of the matrix*

$$B = \begin{bmatrix} 1 & 3 & 1 & 1 \\ 3 & -1 & 0 & 0 \\ 0 & 0 & 1 & -1 \end{bmatrix}.$$

$$\text{RREF}(B) = \begin{bmatrix} 1 & 0 & 0 & \frac{1}{5} \\ 0 & 1 & 0 & \frac{3}{5} \\ 0 & 0 & 1 & -1 \end{bmatrix}.$$

A vector in the null space of B is $\left(\frac{1}{5}, \frac{3}{5}, -1, -1\right)$, but we prefer to use $(1,3,-5,-5)$. Thus we come up with the orthogonal basis for null space A

$$\left\{ (3,-1,0,0), (0,0,1,-1), (1,3,-5,-5) \right\}.$$

It is easy to check that these vectors are mutually orthogonal and all in the null space of A. To get an orothonormal basis, we divide each vector by its length, getting

$$\left\{ \frac{1}{\sqrt{10}} (3,-1,0,0), \frac{1}{\sqrt{2}} (0,0,1,-1), \frac{1}{\sqrt{60}} (1,3,-5,-5) \right\}.$$

3.3.1   Exercises

In problems 1-4, find an orthogonal basis for the subspace spanned by the given vectors.

1. $(1,1,2)$ and $(0,1,0)$

2. $(1,3,1)$ and $(2,1,1)$

3. $(2,1,1,2)$ and $(1,3,1,1)$

4. $(1,0,1,0), (1,1,1,0)$ and $(0,1,1,1)$

5. Find an orthonormal basis for each of the subspaces in problems 1-4.

   In problems 6-10, find an orthogonal basis for the null space of the given matrix.

6. $\begin{bmatrix} 1 & 2 & 2 \end{bmatrix}$

7. $\begin{bmatrix} -1 & 2 & 1 \end{bmatrix}$

8. $\begin{bmatrix} 1 & 1 & 2 & -1 \\ 3 & 1 & 0 & 1 \end{bmatrix}$

9. $\begin{bmatrix} 1 & 0 & 2 & 2 \end{bmatrix}$

10. $\begin{bmatrix} 1 & 2 & 2 & 1 \end{bmatrix}$

11. Find an orthonormal basis for the null space of each matrix in problems 6-10.

3.3.2   Matlab

There are two relevant commands in Matlab. One of them we have already met in earlier sections. The command

$$\boxed{\text{N=null(A)}}$$

returns an orthonormal basis for the null space of A.
   A new command,

$$\boxed{\text{Q=orth(A)}}$$

returns a matrix Q whose columns are an orthonormal basis of the column space of A. This command is useful if our subspace is defined by a spanning set or basis. Simply put the spanning vectors as columns of a matrix A and use the orth(A) command. The columns of the resulting matrix are an orthonormal basis for your subspace. If the columns of A are linearly dependent, orth(A) will return a matrix with fewer columns than A.

Example 3.31 *Find an orthonormal basis for the subspace of R^3 spanned by $(5, 3, -4)$ and $(6, 3, 2)$. The following is input and output from a Matlab session.*

EDU» B=[5 3 -4;6 3 2]

B =

       5   3   −4
       6   3   2

EDU» A=B'

A =

        5   6
        3   3
       −4   2

Comment: The space we are interested in is the column space of A.

EDU» Q=orth(A)

Q =

        0.8662   0.1790
        0.4728   0.0080
       −0.1614   0.9838

Comment: To check that the columns of Q are orthonormal, compute

EDU» Q'*Q

ans =

        1.0000   0
             0   1.0000

Comment: To check that the column space of Q is the same as the column space of A, we compute

EDU» rref(A')

ans =

        1.0000   0   6.0000
             0   1.0000   −11.3333

EDU» rref(Q')

ans =

        1.0000   0   6.0000
             0   1.0000   −11.3333

Thus an orthonormal basis for the given subspace is $(0.8662, 0.4728, −0.1614)$ and $(0.1790, 0.0080, 0.9838)$.

Remark *The reason we go to* RREF(A') *and* RREF (Q') *to check if A and Q have the same column space is because our test for when two subspaces are identical is for row spaces. Recall that two matrices have the same row space if and only if they have the same nonzero rows in their RREF.*

Example 3.32 *Find an orthonormal basis for the space W spanned by the vectors $(1, 1, 2), (1, 3, 2)$, and $(0, −2, 0)$. Notice that $(0, −2, 0) = (1, 1, 2) − (1, 3, 2)$, so this is not a basis, just a spanning set for W. If you notice this, you can just eliminate $(0, −2, 0)$ and use the other two vectors as the columns of A. If you don't happen to notice and you include all three vectors* *as columns of A, Matlab will still return an orthonormal basis of column space A.*

```
EDU» B=[1 1 2;1 3 2;0 -2 0]
B =
     1    1   2
     1    3   2
     0   −2   0
EDU» A=B'
A =
     1   1   0
     1   3   2
     2   2   0
EDU» Q=orth(A)
Q =
     0.2796   −0.3490
     0.7805    0.6252
     0.5592   −0.6981
EDU» Q'*Q
ans =
     1.0000   −0.0000
    −0.0000    1.0000
EDU» C=A(:,1:2)
C =
     1   1
     1   3
     2   2
EDU» R=orth(C)
R =
     0.3162   −0.3162
     0.7071    0.7071
     0.6325   −0.6325
EDU» R'*R
ans =
     1.0000   0.0000
     0.0000   1.0000
```

Comment: This is a different orthonormal basis for column space of *A* than we got before.   We verify below that R and Q do have the same column space.

```
EDU» rref(Q')
ans =
     1.0000        0    2.0000
          0   1.0000   −0.0000
EDU» rref(R')
```

ans =
    1.0000   0   2.0000
       0 1.0000 −0.0000

Comment: This verifies that R and Q have the same column space.

EDU» rref(C')

ans =
   1 0 2
   0 1 0

EDU» rref(A')

ans =
   1 0 2
   0 1 0
   0 0 0

Comment: Verifying that C and A also have the same column space as R and Q.

Example 3.33 *Find an orthonormal basis for the null space of*

$$A = \begin{bmatrix} 3 & -4 & 5 & 10 \end{bmatrix}.$$

EDU» A=[3 -4 5 10]

A =
   3 −4 5 10

EDU» N=null(A)

N =
  −0.9695   0   0
  −0.0825   0.4211   0.8422
   0.1031   0.8674 −0.2653
   0.2063 −0.2653   0.4695

Comment: We check that the columns of N are orthonormal by computing

EDU» N'*N

ans =
   1.0000 −0.0000 −0.0000
  −0.0000   1.0000   0.0000
  −0.0000   0.0000   1.0000

Comment: We check that the columns of N are in the null space of A.

EDU» A*N

ans =

1.0e-014 *
   0.1332 −0.0666 −0.1332

Comment: Zero to within 14-place accuracy.

3.3.3   Matlab Exercises

The first exercise is a worksheet. Go to your computer or computer lab and call up the Matlab program.   Enter the following commands and observe the output.

Worksheet

EDU» b=[1 3 1 3 1;2 2 2 2 2]
EDU» a=b'
EDU» q=orth(a)
EDU» q'*q
EDU» rref(b)
EDU» rref(q')
EDU» n=null(b)
EDU» n'*n
EDU» b*n

In the following problems, use Matlab to find an orthonormal basis for the space spanned by the given vectors.

1. $(1, 2, 5, 4) , (3, 2, 1, 1) , (1, 2, 0, 1)$

2. $(1, 3, 3) , (2, 1, -2) , (-1, 2, 5)$

3. $(2, 1, 3, 0) , (1, 4, -2, 6)$

4. $(1, 1, 0, 1, 2) , (3, 1, 0, 1, 2) , (1, 1, -2, 4, 0)$

5. $\left(\frac{1}{2}, \frac{2}{3}, \frac{1}{5}\right) , \left(\frac{1}{4}, 0, \frac{1}{2}\right)$

In problems 6-10, use Matlab to find an orthonormal basis for the null space of the given matrix.

6. $\begin{bmatrix} 5 & 2 & 13 & 9 \end{bmatrix}$

7. $\begin{bmatrix} 3 & -2 & 5 & 2 \end{bmatrix}$

8. $\begin{bmatrix} 1 & 4 & 2 & 0 & -3 \\ 2 & 0 & 1 & -3 & 4 \end{bmatrix}$

9. $\begin{bmatrix} 1 & 1 & 1 & 1 & 1 \end{bmatrix}$

10. $\begin{bmatrix} 0 & 1 & 0 & 2 \end{bmatrix}$

3.4 Orthogonal Diagonalization

An $n \times n$ matrix P is called **orthogonal** if $P'P = I$. This is equivalent to requiring the columns of P to be an orthonormal basis of R^n. Perhaps it would have been more logical to call such a matrix an orthonormal matrix, but this is not the way the terminology has developed. Thus be careful. For a matrix to be orthogonal, it is not enough that its columns be orthogonal, they must also be of length 1, in other words orthonormal.

Fact   *The following are equivalent:*

1. *P is an orthognonal matrix.*

2. *$P'P = I$.*

3. *The columns of P are an orthonormal basis of R^n.*

4. *$PP' = I$.*

5. *The rows of P are an orthonormal basis of R^n.*

6. *$P^{-1} = P'$*

A matrix A is said to be **orthogonally diagonalizable** if there exists an orthogonal matrix P such that $P^{-1}AP = D$, with D a diagonal matrix.
A matrix A is called **symmetric** if $A' = A$.

Fact   *All the eigenvalues of a real symmetric matrx are real numbers.*

Fact   *A real matrix A is orthogonally diagonalizable if and only if A is symmetric.*

Thus we can easily tell just by looking at a matrix whether or not it is orthogonally diagonalizable.

Example 3.34 *Which of the following matrices is orthogonally diagonalizable?*

$$\begin{bmatrix} 1 & 2 & 4 \\ 2 & 3 & 6 \\ 4 & 6 & -5 \end{bmatrix} \qquad \begin{bmatrix} 1 & -1 & 1 \\ -4 & 7 & -2 \\ -6 & 9 & -2 \end{bmatrix}$$

The first one is orthogonally diagonalizable because it is symmetric. The second is not orthogonally diagonalizable because it is not symmetric.

Remark   *Although it is not obvious just by inspection, the second matrix above is diagonalizable but not orthogonally diagonalizable.*

To find the orthogonal matrix that diagonalizes A, we need to find an orthonormal basis of R^n consisting entirely of eigenvectors of A. If A is symmetric, we can always do this in the following way: Choose an orthonormal basis of each eigenspace and use these as the columns of P. This will be an orthogonal matrix that diagonalizes A.

Fact *For a symmetric matrix A, eigenvectors belonging to different eigenvalues are orthogonal.*

Because of this fact, if there are no repeated roots, we only have to divide each eigenvector by its length before using it as a column of P. Only in the case of repeated roots do we have to use what we learned in the preceding section to choose an orthonormal basis for the eigenspace.

Example 3.35 *Find an orthogonal matrix that diagonalizes the matrix*

$$A = \begin{bmatrix} 4 & 1 \\ 1 & 4 \end{bmatrix}.$$

We start by finding the eigenvalues. Using the ideas in Example 3.7, you may be able to see at once that 3 and 5 are the eigenvalues of this matrix. In the 2×2 case however, it is also easy to compute the charateristic polynomial and find the eigenvalues that way.

$$\begin{aligned} |A - kI| &= \begin{vmatrix} 4 - k & 1 \\ 1 & 4 - k \end{vmatrix} \\ &= (4 - k)^2 - 1 \\ &= k^2 - 8k + 15 \\ &= (k - 3)(k - 5). \end{aligned}$$

We now find a basis for each eigenspace. For $k = 3$, we seek a basis of the null space of

$$(A - 3I) = \begin{bmatrix} 1 & 1 \\ 1 & 1 \end{bmatrix}.$$

We have

$$\text{RREF}\,(A - 3I) = \begin{bmatrix} 1 & 1 \\ 0 & 0 \end{bmatrix},$$

and this is also the Hermite form H; thus

$$H - I = \begin{bmatrix} 0 & 1 \\ 0 & -1 \end{bmatrix},$$

so a basis of the null space is $(1, -1)$. *For the eigenvector* $k = 5$, *we have*

$$(A - 5I) = \begin{bmatrix} -1 & 1 \\ 1 & -1 \end{bmatrix}.$$

Now

$$\text{RREF}\,(A - 5I) = \begin{bmatrix} 1 & -1 \\ 0 & 0 \end{bmatrix} = H;$$

thus

$$H - I = \begin{bmatrix} 0 & -1 \\ 0 & -1 \end{bmatrix},$$

whence $(-1, -1)$, *is a basis for this null space, but we can use* $(1, 1)$ *if we choose. Note that the basis vectors for the two eigenspaces are orthogonal,* $(1, -1) \cdot (1, 1) = 0$. *Now for the matrix* P *to be orthogonal, its columns must be* **orthonormal,** *which means not only orthogonal to each other, but of length 1. Thus we devide each basis vector by its length. In this case they are both of length* $\sqrt{2}$. *The vectors* $\left(\frac{1}{\sqrt{2}}, \frac{-1}{\sqrt{2}}\right)$ *and* $\left(\frac{1}{\sqrt{2}}, \frac{1}{\sqrt{2}}\right)$ *become the columns of* P. *For*

$$P = \begin{bmatrix} \frac{1}{\sqrt{2}} & \frac{1}{\sqrt{2}} \\ \frac{-1}{\sqrt{2}} & \frac{1}{\sqrt{2}} \end{bmatrix}$$

we have

$$P'AP = \begin{bmatrix} 3 & 0 \\ 0 & 5 \end{bmatrix}$$

and

$$P'P = I.$$

Example 3.36 *Find an orthogonal matrix* P *such that* $P^{-1}AP$ *is diagonal if*

$$A = \begin{bmatrix} 3 & -2 & -4 \\ -2 & -2 & -6 \\ -4 & -6 & -1 \end{bmatrix}.$$

The eigenvalues of this matrix aren't easy to find by hand, but if you expand the determinant $|A - kI|$ *correctly, you will find that* $|A - kI| = -k^3 + 63k - 162$. *Testing possible rational roots (divisors of 162), one discovers that* $k = 3$ *is a root. Dividing by* $(k - 3)$, *one is left with a quadratic and finds that the other two roots are −9 and 6.   Thus the eigenvalues of A are −9, 3, 6.   We find an eigenvector for each eigenvalue.*

$$A + 9I = \begin{bmatrix} 12 & -2 & -4 \\ -2 & 7 & -6 \\ -4 & -6 & 8 \end{bmatrix}.$$

$$\text{RREF}(A + 9I) = \begin{bmatrix} 1 & 0 & -\frac{1}{2} \\ 0 & 1 & -1 \\ 0 & 0 & 0 \end{bmatrix}.$$

This is also the Hermite form, and we see that a basis for the null space is $\left(-\frac{1}{2}, -1, -1\right)$, *or we may use* $(1, 2, 2)$.

$$A - 3I = \begin{bmatrix} 0 & -2 & -4 \\ -2 & -5 & -6 \\ -4 & -6 & -4 \end{bmatrix}$$

$$\text{RREF}\,(A - 3I) = \begin{bmatrix} 1 & 0 & -2 \\ 0 & 1 & 2 \\ 0 & 0 & 0 \end{bmatrix},$$

so a basis for the null space is $(-2, 2, -1)$.   *Last we consider*

$$A - 6I = \begin{bmatrix} -3 & -2 & -4 \\ -2 & -8 & -6 \\ -4 & -6 & -7 \end{bmatrix}$$

$$\text{RREF}\,(A - 6I) = \begin{bmatrix} 1 & 0 & 1 \\ 0 & 1 & \frac{1}{2} \\ 0 & 0 & 0 \end{bmatrix},$$

so a basis for the null space is $\left(1, \frac{1}{2}, -1\right)$ *or if we prefer,* $(2, 1, -2)$.   *Now we have three eigenvectors,*

$$(1, 2, 2),\ \ (-2, 2, -1),\ \text{and}\ (2, 1, -2).$$

You can check that they are orthogonal.   Note also that each has length $\sqrt{9}$, *or 3.   Dividing each vector by its length and using them as the columns of a matrix P, we get*

$$P = \begin{bmatrix} \frac{1}{3} & -\frac{2}{3} & \frac{2}{3} \\ \frac{2}{3} & \frac{2}{3} & \frac{1}{3} \\ \frac{2}{3} & -\frac{1}{3} & -\frac{2}{3} \end{bmatrix}.$$

You can check that

$$AP = PD,$$

where

$$D = \begin{bmatrix} -9 & 0 & 0 \\ 0 & 3 & 0 \\ 0 & 0 & 6 \end{bmatrix}.$$

Example 3.37 *Find an orthogonal P such that $P'AP$ is diagonal for*

$$A = \begin{bmatrix} 3 & 1 & 1 \\ 1 & 3 & 1 \\ 1 & 1 & 3 \end{bmatrix}.$$

The eigenvalues of this matrix are 2, 2, and 5. We look for eigenvectors.

$$A - 2I = \begin{bmatrix} 1 & 1 & 1 \\ 1 & 1 & 1 \\ 1 & 1 & 1 \end{bmatrix}.$$

We need an orthogonal basis of the two-dimensional null space of this matrix.

$$\text{RREF}\,(A - 2I) = \begin{bmatrix} 1 & 1 & 1 \\ 0 & 0 & 0 \\ 0 & 0 & 0 \end{bmatrix},$$

so a basis for the null space is $(1, -1, 0)$ and $(1, 0, -1)$. These vectors are not orthogonal; however, using the Gram-Schmidt process, we let

$$v_1 = (1, -1, 0)$$

and

$$
\begin{aligned}
v_2 &= (1, 0, -1) - \left(\frac{(1, 0, -1) \cdot (1, -1, 0)}{(1, -1, 0) \cdot (1, -1, 0)} \right)(1, -1, 0) \\
&= (1, 0, -1) - \frac{1}{2}(1, -1, 0) \\
&= \left(\frac{1}{2}, \frac{1}{2}, -1 \right),
\end{aligned}
$$

so we choose

$$v_2 = (1, 1, -2).$$

Thus an orthogonormal basis of the eigenspace for $k = 2$ is

$$\left(\frac{1}{\sqrt{2}}, -\frac{1}{\sqrt{2}}, 0\right) \quad and \quad \left(\frac{1}{\sqrt{6}}, \frac{1}{\sqrt{6}}, -\frac{2}{\sqrt{6}}\right).$$

It is easy to check that $(1, 1, 1)$ is an eigenvector for $k = 5$. Dividing by its length, we get

$$\left(\frac{1}{\sqrt{3}}, \frac{1}{\sqrt{3}}, \frac{1}{\sqrt{3}}\right).$$

Using these three vectors as the columns of a matrix P, we get

$$P = \begin{bmatrix} \frac{1}{\sqrt{2}} & \frac{1}{\sqrt{6}} & \frac{1}{\sqrt{3}} \\ -\frac{1}{\sqrt{2}} & \frac{1}{\sqrt{6}} & \frac{1}{\sqrt{3}} \\ 0 & -\frac{2}{\sqrt{6}} & \frac{1}{\sqrt{3}} \end{bmatrix}.$$

This matrix will satisfy

$$P'AP = \begin{bmatrix} 2 & 0 & 0 \\ 0 & 2 & 0 \\ 0 & 0 & 5 \end{bmatrix}.$$

3.4.1   Exercises

For each of the following symmetric matrices, find the eigenvalues and find an orthogonal matrix P that diagonalizes the given matrix.

1. $\begin{bmatrix} 2 & -2 \\ -2 & 5 \end{bmatrix}$ 2. $\begin{bmatrix} 3 & 2 \\ 2 & 3 \end{bmatrix}$ 3. $\begin{bmatrix} 3 & 2 & 2 \\ 2 & 1 & 0 \\ 2 & 0 & 1 \end{bmatrix}$

4. $\begin{bmatrix} 6 & 2 & 2 \\ 2 & 6 & 2 \\ 2 & 2 & 6 \end{bmatrix}$ 5. $\begin{bmatrix} 2 & 2 & 1 \\ 2 & -1 & -2 \\ 1 & -2 & 2 \end{bmatrix}$ 6. $\begin{bmatrix} 5 & -2 & 2 \\ -2 & 2 & 4 \\ 2 & 4 & 2 \end{bmatrix}$

7. $\begin{bmatrix} -1 & 0 & 0 \\ 0 & 1 & 1 \\ 0 & 1 & 1 \end{bmatrix}$ 8. $\begin{bmatrix} 3 & 0 & 0 \\ 0 & 2 & 2 \\ 0 & 2 & 2 \end{bmatrix}$ 9. $\begin{bmatrix} 8 & -1 & 1 \\ -1 & 8 & 1 \\ 1 & 1 & 8 \end{bmatrix}$

10. $\begin{bmatrix} 5 & 1 & 1 & 1 \\ 1 & 5 & 1 & 1 \\ 1 & 1 & 5 & 1 \\ 1 & 1 & 1 & 5 \end{bmatrix}$ 11. $\begin{bmatrix} 2 & 1 & 0 & 0 \\ 1 & 2 & 0 & 0 \\ 0 & 0 & 4 & 3 \\ 0 & 0 & 3 & 4 \end{bmatrix}$ 12. $\begin{bmatrix} 5 & 2 & 2 \\ 2 & -1 & 4 \\ 2 & 4 & -1 \end{bmatrix}$

3.4.2 Matlab

When the matrix A is symmetric, we know that A is orthogonally diagonalizable. The matlab command

$$[P,D]=eig(A)$$

returns an orthogonal matrix P and a diagonal matrix D satisfying $P'AP = D$.

Example 3.38 *Here is Matlab input and output using the same matrix we calculated manually in our first example above.*

```
EDU» A=[3 -2 -4;-2 -2 -6;-4 -6 -1]
A =
        3   -2   -4
       -2   -2   -6
       -4   -6   -1
EDU» eig(A)
ans =
        3.0000
        6.0000
       -9.0000
EDU [P,D]=eig(A)
P =
        0.6667      0.6667    -0.3333
       -0.6667      0.3333    -0.6667
        0.3333     -0.6667    -0.6667
D =
        3.0000        0           0
             0      6.0000        0
             0        0       -9.0000
EDU» P'*P
ans =
        1.0000    -0.0000     0.0000
       -0.0000     1.0000    -0.0000
        0.0000    -0.0000     1.0000
EDU» P'*A*P
ans =
        3.0000    -0.0000     0.0000
             0      6.0000     0.0000
        0.0000     0.0000    -9.0000
```

Example 3.39 *Here we repeat the second example we calculated manually above.*

```
EDU» A=[3 1 1;1 3 1;1 1 3]
A =
      3   1   1
      1   3   1
      1   1   3
EDU» eig(A)
ans =
      2.0000
      2.0000
      5.0000
EDU [P,D]=eig(A)
P =
     −0.8164   −0.0137   0.5774
      0.3963    0.7139   0.5774
      0.4201   −0.7001   0.5774
D =
      2.0000        0        0
           0   2.0000        0
           0        0   5.0000
EDU» P'*P
ans =
      1.0000    0.0000   −0.0000
      0.0000    1.0000   −0.0000
     −0.0000   −0.0000    1.0000
```

3.4.3   Matlab Exercises

Worksheet

```
EDU» a=[5 2 2 2;2 5 2 2;2 2 5 2;2 2 2 5]
EDU» p=poly(a)
EDU» r=roots(p)
EDU» e=eig(a)
EDU [p,d]=eig(a)
EDU» a*p-p*d
EDU» det(p)
EDU» p'*p
EDU» p'*a*p
EDU» quit
```

For each of the given matrices, use Matlab to find the eigenvalues and to find an orthogonal matrix P such that P′AP is diagonal. Then use Matlab to check that P is orthogonal and that $P'AP$ is diagonal.

1. $\begin{bmatrix} 3 & 2 & 0 \\ 2 & 4 & 2 \\ 0 & 2 & 5 \end{bmatrix}$ 2. $\begin{bmatrix} 11 & -8 & 4 \\ -8 & -1 & -2 \\ 4 & -2 & -4 \end{bmatrix}$ 3. $\begin{bmatrix} 2 & 2 & -2 \\ 2 & -1 & 4 \\ -2 & 4 & -1 \end{bmatrix}$

4. $\begin{bmatrix} 4 & 1 \\ 1 & 2 \end{bmatrix}$ 5. $\begin{bmatrix} 2 & 4 \\ 4 & 3 \end{bmatrix}$ 6. $\begin{bmatrix} 0 & 2 & -1 \\ 2 & 3 & -2 \\ -1 & -2 & 0 \end{bmatrix}$

7. $\begin{bmatrix} 4 & -2 & 0 \\ -2 & 3 & 2 \\ 0 & 2 & 2 \end{bmatrix}$ 8. $\begin{bmatrix} 0 & -1 & -2 \\ -1 & \frac{4}{3} & 1 \\ -2 & 1 & \frac{15}{4} \end{bmatrix}$ 9. $\begin{bmatrix} 1 & 2 & 3 \\ 2 & 0 & 4 \\ 3 & 4 & 7 \end{bmatrix}$

10. $\begin{bmatrix} 2 & 2 & 1 & 0 \\ 2 & -1 & -2 & 0 \\ 1 & -2 & 2 & 0 \\ 0 & 0 & 0 & 3 \end{bmatrix}$ 11. $\begin{bmatrix} 7 & 3 & 3 & 3 \\ 3 & 7 & 3 & 3 \\ 3 & 3 & 7 & 3 \\ 3 & 3 & 3 & 7 \end{bmatrix}$

Chapter 4

Applications

4.1 Differential Equations

Problem *Hyenas and lions are coexisting in an enclosed space. Suppose that $x(t)$ equals the number of hyenas t years from now and that $y(t)$ equals the number of lions t years from now. Also, we are told that the functions $x(t)$, $y(t)$, and their derivatives $\dfrac{dx}{dt}$ and $\dfrac{dy}{dt}$ satisfy the equations*

$$
\begin{aligned}
\frac{dx}{dt} &= -4x(t) + 2y(t) \\
\frac{dy}{dt} &= 6x(t) - 3y(t).
\end{aligned}
$$

Solve for $x(t)$ and $y(t)$ and use this information to predict an eventual outcome for the populations of hyenas and lions given the side conditions that at present there are 400 hyenas and 100 lions.

Solution *Put the differential equations in matrix form:*

$$
\left[\begin{array}{c} \dfrac{dx}{dt} \\[2ex] \dfrac{dy}{dt} \end{array} \right]
= \left[\begin{array}{cc} -4 & 2 \\ 6 & -3 \end{array} \right]
\left[\begin{array}{c} x(t) \\ y(t) \end{array} \right].
$$

We use diagonalization of this matrix, if that is possible, to separate the variables. We solve for the eigenvalues and then for the matrix P which diagonalizes this matrix:

$$
\left| \begin{array}{cc} -4 - k & 2 \\ 6 & -3 - k \end{array} \right| = k^2 + 7k,
$$

129

so the eigenvalues are 0 and −7. The vectors $\begin{bmatrix} 1 \\ 2 \end{bmatrix}$ *and* $\begin{bmatrix} -2 \\ 3 \end{bmatrix}$ *are eigen-*
vectors for 0 and −7 respectively, so

$$P = \begin{bmatrix} 1 & -2 \\ 2 & 3 \end{bmatrix}$$

diagonalizes this matrix.   We then do the change of variable

$$\begin{bmatrix} x \\ y \end{bmatrix} = \begin{bmatrix} 1 & -2 \\ 2 & 3 \end{bmatrix} \begin{bmatrix} w \\ z \end{bmatrix},$$

whence

$$\begin{bmatrix} \dfrac{dx}{dt} \\ \dfrac{dy}{dt} \end{bmatrix} = \begin{bmatrix} 1 & -2 \\ 2 & 3 \end{bmatrix} \begin{bmatrix} \dfrac{dw}{dt} \\ \dfrac{dz}{dt} \end{bmatrix}$$

and substituting this in our original equation, we obtain

$$\begin{bmatrix} \dfrac{dw}{dt} \\ \dfrac{dz}{dt} \end{bmatrix} = \begin{bmatrix} 0 & 0 \\ 0 & -7 \end{bmatrix} \begin{bmatrix} w \\ z \end{bmatrix}.$$

The equations

$$\begin{aligned} \frac{dw}{dt} &= 0 \\ \frac{dz}{dt} &= -7z \end{aligned}$$

have separate variables for the new variables w and z.   From calculus these
have the general solutions

$$\begin{aligned} w &= c_1 \\ z &= c_2 e^{-7t}, \end{aligned}$$

where c_1 and c_2 are constants of integration.   This allows us to solve for x
and y:

$$\begin{bmatrix} x \\ y \end{bmatrix} = \begin{bmatrix} 1 & -2 \\ 2 & 3 \end{bmatrix} \begin{bmatrix} w \\ z \end{bmatrix} = \begin{bmatrix} 1 & -2 \\ 2 & 3 \end{bmatrix} \begin{bmatrix} c_1 \\ c_2 e^{-7t} \end{bmatrix}.$$

Thus by matrix multiplication we see that the following two functions are a solution to the original system of differential equations

$$\begin{aligned} x\,(t) &= c_1 - 2c_2 e^{-7t} \\ y\,(t) &= 2c_1 + 3c_2 e^{-7t}. \end{aligned}$$

To check our solution, we differentiate our solution functions to get

$$\begin{aligned} \frac{dx}{dt} &= 14c_2 e^{-7t} \\ \frac{dy}{dt} &= -21c_2 e^{-7t}. \end{aligned}$$

We now verify that the original equations are satisfied.

$$\begin{aligned} -4x + 2y &= -4(c_1 - 2c_2 e^{-7t}) + 2(2c_1 + 3c_2 e^{-7t}) \\ &= 8c_2 e^{-7t} + 6c_2 e^{-7t} \\ &= 14c_2 e^{-7t} = \frac{dx}{dt} \end{aligned}$$

and

$$\begin{aligned} 6x - 3y &= 6(c_1 - 2c_2 e^{-7t}) - 3(2c_1 + 3c_2 e^{-7t}) \\ &= -12c_2 e^{-7t} - 9c_2 e^{-7t} \\ &= -21c_2 e^{-7t} = \frac{dy}{dt}. \end{aligned}$$

The calculations above check that we have found solutions to the original differential equations.   By use of the initial conditions, $x\,(0) = 400$, and $y\,(0) = 100$, we can compute c_1 and c_2. Substitiuting $t = 0$ into the solutions we have

$$\begin{aligned} 400 &= x\,(0) = c_1 - 2c_2 \\ 100 &= y\,(0) = 2c_1 + 3c_2. \end{aligned}$$

This system of equations has solutions $c_1 = 200$, $c_2 = -100$.   Then

$$\begin{aligned} x &= 200 + 200e^{-7t} \\ y &= 400 - 300e^{-7t} \end{aligned}$$

tells the whole story.   As t is positive, we see that x gets smaller as t increases.   When $t \to \infty$, $x \to 200$.   The hyena population is decreasing gradually from 400 this year to 200 eventually.   The lion population, on the other hand, is increasing from 100 this year to 400 eventually as $t \to \infty$. This tells us that under these conditions both species will survive.

In general, if we have a system of linear first-order differential equations of the form

$$
\begin{bmatrix} x_1'(t) \\ x_2'(t) \\ \vdots \\ x_n'(t) \end{bmatrix} = A \begin{bmatrix} x_1(t) \\ x_2(t) \\ \vdots \\ x_n(t) \end{bmatrix}
$$

and if we can diagonalize the coefficient matrix A, say $P^{-1}AP = D$, then the solution is given by

$$
\begin{bmatrix} x_1(t) \\ x_2(t) \\ \vdots \\ x_n(t) \end{bmatrix} = P \begin{bmatrix} c_1 e^{k_1 t} \\ c_2 e^{k_2 t} \\ \vdots \\ c_n e^{k_n t} \end{bmatrix},
$$

where $c_1, c_2, \ldots, c_n$ are any constants and $k_1, k_2, \ldots, k_n$ are the eigenvalues of A.

We have just seen how one can solve a system of linear first-order differential equations by diagonalizing the coefficient matrix and making a clever substitution.

Remark   *An orthonormal P is not needed for this application! All you need to do is diagonalize as in Section 3.2.*

Example 4.1 *Solve the following system of differential equations:*

$$
\begin{bmatrix} x'(t) \\ y'(t) \\ z'(t) \end{bmatrix} = \begin{bmatrix} 3 & 2 & 0 \\ 2 & 4 & 2 \\ 0 & 2 & 5 \end{bmatrix} \begin{bmatrix} x(t) \\ y(t) \\ z(t) \end{bmatrix}.
$$

Using the techniques of Section 3.2, we find that the eigenvalues of the coefficient matrix are $1, 4$, and 7, and that a matrix which diagonalizes it is

$$
P = \begin{bmatrix} 2 & -2 & 1 \\ -2 & -1 & 2 \\ 1 & 2 & 2 \end{bmatrix}.
$$

You can check that

$$
\begin{bmatrix} 2 & -2 & 1 \\ -2 & -1 & 2 \\ 1 & 2 & 2 \end{bmatrix}^{-1} \begin{bmatrix} 3 & 2 & 0 \\ 2 & 4 & 2 \\ 0 & 2 & 5 \end{bmatrix} \begin{bmatrix} 2 & -2 & 1 \\ -2 & -1 & 2 \\ 1 & 2 & 2 \end{bmatrix} = \begin{bmatrix} 1 & 0 & 0 \\ 0 & 4 & 0 \\ 0 & 0 & 7 \end{bmatrix}.
$$

With this information we can write down the complete solution to the system of differential equations as

$$
\begin{bmatrix} x(t) \\ y(t) \\ z(t) \end{bmatrix} = \begin{bmatrix} 2 & -2 & 1 \\ -2 & -1 & 2 \\ 1 & 2 & 2 \end{bmatrix} \begin{bmatrix} c_1 e^t \\ c_2 e^{4t} \\ c_3 e^{7t} \end{bmatrix}
$$

or

$$
\begin{array}{rcrcrcr}
x(t) & = & 2c_1 e^t & - & 2c_2 e^{4t} & + & c_3 e^{7t} \\
y(t) & = & -2c_1 e^t & - & c_2 e^{4t} & + & 2c_3 e^{7t} \\
z(t) & = & c_1 e^t & + & 2c_2 e^{4t} & + & 2c_3 e^{7t}.
\end{array}
$$

If initial conditions were given, we could determine the constants by plugging in $t = 0$ and solving for $c_1, c_2,$ and c_3. For example, suppose we are told that $x(0) = 400$, $y(0) = 800$, and $z(0) = 300$. Then we would have the system

$$
\begin{array}{rcrcrcr}
400 & = & 2c_1 & - & 2c_2 & + & c_3 \\
800 & = & -2c_1 & - & c_2 & + & 2c_3 \\
300 & = & c_1 & + & 2c_2 & + & 2c_3
\end{array}
$$

or

$$
\begin{bmatrix} 2 & -2 & 1 \\ -2 & -1 & 2 \\ 1 & 2 & 2 \end{bmatrix} \begin{bmatrix} c_1 \\ c_2 \\ c_3 \end{bmatrix} = \begin{bmatrix} 400 \\ 800 \\ 300 \end{bmatrix}.
$$

The coefficient matrix here is P, so we already know that it is invertible; hence a unique solution for the constants exists:

$$
\begin{bmatrix} c_1 \\ c_2 \\ c_3 \end{bmatrix} = \begin{bmatrix} 2 & -2 & 1 \\ -2 & -1 & 2 \\ 1 & 2 & 2 \end{bmatrix}^{-1} \begin{bmatrix} 400 \\ 800 \\ 300 \end{bmatrix}
$$

Using Matlab to do the computation, we get

$$
\begin{bmatrix} c_1 \\ c_2 \\ c_3 \end{bmatrix} \cong \begin{bmatrix} -55.5556 \\ -111.1111 \\ 288.8889 \end{bmatrix}.
$$

Another kind of differential equation that we can solve is one with higher-order deriviatives but where the coefficients are all constant. We can solve this by substitutions that change it into a system of the kind we just did.

Example 4.2 *Solve the differential equation*

$$\frac{d^3x}{dt^3} - 7\frac{d^2x}{dt^2} + 14\frac{dx}{dt} - 8x = 0.$$

Make the following substitutions:

$$y = \frac{dx}{dt}$$

$$z = \frac{dy}{dt} = \frac{d^2x}{dt^2}.$$

Then using the original differential equation, we have

$$\frac{dz}{dt} = \frac{d^3x}{dt^3} = 7\frac{d^2x}{dt^2} - 14\frac{dx}{dt} + 8x.$$

Now we have the following system of differential equations with the three variables x, y, z:

$$\frac{dx}{dt} = y$$

$$\frac{dy}{dt} = z$$

$$\frac{dz}{dt} = 8x - 14y + 7z.$$

In matrix form this becomes

$$\begin{bmatrix} \dfrac{dx}{dt} \\ \dfrac{dy}{dt} \\ \dfrac{dz}{dt} \end{bmatrix} = \begin{bmatrix} 0 & 1 & 0 \\ 0 & 0 & 1 \\ 8 & -14 & 7 \end{bmatrix} \begin{bmatrix} x \\ y \\ z \end{bmatrix}.$$

The characteristic equation of this matrix is

$$\begin{vmatrix} -k & 1 & 0 \\ 0 & -k & 1 \\ 8 & -14 & 7-k \end{vmatrix} = -k^3 + 7k^2 - 14k + 8.$$

Since $k = 1$ *is a root of the characteristic equation, we can factor out* $k - 1$, *obtaining*

$$-k^3 + 7k^2 - 14k + 8 = -(k-1)\left(k^2 - 6k + 8\right).$$

Then we solve the quadratic equation $(k^2 - 6k + 8) = 0$ *to obtain the other two roots, 2 and 4. The eigenvalues of the matrix are 1, 2, and 4. By finding an eigenvector for each of these eigenvalues and putting them as columns of a matrix, we obtain the matrix P, which diagonalizes the coefficient matrix of our system. One such matrix P that will work is*

$$P = \begin{bmatrix} 1 & 1 & 1 \\ 1 & 2 & 4 \\ 1 & 4 & 16 \end{bmatrix}.$$

You can check that

$$\begin{bmatrix} 1 & 1 & 1 \\ 1 & 2 & 4 \\ 1 & 4 & 16 \end{bmatrix}^{-1} \begin{bmatrix} 0 & 1 & 0 \\ 0 & 0 & 1 \\ 8 & -14 & 7 \end{bmatrix} \begin{bmatrix} 1 & 1 & 1 \\ 1 & 2 & 4 \\ 1 & 4 & 16 \end{bmatrix} = \begin{bmatrix} 1 & 0 & 0 \\ 0 & 2 & 0 \\ 0 & 0 & 4 \end{bmatrix}.$$

Once we have the matrix eigenvalues and the matrix P, we can immediately write down the complete solution,

$$\begin{bmatrix} x \\ y \\ z \end{bmatrix} = \begin{bmatrix} 1 & 1 & 1 \\ 1 & 2 & 4 \\ 1 & 4 & 16 \end{bmatrix} \begin{bmatrix} c_1 e^t \\ c_2 e^{2t} \\ c_3 e^{4t} \end{bmatrix},$$

so that

$$x = c_1 e^t + c_2 e^{2t} + c_3 e^{4t}$$

is the general solution to the original differential equation.

Remark *This is not the quickest way to obtain a solution to this problem. If your intuition tells you that* $x = e^{kt}$ *ought to be a solution, substituting this into the differential equation gives*

$$k^3 e^{kt} - 7k^2 e^{kt} + 14k e^{kt} - 8 e^{kt} = 0$$
$$(k^3 - 7k^2 + 14k - 8) e^{kt} = 0,$$

which will be satisfied if k is a root of $(k^3 - 7k^2 + 14k - 8)$, *in other words, if k is 1, 2, or 4. Thus we see that* $x = e^t, x = e^{2t}$, *and* $x = e^{4t}$ *are all solutions to the given differential equation. Therefore, any linear combination of these functions will also be a solution, giving again the solution we arrived at before. There is often more than one way to solve a mathematics problem. The second method, however, depends on making a good guess and does not guarantee that you have found all solutions.*

4.1.1   Matlab

You can use the Matlab eig(A) and null(A-k*eye(n),'r') commands to diagonalize the coefficient matrix, as we did in Section 3.2. It is preferable not to use the [P,D]=eig(A) command when all the eigenvalues are rational, since the P produced by this command is normalized and thus often involves decimal approximations of irrational numbers. You can also use Matlab to solve for the constants if initial conditions are given. We demonstrate with an example.

Example 4.3 *Solve the system*

$$\begin{array}{rclcrcl} x'(t) & = & 7x(t) & & & - & 8z(t) \\ y'(t) & = & 8x(t) & - & y(t) & - & 8z(t) \\ z'(t) & = & 4x(t) & & & - & 5z(t) \end{array}$$

or, equivalently,

$$\begin{bmatrix} x'(t) \\ y'(t) \\ z'(t) \end{bmatrix} = \begin{bmatrix} 7 & 0 & -8 \\ 8 & -1 & -8 \\ 4 & 0 & -5 \end{bmatrix} \begin{bmatrix} x(t) \\ y(t) \\ z(t) \end{bmatrix}.$$

We use Matlab to find the eigenvalues and a diagonalizing matrix P.

```
EDU» A=[7 0 -8;8 -1 -8;4 0 -5]
A =
     7    0   -8
     8   -1   -8
     4    0   -5
EDU» eig(A)
ans =
    -1
     3
    -1
EDU» I=eye(3)
I =
     1   0   0
     0   1   0
     0   0   1
EDU» N1=null(A+I,'r')
N1 =
     0   1
     1   0
     0   1
EDU» N2=null(A-3*I,'r')
```

N2 =
        2
        2
        1
EDU» P=[N1 N2]
P =
        0   1   2
        1   0   2
        0   1   1
EDU» inv(P)*A*P
ans =
       −1   0   0
        0   −1   0
        0   0   3

Comment: We can now write the general solution as

$$
\begin{bmatrix} x(t) \\ y(t) \\ z(t) \end{bmatrix} = \begin{bmatrix} 0 & 1 & 2 \\ 1 & 0 & 2 \\ 0 & 1 & 1 \end{bmatrix} \begin{bmatrix} c_1 e^{-t} \\ c_2 e^{-t} \\ c_3 e^{3t} \end{bmatrix}.
$$

If we are given initial conditions, say $x(0) = 5$, $y(0) = 20$, $z(0) = 0$, then putting $t = 0$ in the equation above gives

$$
\begin{bmatrix} 5 \\ 20 \\ 0 \end{bmatrix} = \begin{bmatrix} 0 & 1 & 2 \\ 1 & 0 & 2 \\ 0 & 1 & 1 \end{bmatrix} \begin{bmatrix} c_1 \\ c_2 \\ c_3 \end{bmatrix}.
$$

In general, we can solve for the constants by taking P^{-1} times the column of initial conditions. We use Matlab to do this.

EDU» ini=[5;20;0]
ini =
        5
       20
        0
EDU» C=inv(P)*ini
C =
       10
       −5
        5

Substituting this in the solution above, we get

$$
\begin{bmatrix} x(t) \\ y(t) \\ z(t) \end{bmatrix} = \begin{bmatrix} 0 & 1 & 2 \\ 1 & 0 & 2 \\ 0 & 1 & 1 \end{bmatrix} \begin{bmatrix} 10e^{-t} \\ -5e^{-t} \\ 5e^{3t} \end{bmatrix}.
$$

We can leave the solution in this form, or multiply it out, getting

$$
\begin{aligned}
x(t) &= & - 5e^{-t} &+ 10e^{3t} \\
y(t) &= 10e^{-t} & &+ 10e^{3t} \\
z(t) &= & - 5e^{-t} &+ 5e^{3t}.
\end{aligned}
$$

4.1.2   Exercises

Solve the following systems of differential equations.   These problems can be done with or without the help of Matlab.

1.

$$
\begin{aligned}
\frac{dx}{dt} &= 4x - y \\
\frac{dt}{dt} &= -2x + 3y
\end{aligned}
$$

2.

$$
\begin{aligned}
\frac{dx}{dt} &= x - 2y \\
\frac{dy}{dt} &= -x - 2y - z \\
\frac{dz}{dt} &= -2y + z
\end{aligned}
$$

3.

$$
\begin{aligned}
\frac{dx}{dt} &= -3x + 6y \\
\frac{dy}{dt} &= x - 2y
\end{aligned}
$$

with initial conditions $x(0) = 500$, $y(0) = 200$.

4.

$$
\begin{aligned}
\frac{dx}{dt} &= 4x + z \\
\frac{dy}{dt} &= 2x + y \\
\frac{dz}{dt} &= -2x + z
\end{aligned}
$$

with initial conditions $x(0) = -1$, $y(0) = 1$, $z(0) = 0$.

5.

$$\frac{dx}{dt} = 7x + 6y$$

$$\frac{dy}{dt} = 2x + 6y$$

6.

$$\frac{dx}{dt} = 2x + y + 2z$$

$$\frac{dy}{dt} = -x - 2z$$

$$\frac{dz}{dt} = 2x + 2y + 5z$$

7.

$$\frac{dx}{dt} = 5x + 2y + 2z$$

$$\frac{dy}{dt} = 2x - y + 4z$$

$$\frac{dz}{dt} = -2x + 4y - z$$

8.

$$\frac{dx}{dt} = x + y + z$$

$$\frac{dy}{dt} = -4x + 5y + 2z$$

$$\frac{dz}{dt} = 4x + 3z$$

9.

$$\frac{d^3x}{dt^3} - \frac{d^2x}{dt^2} - 4\frac{dx}{dt} + 4x = 0.$$

10.

$$\frac{d^3x}{dt^3} - 2\frac{d^2x}{dt^2} - \frac{dx}{dt} + 2x = 0.$$

11.

$$\frac{d^3x}{dt^3} - 6\frac{d^2x}{dt^2} + 11\frac{dx}{dt} - 6x = 0.$$

4.2   Least Squares Approximation

The system of linear equations $Ax = b$ has a solution if and only if b is in the column space of A. If the system has no solution, we can solve $A'Ax = A'b$ (this is called the **normal equation**, and it can be shown that it always has a solution for any matrix A and any vector b). A solution v to $A'Ax = A'b$ is called a **least squares approximate solution** or just a **least squares solution** to $Ax = b$, and the vector Av is the projection of b on the column space of A (the closest vector to b in the column space of A.) We can use the normal equation to find the least squares fit line to a set of points in a plane. We can also use it to find the projection of a vector on a subspace. Several examples will illustrate these techniques.

Problem   *Find the least squares fit line throught the points*
$(0,5),(1,4),(2,7),(3,9),(4,10)$.

Solution   *Let $c_1 x + c_0 = y$ be the equation of a line.   If this line were to pass through all of the given points, then c_1 and c_0 would have to satisfy the following system of equations:*

$$\begin{array}{rcrcr}
 & & c_0 & = & 5 \\
c_1 & + & c_0 & = & 4 \\
2c_1 & + & c_0 & = & 7 \\
3c_1 & + & c_0 & = & 9 \\
4c_1 & + & c_0 & = & 10.
\end{array}$$

This system of equations has no solution for c_1 and c_0 (the points do not lie on a line).   We set up the system in matrix form:

$$\begin{bmatrix} 0 & 1 \\ 1 & 1 \\ 2 & 1 \\ 3 & 1 \\ 4 & 1 \end{bmatrix} \begin{bmatrix} c_1 \\ c_0 \end{bmatrix} = \begin{bmatrix} 5 \\ 4 \\ 7 \\ 9 \\ 10 \end{bmatrix}.$$

Now we solve the normal equation:

$$\begin{bmatrix} 0 & 1 & 2 & 3 & 4 \\ 1 & 1 & 1 & 1 & 1 \end{bmatrix} \begin{bmatrix} 0 & 1 \\ 1 & 1 \\ 2 & 1 \\ 3 & 1 \\ 4 & 1 \end{bmatrix} \begin{bmatrix} c_1 \\ c_0 \end{bmatrix} = \begin{bmatrix} 0 & 1 & 2 & 3 & 4 \\ 1 & 1 & 1 & 1 & 1 \end{bmatrix} \begin{bmatrix} 5 \\ 4 \\ 7 \\ 9 \\ 10 \end{bmatrix}$$

$$\begin{bmatrix} 30 & 10 \\ 10 & 5 \end{bmatrix} \begin{bmatrix} c_1 \\ c_0 \end{bmatrix} = \begin{bmatrix} 85 \\ 35 \end{bmatrix}.$$

The augmented matrix $\begin{bmatrix} 30 & 10 & 85 \\ 10 & 5 & 35 \end{bmatrix}$ *has reduced row echelon form*

$\begin{bmatrix} 1 & 0 & \frac{3}{2} \\ 0 & 1 & 4 \end{bmatrix}$, *so a solution is $c_1 = 1.5$ and $c_0 = 4$. Thus the least squares fit line is*

$$y = 1.5x + 4.$$

The numbers do not always come out so nicely.

Problem   *Find the least squares fit line through the points $(1,4), (2,0),$ $(3,6), (5,10)$.*

Solution   *We can set up the matrix form of the equation at once. The coefficients c_1 and c_0 of a line through these points would have to satisfy the system*

$$\begin{bmatrix} 1 & 1 \\ 2 & 1 \\ 3 & 1 \\ 5 & 1 \end{bmatrix} \begin{bmatrix} c_1 \\ c_0 \end{bmatrix} = \begin{bmatrix} 4 \\ 0 \\ 6 \\ 10 \end{bmatrix}.$$

The normal equation that we get from this is

$$\begin{bmatrix} 1 & 2 & 3 & 5 \\ 1 & 1 & 1 & 1 \end{bmatrix} \begin{bmatrix} 1 & 1 \\ 2 & 1 \\ 3 & 1 \\ 5 & 1 \end{bmatrix} \begin{bmatrix} c_1 \\ c_0 \end{bmatrix} = \begin{bmatrix} 1 & 2 & 3 & 5 \\ 1 & 1 & 1 & 1 \end{bmatrix} \begin{bmatrix} 4 \\ 0 \\ 6 \\ 10 \end{bmatrix} \quad or$$

$$\begin{bmatrix} 39 & 11 \\ 11 & 4 \end{bmatrix} \begin{bmatrix} c_1 \\ c_0 \end{bmatrix} = \begin{bmatrix} 72 \\ 20 \end{bmatrix}.$$

The augmented matrix $\begin{bmatrix} 39 & 11 & 72 \\ 11 & 4 & 20 \end{bmatrix}$ *has reduced row echelon form*

$\begin{bmatrix} 1 & 0 & \frac{68}{35} \\ 0 & 1 & -\frac{12}{35} \end{bmatrix}$, *so the least squares fit line is*

$$y = \frac{68}{35}x - \frac{12}{35}.$$

Problem   *Find a least squares solution to the system $Ax = b$, where*

$$A = \begin{bmatrix} -1 & 1 \\ 1 & -2 \\ 1 & 1 \end{bmatrix} \text{ and } b = \begin{bmatrix} 2 \\ 7 \\ 8 \end{bmatrix}.$$

Solution   *The system of equations is*

$$\begin{bmatrix} -1 & 1 \\ 1 & -2 \\ 1 & 1 \end{bmatrix} \begin{bmatrix} x_1 \\ x_2 \end{bmatrix} = \begin{bmatrix} 2 \\ 7 \\ 8 \end{bmatrix}.$$

First we check that there is no solution.   (If there are solutions, however, the solutions to the original system and the normal system will be the same.) We form the augmented matrix $\begin{bmatrix} -1 & 1 & 2 \\ 1 & -2 & 7 \\ 1 & 1 & 8 \end{bmatrix}$, *which has reduced row echelon form* $\begin{bmatrix} 1 & 0 & 0 \\ 0 & 1 & 0 \\ 0 & 0 & 1 \end{bmatrix}$, *showing that there are no solutions to the given system.   Now we form the normal equations:*

$$\begin{bmatrix} -1 & 1 & 1 \\ 1 & -2 & 1 \end{bmatrix} \begin{bmatrix} -1 & 1 \\ 1 & -2 \\ 1 & 1 \end{bmatrix} \begin{bmatrix} x_1 \\ x_2 \end{bmatrix} = \begin{bmatrix} -1 & 1 & 1 \\ 1 & -2 & 1 \end{bmatrix} \begin{bmatrix} 2 \\ 7 \\ 8 \end{bmatrix} \quad or$$

$$\begin{bmatrix} 3 & -2 \\ -2 & 6 \end{bmatrix} \begin{bmatrix} x_1 \\ x_2 \end{bmatrix} = \begin{bmatrix} 13 \\ -4 \end{bmatrix}.$$

The augmented matrix of this system is $\begin{bmatrix} 3 & -2 & 13 \\ -2 & 6 & -4 \end{bmatrix}$, *which has reduced row echelon form* $\begin{bmatrix} 1 & 0 & 5 \\ 0 & 1 & 1 \end{bmatrix}$, *so that a least square solution to the system is*

$$v = \begin{bmatrix} 5 \\ 1 \end{bmatrix}.$$

Remark   *From this we can also compute the projection of the vector* $b = \begin{bmatrix} 2 \\ 7 \\ 8 \end{bmatrix}$ *on the column space of A, which is the plane spanned by the two column vectors of A.   The projection of b on this plane is given by Av (A times the least squares solution vector).   Thus we compute that the projection of b on the column space of A is*

$$\begin{bmatrix} -1 & 1 \\ 1 & -2 \\ 1 & 1 \end{bmatrix} \begin{bmatrix} 5 \\ 1 \end{bmatrix} = \begin{bmatrix} -4 \\ 3 \\ 6 \end{bmatrix}.$$

4.2.1 Exercises

In problems 1-6, find the least squares line solution for each set of points.

1. $(0,3),(1,4),(2,7),(3,11),(4,14)$

2. $(-1,8),(0,4),(1,5),(2,11)$

3. $(1,4),(2,7),(3,6),(4,8)$

4. $(0,3),(1,6),(2,5)$

5. $(0,1),(2,0),(3,1),(4,7)$

6. $(-1,8),(0,5),(1,4),(2,3),(3,0)$

7. Find the least squares solution to the system $Ax = b$, where $A = \begin{bmatrix} 1 & 1 \\ 3 & 1 \\ 0 & 2 \\ 1 & 1 \end{bmatrix}$ and $b = \begin{bmatrix} 5 \\ 2 \\ 1 \\ 3 \end{bmatrix}$.

8. Using A and b as in problem 7, find the projection of b on the column space of A.

9. Find the projection of the vector $(5,10,-4)$ on the plane $W = sp\{(3,1,1),(2,-1,4)\}$.

10. Find the projection of the vector $(1,-1,1)$ on the plane $W = sp\{(1,0,-3),(3,5,1)\}$.

4.2.2 Matlab

We can use Matlab to do the computations in these problems just using commands we already know. There are also some special commands in Matlab that will take us directly to the answer. The command

$$\boxed{\text{p=polyfit }(X,Y,n)}$$

will return a row vector p whose components are the coefficients of a polynomial of degree n, which is the least squares fit polynomial to the set of points whose first coordinates come from the vector X and whose second coordinates come from the corresponding components of the vector Y. When n is 1, this command returns the row vector (c_1, c_2), where $y = c_1 x + c_0$ is the least square fit line to the points (x_i, y_i). The vectors X and Y can be entered either as row vectors or as column vectors when using the polyfit command, but they must both be the same, either both entered as rows or both entered as columns.

The left divide command

$$\boxed{\text{x=A\textbackslash b}}$$

will return a least squares solution to $Ax = b$ in the case where no solution exists and the columns of A are linearly independent. This is the same solution we get by solving the normal equation $A'Ax = A'b$.

Example 4.4 *We repeat the first problem worked in the preceding section using the **polyfit** command. Find the least squares fit line through the points* $(0,5), (1,4), (2,7), (3,9), (4,10)$.

```
EDU» X=[0 1 2 3 4]
    X =  0  1  2  3  4
EDU» Y=[5 4 7 9 10]
    Y =  5  4  7  9  10
EDU» p=polyfit(X,Y,1)
    p =  1.5000  4.000
```
Comment: The least squares fit line is

$$y = 1.5x + 4.$$

Example 4.5 *We repeat the third problem worked in the preceding section using the left divide command. Find the least squares solution to* $Ax = b$, *where* $A = \begin{bmatrix} -1 & 1 \\ 1 & -2 \\ 1 & 1 \end{bmatrix}$ *and* $b = \begin{bmatrix} 2 \\ 7 \\ 8 \end{bmatrix}$.

```
EDU» A=[-1 1;1 -2;1 1]
              -1   1
        A =   1  -2
              1   1
EDU» b=[2;7;8]
             2
        b =  7
             8
EDU» v=A\b
```

$$v = \begin{matrix} 5 \\ 1 \end{matrix}$$

EDU» A*v

$$ans = \begin{matrix} -4 \\ 3 \\ 6 \end{matrix} \quad .$$

We see that $Av \neq b$, so v is not a solution of $Ax = b$. Av is the projection of b on column space A, and v is the least square solution of $Ax = b$.

4.2.3 Matlab Exercises

In problems 1-5, find the least squares fit line through the given points.

1. $(-1, 3), (0, 1), (1, 3), (2, 7), (3, 9)$

2. $(0, 1), (1, 2), (2, 4), (3, 3), (4, 5)$

3. $(0, 0), (1, 3), (2, 5), (3, 6), (4, 8)$

4. $(0, 2), (1, 5), (2, 3), (3, 7), (4, 9)$

5. $(-1, 5), (0, 4), (1, 8), (2, 13), (3, 15)$

6. Find a least squares solution of

$$\begin{bmatrix} -1 & 2 \\ 2 & -3 \\ -1 & 3 \end{bmatrix} \begin{bmatrix} x_1 \\ x_2 \end{bmatrix} = \begin{bmatrix} 4 \\ 1 \\ 2 \end{bmatrix} .$$

7. Use the answer to the preceding problem to find the projection of the vector $(4, 1, 2)$ on the plane spanned by the vectors $(-1, 2, -1)$ and $(2, -3, 3)$.

8. Find a least squares solution of

$$\begin{bmatrix} 1 & 3 \\ 2 & 1 \\ 1 & 1 \end{bmatrix} \begin{bmatrix} x_1 \\ x_2 \end{bmatrix} = \begin{bmatrix} 1 \\ -1 \\ 2 \end{bmatrix} .$$

9. Use the answer to the preceding problem to find the projection of the vector $(1, -1, 2)$ on the plane spanned by the vectors $(1, 2, 1)$ and $(3, 1, 1)$.

10. Find the projection of $(3, 5, -2, 4)$ on the subspace $W = sp\{(2, 1, 1, 2), (1, 3, 1, 1)\}$.

4.2.4   Optional Matlab: Vandermonde Matrices and Curve Fitting

If x is a vector in R^n, the Matlab command

$$\boxed{\text{vander}(X)}$$

returns an $n \times n$ Vandermonde matrix. The vector X can be given as a row or column vector. The Vandermonde matrix that Matlab returns has its rightmost column all 1's. The next column to the left has as entries the components of X. Next left is a column whose entries are the squares of the components of X. The next column has as entries the cubes of the components of X, and so on, until the matrix is square, thus ending with the $(n-1)$st powers of the components of X.

Example 4.6 *Here we find the Vandermonde matrix for* $X = (1, 2, 3, 4)$.

```
EDU» X=[1 2 3 4]
X =
     1   2   3   4
EDU» V=vander(X)
V =
      1    1   1   1
      8    4   2   1
     27    9   3   1
     64   16   4   1
EDU» det(V)
ans =
     12
```

It can be shown that if $X = (x_1, x_2, \dots , x_{n+1})$, and if $V = \text{Vander}(X)$, then

$$|V| = \prod_{i<j} (x_i - x_j) \, ,$$

where $\prod$ stands for product. Thus $|V|$ is never 0 if the components of X are all distinct. Because this determinant is nonzero, we have the following fact.

Fact   *If* $X = (x_1, x_2, \dots , x_{n+1})$ *and* $Y = (y_1, y_2, \dots , y_{n+1})$ *are both vectors in* R^{n+1}, *with all components of* X *being distinct, and if* $V = Vander(X)$, *then the system of equations* $Vp = Y'$ *has a unique solution for* p. *This* *vector p gives the coefficients of the unique polynomial of degree n or less going through the n + 1 points (x_i, y_i). The command polyfit(X, Y, n) will give this polynomial.*

Example 4.7 *Let us consider the points (1,4),(2,8),(3,3),(4,1). We let $X = (1, 2, 3, 4)$ and $Y = (4, 8, 3, 1)$. Now*

$$Vp = Y'$$

becomes

$$\begin{bmatrix} 1 & 1 & 1 & 1 \\ 8 & 4 & 2 & 1 \\ 27 & 9 & 3 & 1 \\ 64 & 16 & 4 & 1 \end{bmatrix} \begin{bmatrix} p_3 \\ p_2 \\ p_1 \\ p_0 \end{bmatrix} = \begin{bmatrix} 4 \\ 8 \\ 3 \\ 1 \end{bmatrix}.$$

This matrix equation is equivalent to requiring that all four of the given points lie on the graph of the polynomial p, or in other words, that all pairs (x_i, y_i) satisfy the equation

$$p_3 x^3 + p_2 x^2 + p_1 x + p_0 = y.$$

Since we know that the Vandermonde matrix has a nonzero determinant, we know that there is a unique solution for the coefficients of the polynomial. We use Matlab.

```
EDU» X=[1 2 3 4]
X =
     1   2   3   4
EDU» Y=[4 8 3 1]
Y =
     4   8   3   1
EDU» V=vander(X)
V =
     1    1   1   1
     8    4   2   1
    27    9   3   1
    64   16   4   1
EDU» p=inv(V)*Y'
p =
       2.0000
     -16.5000
      39.5000
     -21.0000
```

EDU» p=polyfit(X,Y,3)

p =

    2.0000   −16.5000   39.5000   −21.0000

Comment: Thus we have the cubic polynomial

$$p(x) = 2x^3 - 16.5x^2 + 39.5x - 21,$$

fitting the four given points exactly.

If we try to put a degree 2 polynomial (parabola) through these for points, we would need the coefficients of the polynomial to satisfy the matrix equation

$$\begin{bmatrix} 1 & 1 & 1 \\ 4 & 2 & 1 \\ 9 & 3 & 1 \\ 16 & 4 & 1 \end{bmatrix} \begin{bmatrix} p_2 \\ p_1 \\ p_0 \end{bmatrix} = \begin{bmatrix} 4 \\ 8 \\ 3 \\ 1 \end{bmatrix}.$$

This system of equations is equivalent to requiring that all four of the given points lie on the graph of the polynomial

$$p_2 x^2 + p_1 x + p_0 = y.$$

But now we have more equations than unknowns, so there may not be a solution. In this case we can find the least squares approximate solution, and that will be the least squares fit degree 2 polynomial. We can do it with the truncated Vandermonde matrix, solving the normal equation $V'Vp = V'Y'$. If we are using Matlab, we can get the least squares solution to $Vp = Y'$ using the left divide command p=V\Y'. Or we can go directly to the Matlab command polyfit(X,Y,2), which will return the least squares fit polynimial of degree 2.

Example 4.8 *We illustrate using Matlab. Assuming that we have X, Y, and V = Vander(X) already entered as before, we truncate the Vandermonde matrix.*

EDU» v=V(:,2:4)

v =

     1   1   1

     4   2   1

     9   3   1

   16   4   1

EDU» a=v'*v

a =

$$\begin{array}{ccc} 354 & 100 & 30 \\ 100 & 30 & 10 \\ 30 & 10 & 4 \end{array}$$

EDU» b=v'*Y'

b =

$$\begin{array}{c} 79 \\ 33 \\ 16 \end{array}$$

EDU» rref([a b])

ans =

$$\begin{array}{cccc} 1.0000 & 0 & 0 & -1.5000 \\ 0 & 1.0000 & 0 & 6.1000 \\ 0 & 0 & 1.0000 & 0 \end{array}$$

Comment: The sequence above is the best way to do this problem if working without aid of computer or calculator. With Matlab, the following commands will also solve for the polynomial coefficients.

EDU» p=inv(a)*b

p =

$$\begin{array}{c} -1.5000 \\ 6.1000 \\ -0.0000 \end{array}$$

EDU» p=v\Y'

p =

$$\begin{array}{c} -1.5000 \\ 6.1000 \\ -0.0000 \end{array}$$

EDU» p=polyfit(X,Y,2)

p =

$$\begin{array}{ccc} -1.5000 & 6.1000 & -0.0000 \end{array}$$

Comment: Thus we have the quadratic polynomial

$$p(x) = -1.5x^2 + 6.1x$$

as the best fit (in the least squares sense) to the four given points.

Now suppose that we want the least squares fit line to these same points. In this case we would need the coefficients of the polynomial to satisfy the matrix equation

$$\begin{bmatrix} 1 & 1 \\ 2 & 1 \\ 3 & 1 \\ 4 & 1 \end{bmatrix} \begin{bmatrix} p_1 \\ p_0 \end{bmatrix} = \begin{bmatrix} 4 \\ 8 \\ 3 \\ 1 \end{bmatrix}.$$

This system of equations is equivalent to requiring that all four of the given points lie on the line

$$p_1 x + p_0 = y.$$

Once again there is no exact solution. We have more equations than unknowns. Thus we seek the least squares solution. Again we have the same methods available. Let v equal the 4×2 matrix above. We can solve the normal equation $(v'v)\,p = v'Y'$, use the Matlab command p=v\Y', or use the Matlab command polyfit(X,Y,1). You can check that all these methods give the same answer as we get in the following example.

Example 4.9 *Assuming again that we have entered $X = (1, 2, 3, 4)$ and $Y = (4, 8, 3, 1)$, we use the **polyfit** command.*

EDU» polyfit(X,Y,1)
ans =
        −1.4000   7.5000
Comment: The least squares fit line is

$$y = -1.4x + 7.5.$$

Given a set of points, the power of Matlab makes it very easy to find the least squares fit and exact fit polynomials of various degrees. But it is even more fun if you can see the points and the curves on a graph. For the following command to work, you need to have the m-file "lspolygr.m" accessible to your Matlab program. This m-file was written by the authors, and you can find it at the end of this section. You can type it in any word processing program and save it as a file named "lspolygr.m" in the same directory with your Matlab program. Then you can use the command

$$\boxed{\text{lspolygr(X,Y,n)}}$$

This command returns
  $p =$ coefficients of the least squares fit polynomial of degree n, to points (x_i, y_i) and
  $d =$ sum of the squares of the vertical distances of the given points to the curve, and
  a graph showing the curve, the points, and vertical lines from the points to the curve.

The lspolygr m-file uses the polyfit command, so the same requirements for the input arguments apply. You can download the m-file **lspolygr.m** from the following Web site: http://www.math.uiowa.edu/~mkleinf/. After copying the m-file onto your system, try the **lspolygr** command on the X and Y of the preceding example with $n = 1, 2,$ and 3.

```
function ans=lspolygr3(x,y,n)
% This function computes and graphs the least square fit
% polynomial of degree n through k given points in 2-space.
% It requires as input vectors x giving the first components
% and y giving the second components of the points,
% and a positive integer n. Then the graph is drawn
% showing the polynomial, the given points,
% and the points on the graph for the same x values.
% Vertical lines are drawn from the given points to the points
% on the graph, and the sum of the squares of the
% lengths of these lines is computed and given as d.
k=length(x);
xm=max(x);
xmi=min(x);
ym=max(y);
ymi=min(y);
axis([xmi-1,xm+1,ymi-1,ym+1]);
hold on
p=polyfit(x,y,n)
xi=linspace(xmi-1,xm+1,100);
z=polyval(p,xi);
w=polyval(p,x);
q=norm(y-w);
d=q*q
plot(x,y,'*',xi,z,x,w,'o')
for i=1:k
plot([x(i),x(i)],[y(i),w(i)],'b')
end
```

We have seen that the p=polyfit(X,Y,n) command returns the exact fit polynomial if the number of points is $n + 1$, and the least squares fit polynomial if the number of points is greater than $n + 1$. But what will happen if you use fewer than $n + 1$ points, for example, if you ask for the least squares fit polynomial of degree 3 through three points? We know that three points determine a parabola or degree 2 polynomial. We can fit three points exactly with degree 2. If we are allowed a cubic, then of course we can find an exact fit; in fact we can find many. The solution is not unique. However, the polyfit command will still work. It will give one of the possible exact fit polynomials. Since the **lspolygr** command is based on the **polyfit** command, it will also work in this case, graphing the polynomial chosen by the **polyfit** command.

Example 4.10 *Here is an example where we ask for a quadratic, a cubic, and a quartic thorough three given points,* $(1, 2), (2, 4), (3, 1)$. *We know that we can fit the points exactly with a quadratic, but we ask for the degree 3 and degree 4 polynomials just to test the* **polyfit** *command.*

```
EDU» X=[1 2 3]
X =
      1   2   3
EDU» Y=[2 4 1]
Y =
      2   4   1
EDU» p=polyfit(X,Y,2)
p =
      -2.5000   9.5000   -5.0000
EDU» p=polyfit(X,Y,3)
p =
      -0.8636   2.6818   0   0.1818
EDU» p=polyfit(X,Y,4)
p =
      -0.3471   1.0294   0   0   1.3176
```

Comment: We see that the **polyfit** command finds polynomials with some of the lower-order coefficients equal to zero when the polynomial is "underdetermined."

4.2.5   Optional Matlab Exercises

In the following problemss use the vander(X) and the polyfit(X,Y,n) commands. If you have downloaded the lspolygr.m file, use the lspolygr(X,Y,n) command in problems 3-15 to view the graphs and compute d, the sum of the squares of the vertical distances from the given points to the curve.

1. Form the Vandermonde matrix built from $X = (5, 3, -2, 4)$.

2. Find the determinant of the matrix in problem 1.

3. Find the equation of a parabola through the points $(1, 5), (2, -1), (3, 1)$.

4. Find the equation of a parabola through the points $(1, 2), (2, 8), (3, 6)$.

5. Find the equation of a parabola through the points $(1, 0), (3, 5), (6, 4)$.

6. Find the least square fit line to the points
   $(-1, 3), (0, 2), (1, -4), (2, -7)$.

7. Find the equation of the least square fit parabola to the points given in problem 6.

8. Find the polynomial of degree 3 that goes through all the points given in problem 6.

9. Find the exact fit polynomial of degree 3 or less through the points
   $(-1, 8), (0, 4), (1, 5), (2, 11)$.

10. Find the least square fit line to the points
    $(-1, 1), (0, 3), (1, 6), (2, 10), (3, 13)$.

11. Find an exact fit polynomial of degree 4 through the points in problem 10.

12. Find the least square fit line to the points
    $(0, 12), (1, 8), (2, 6), (3, 3), (4, -1)$.

13. Find the least square fit quadratic polynomial to the points in problem 12.

14. Find the least square fit cubic polynomial to the points in problem 12.

15. Find the exact fit polynomial of degree 4 through the points in problem 12.

4.3 Markov Chains

In many applications we encounter a situation where we can get from one set of values to the next by multiplying by the same matrix.

Problem *In a certain town of fairly constant population, adults are classified as using either public or private transportation. It has been observed yearly that 10% switch from public to private, while 5% switch from private to public. What prediction about the eventual distrubution of public and private users can we make?*

Solution *If x_0 now use private and y_0 use public transportation, while x_1 and y_1, are, respectively, private and public users one year from now, then*

$$\begin{bmatrix} .95 & .10 \\ .05 & .90 \end{bmatrix} \begin{bmatrix} x_0 \\ y_0 \end{bmatrix} = \begin{bmatrix} x_1 \\ y_1 \end{bmatrix}.$$

*If we call the 2×2 matrix in the equation P, then P is a **probability matrix**. Such matrices have nonnegative entries and satisfy the condition that the sum of the entries in each column equals 1. Also, if x_k and y_k are, respectively, private and public users k years from now, then*

$$\begin{bmatrix} .95 & .10 \\ .05 & .90 \end{bmatrix} \begin{bmatrix} x_k \\ y_k \end{bmatrix} = \begin{bmatrix} x_{k+1} \\ y_{k+1} \end{bmatrix},$$

so that

$$P^n \begin{bmatrix} x_0 \\ y_0 \end{bmatrix} = \begin{bmatrix} x_n \\ y_n \end{bmatrix}.$$

To obtain an exact formula for P^n, we diagonalize P if that is possible. If

$$Q^{-1}PQ = D,$$

then

$$Q^{-1}P^nQ = D^n$$

and

$$P^n = QD^nQ^{-1}.$$

D is a diagonal matrix, so D^n is easy once we have obtained the eigenvalues of P. Then all we need is a basis of eigenvectors and we have Q. Note that 1 will always be an eigenvalue of a probability matrix like P since the sum of the rows of $P - I$ will be the zero vector. Thus $|P - I| = 0$, showing that 1 must be an eigenvalue. In this example the eigenvalues of P are 1 and .85 and $\begin{bmatrix} 2 \\ 1 \end{bmatrix}$ and $\begin{bmatrix} -1 \\ 1 \end{bmatrix}$ are eigenvectors that correspond to these eigenvalues. Thus

$$Q = \begin{bmatrix} 2 & -1 \\ 1 & 1 \end{bmatrix}, \quad D = \begin{bmatrix} 1 & 0 \\ 0 & .85 \end{bmatrix}$$

$$D^n = \begin{bmatrix} 1 & 0 \\ 0 & (.85)^n \end{bmatrix}, \quad Q^{-1} = \begin{bmatrix} \frac{1}{3} & \frac{1}{3} \\ -\frac{1}{3} & \frac{2}{3} \end{bmatrix}.$$

Thus

$$\begin{aligned}
P^n &= \begin{bmatrix} 2 & -1 \\ 1 & 1 \end{bmatrix} \begin{bmatrix} 1 & 0 \\ 0 & (.85)^n \end{bmatrix} \begin{bmatrix} \frac{1}{3} & \frac{1}{3} \\ -\frac{1}{3} & \frac{2}{3} \end{bmatrix} \\
&= \begin{bmatrix} 2 & -(.85)^n \\ 1 & (.85)^n \end{bmatrix} \begin{bmatrix} \frac{1}{3} & \frac{1}{3} \\ -\frac{1}{3} & \frac{2}{3} \end{bmatrix} \\
&= \begin{bmatrix} \frac{2}{3} + \frac{1}{3}(.85)^n & \frac{2}{3} - \frac{2}{3}(.85)^n \\ \frac{1}{3} - \frac{1}{3}(.85)^n & \frac{1}{3} + \frac{2}{3}(.85)^n \end{bmatrix}.
\end{aligned}$$

As n becomes large, $(.85)^n$ becomes small; in fact, by choosing n large enough, we can make $(.85)^n$ as close to 0 as we like. Therefore,

$$P^n \to \begin{bmatrix} \frac{2}{3} & \frac{2}{3} \\ \frac{1}{3} & \frac{1}{3} \end{bmatrix},$$

so

$$P^n \begin{bmatrix} x_0 \\ y_0 \end{bmatrix} = \begin{bmatrix} \frac{2}{3} & \frac{2}{3} \\ \frac{1}{3} & \frac{1}{3} \end{bmatrix} \begin{bmatrix} x_0 \\ y_0 \end{bmatrix}$$
$$= \begin{bmatrix} \frac{2}{3}(x_0 + y_0) \\ \frac{1}{3}(x_0 + y_0) \end{bmatrix}.$$

*We conclude that in the long run (no matter what the present division is) $\frac{2}{3}$ of the total population will use private transportation and $\frac{1}{3}$ of the population will use public transportation. The vector $\begin{bmatrix} \frac{2}{3} \\ \frac{1}{3} \end{bmatrix}$ is called the **steady-state vector** since*

$$\begin{bmatrix} .95 & .10 \\ .05 & .90 \end{bmatrix} \begin{bmatrix} \frac{2}{3} \\ \frac{1}{3} \end{bmatrix} = \begin{bmatrix} \frac{2}{3} \\ \frac{1}{3} \end{bmatrix}.$$

In other words, if $\frac{2}{3}$ are using private transportation and $\frac{1}{3}$ are using public transportation, this will also be true in each successive year. Even if that is not the starting distruibution, eventually the system will tend to the steady state-vector, as we have seen above.

Definition *The **steady-state vector** of a probability matrix P is an eigenvector for the eigenvalue 1 of P which also has the sum of its components equal to 1.*

Definition *A matrix P is called **regular** if for some positive integer n there are no zero entries in P^n.*

Procedure *If P is regular, all we have to do is find the steady state-vector and it can be shown that in the long run the system will tend to this distribution.*

Fact *It can be shown that for regular matrices P, $P^n \to$ a matrix with all columns equal to the steady state-vector, just as it did in our example, and the long-range distribution equals the steady-state vector. If the matrix is not regular, however, these results do not hold, as shown in the next example.*

156   CHAPTER 4.   APPLICATIONS

Example 4.11 *In another town (population 100), 60 voted Republican and
40 voted Democratic.   The population is so critical of its elected officials
that they all switch parties every year in an attempt to "vote the rascals
out."   Thus the matrix relating this year's distribution of voters to next
year's distribution is*

$$P = \begin{bmatrix} 0 & 1 \\ 1 & 0 \end{bmatrix},$$

which gives

$$\begin{bmatrix} x_1 \\ y_1 \end{bmatrix} = \begin{bmatrix} 0 & 1 \\ 1 & 0 \end{bmatrix} \begin{bmatrix} x_0 \\ y_0 \end{bmatrix} = \begin{bmatrix} y_0 \\ x_0 \end{bmatrix}.$$

The steady-state vector for this P is $\begin{bmatrix} \frac{1}{2} \\ \frac{1}{2} \end{bmatrix}$, *since*

$$\begin{bmatrix} 0 & 1 \\ 1 & 0 \end{bmatrix} \begin{bmatrix} \frac{1}{2} \\ \frac{1}{2} \end{bmatrix} = \begin{bmatrix} \frac{1}{2} \\ \frac{1}{2} \end{bmatrix}.$$

*However, if the division starts at 60 for one party and 40 for the other, the
system never approaches the steady state as it did in the preceding problem.*

Example 4.12 *Let us suppose that we have a situation where the transition
matrix is*

$$\begin{array}{cc} & R \quad D \\ \begin{array}{c} R \\ D \end{array} & \begin{bmatrix} .2 & .6 \\ .8 & .4 \end{bmatrix}. \end{array}$$

*The first column gives the split next time of those who voted R this time.
The second column gives the split next time of those who voted D this time.
This transition matrix represents the case where 20% of those who vote Republican in one presidential election vote Republican in the next presidential
election also, while 80% switch their vote to Democrat.   Of those who vote
Democrat in one presidential election, 40% remain loyal in the next presidential election and 60% switch to Republican.   We have*

$$\begin{bmatrix} R_{n+1} \\ D_{n+1} \end{bmatrix} = \begin{bmatrix} .2 & .6 \\ .8 & .4 \end{bmatrix} \begin{bmatrix} R_n \\ D_n \end{bmatrix}$$

or

$$\begin{bmatrix} R_{n+1} \\ D_{n+1} \end{bmatrix} = \begin{bmatrix} .2R_n + .6D_n \\ .8R_n + .4D_n \end{bmatrix},$$

where R_{n+1}, stands for the number voting Republican in the $(n+1)$st election, and R_n stands for the number voting Republican in the nth election (similarly for D_{n+1} and D_n). The question could be asked: What will happen in the long run? We note that P is regular, since P^1 already has no zero entries. Therefore, we can solve this by finding an eigenvector for the matrix P for the eigenvalue 1.

$$P - I = \begin{bmatrix} -.8 & .6 \\ .8 & -.6 \end{bmatrix}.$$

The RREF of this matrix is

$$\text{RREF}\,(P - I) = \begin{bmatrix} 1 & -\frac{3}{4} \\ 0 & 0 \end{bmatrix}.$$

This is also the Hermite form, so

$$H - I = \begin{bmatrix} 0 & -\frac{3}{4} \\ 0 & -1 \end{bmatrix}.$$

This a basis for the eigenspace for 1 is the vector $\left(-\frac{3}{4}, -1\right)$. Now all nonzero multiples of this vector are eigenvectors for $k = 1$. Usually, for our basis vector we prefer to pick one with no fractions, such as in this case $(3, 4)$, which is just $-4\left(-\frac{3}{4}, -1\right)$. But for our steady-state vector, we want an eigenvector with positive components that add up to 1 (so that it will be a probability vector). Thus we can use $\frac{1}{7}(3, 4) = \left(\frac{3}{7}, \frac{4}{7}\right)$. This would be the long-run distribution, predicting that if this kept up for some time, Democrats would start winning every time, garnering $\frac{4}{7}$, or approximately 57% of the votes.

Remark *The way we are setting these problems up, the entry in the i, j position of the transition matrix is the probability of going from state j to state i in one transition. Another way of stating this is that the entries in column j give the probabilities of going to the other states if you start in state j.*

4.3.1 Matlab

Problem *In a certain town, review of weather data reveals that if it rains one day, it is three times as likely to rain again the next day as it is to be sunny. If it is sunny one day, the next day is equally likely to have rain or sunshine. Assuming that all days can be classified as either rainy or sunny, determine the long-term distribution of rainy and sunny days.*

Solution   *Following a rainy day, let x be the probability of sunshine.   Then 3x is the probability of rain.   We must have one or the other so that the probabilities must add up to 1.   Thus $x + 3x = 1$, so we get $x = 1/4$.   Thus following a rainy day, the probabilities are: rain again 3/4, sunshine 1/4. Following a sunny day, rain or sun are equally likely, so we have probabilities 1/2 and 1/2.   This gives a transition matrix of*

$$
\begin{array}{cc}
 & \begin{array}{cc} rain & sun \end{array} \\
\begin{array}{c} rain \\ sun \end{array} &
\left[\begin{array}{cc} \frac{3}{4} & \frac{1}{2} \\ \frac{1}{4} & \frac{1}{2} \end{array} \right]
\end{array} \; .
$$

We can use Matlab to verify that 1 is an eigenvalue and to find a steady state vector (eigenvector for 1).

```
EDU» a=[3/4 1/2;1/4 1/2]
a =
      0.7500   0.5000
      0.2500   0.5000
EDU» eig(a)
ans =
      1.0000
      0.2500
EDU» i=eye(2)
i =
      1   0
      0   1
EDU» v=null(a-i,'r')
v =
      2
      1
```
Comment: We check that $(2, 1)$ is a fixed vector of a.
```
EDU» a*v
ans =
      2
      1
```

This is a fixed vector but not yet a probability vector.   We want the components to add up to 1.   They currently add up to 3, so if we multiply this vector v by $\frac{1}{3}$, the result will be what we want.   Thus we get $\left(\frac{2}{3}, \frac{1}{3}\right)$ as the long-range distribution of rainy days and sunny days.   We conclude that in this town over the long term, there are twice as many rainy days as sunny days.

To test a matrix A to see if it is regular, you can use the Matlab command

$$\boxed{\text{A\textasciicircum n}}$$

This command multiplies the matrix A times itself n times, where n is a positive integer.

4.3.2 Exercises

1. Determine which of the following matrices are regular.

   (a) $\begin{bmatrix} .5 & 1 \\ .5 & 0 \end{bmatrix}$

   (b) $\begin{bmatrix} .5 & 0 \\ .5 & 1 \end{bmatrix}$

   (c) $\begin{bmatrix} \frac{1}{3} & \frac{1}{4} & 0 \\ \frac{2}{3} & 0 & 1 \\ 0 & \frac{3}{4} & 0 \end{bmatrix}$

   (d) $\begin{bmatrix} \frac{1}{3} & 0 & \frac{1}{2} \\ \frac{2}{3} & \frac{1}{4} & 0 \\ 0 & \frac{3}{4} & \frac{1}{2} \end{bmatrix}$

2. In a certain town, if it rains one day, the next day is twice as likely to be rainy as sunny. If it is sunny one day, it is equally likely to be rainy or sunny the next day. Assuming that every day can be classified as either rainy or sunny, write down the transition matrix for this situation and find the long-term distribution of rainy and sunny days in this town.

3. A certain man eats three different cereals for breakfast. Each morning he eats either oatmeal, bran flakes, or cornflakes. He never eats the same cereal two days in a row. If he eats oatmeal one morning, it is equally likely that he will chose bran flakes or cornflakes the next day. If he eats bran flakes one day, he is twice as likely to eat cornflakes the next day as to eat bran flakes. If he eats cornflakes one day, he always eats oatmeal the next day. Set up the transition matrix and find the steady-state vector.

4. Find the steady-state vector for each of the following matrices.

   (a) $\begin{bmatrix} .6 & .7 \\ .4 & .3 \end{bmatrix}$

(b) $\begin{bmatrix} .65 & .45 \\ .35 & .55 \end{bmatrix}$

(c) $\begin{bmatrix} .2 & .1 & .3 \\ .1 & .1 & .7 \\ .7 & .8 & 0 \end{bmatrix}$

(d) $\begin{bmatrix} .4 & .3 & .5 \\ .6 & .3 & .2 \\ 0 & .4 & .3 \end{bmatrix}$

4.4   Applications of the Null Space

Assuming that A is size $k \times n$, we have the following:

Fact *A basis of Rowsp(A) together with a basis of Nullsp(A) is a basis of $\mathbf{R}^n$.*

This gives us a good way to extend a linearly independent set in R^n to a basis of R^n.

Example 4.13 *Problem*   *Extend the set $\{(1,2,1,-1),(1,1,3,1)\}$ to a basis or R^4.*

Solution   *Let*

$$A = \begin{bmatrix} 1 & 2 & 1 & -1 \\ 1 & 1 & 3 & 1 \end{bmatrix}.$$

We find that

$$\mathrm{RREF}(A) = \begin{bmatrix} 1 & 0 & 5 & 3 \\ 0 & 1 & -2 & -2 \end{bmatrix}.$$

Thus a basis for the null space of A is $(5,-2,-1,0)$ and $(3,-2,0,-1)$. These two vectors extend the given vectors to a basis of R^n.

Remark   *The solution is not unique.   There are many ways to extend the given set to a basis of R^4.*

Problem   *Find a basis for R^3 such that the first vector of that basis is $(1,4,-2)$.*

Solution *We form the matrix*

$$A = \begin{bmatrix} 1 & 4 & -2 \end{bmatrix}.$$

A basis of the null space is $(4, -1, 0)$ *and* $(-2, 0, -1)$.
Thus $\{(1, 4, -2), (4, -1, 0), (-2, 0, -1)\}$ *is a basis of* R^3 *with the desired property.*

Remark *The solution is not unique; for example,*
$\{(1, 4, -2), (1, 0, 0), (0, 0, 1)\}$ *is also a basis of* R^3 *with the desired property. All you need is two more triples which together with the given one will form a* 3×3 *matrix whose rref is the identity matrix. However, it's interesting to know that the null space basis will always work and in fact will extend with vectors orthogonal to the original vector.*

Fact **Every vector in the null space of A is orthogonal to every vector in the row space of A.**

This gives us a method for finding a vector orthogonal to a set of vectors.

Problem *Find a vector that is orthogonal to both the vectors* $(1, 1, 1)$ *and* $(1, 2, 3)$.

Solution *Let* $A = \begin{bmatrix} 1 & 1 & 1 \\ 1 & 2 & 3 \end{bmatrix}$. $\mathrm{RREF}(A) = \begin{bmatrix} 1 & 0 & -1 \\ 0 & 1 & 2 \end{bmatrix}$, *so a vector in the null space of* A *is* $(-1, 2, -1)$. *This is a vector orthogonal to both given vectors.*

Problem *Find a vector in* R^4 *that is orthogonal to both* $(1, 2, 1, -1)$ *and* $(1, 1, 3, 1)$.

Solution *Let*

$$A = \begin{bmatrix} 1 & 2 & 1 & -1 \\ 1 & 1 & 3 & 1 \end{bmatrix};$$

then

$$\mathrm{RREF}(A) = \begin{bmatrix} 1 & 0 & 5 & 3 \\ 0 & 1 & -2 & -2 \end{bmatrix}.$$

A basis of the null space of A is $(5, -2, -1, 0)$ *and* $(3, -2, 0, -1)$. *Either one of these vectors (or any linear combination of them) is a correct answer to the problem.*

Fact *If B is a matrix whose rows are a basis of Nullsp(A), then Nullsp(B)=Rowsp(A).*

This gives us a way to pass from a description of a subspace by a spanning set or basis to a description of the space by a system of equations.

Problem *Find equations describing the subspace W of R^4 spanned by the vectors $(1, 2, 1, -1)$ and $(1, 1, 3, 1)$.*

Solution *We put the spanning set of W as the rows of a matrix A*

$$A = \begin{bmatrix} 1 & 2 & 1 & -1 \\ 1 & 1 & 3 & 1 \end{bmatrix}.$$

Then $W = Rowsp\,(A)$. In a previous example we found that a basis of $Nullsp\,(A)$ is $(5, -2, -1, 0)$ and $(3, -2, 0, -1)$. Putting these as the rows of a matrix B, we get

$$B = \begin{bmatrix} 5 & -2 & -1 & 0 \\ 3 & -2 & 0 & -1 \end{bmatrix}.$$

Now $Nullsp\,(B) = W$, so we conclude that the vector (w, x, y, z) is in W if and only if

$$\begin{bmatrix} 5 & -2 & -1 & 0 \\ 3 & -2 & 0 & -1 \end{bmatrix} \begin{bmatrix} w \\ x \\ y \\ z \end{bmatrix} = \begin{bmatrix} 0 \\ 0 \end{bmatrix}$$

or, in other words, if w, x, y, z satisfy the equations

$$\begin{aligned} 5w - 2x - y &= 0 \\ 3w - 2x - z &= 0. \end{aligned}$$

Fact *The basis vectors of the null space give the coefficients of equations describing the row space.*

In R^3 the equation of a plane through the origin is $ax + by + cz = 0$, where (a, b, c) is a vector orthogonal to the plane. This is a special case of the fact just stated.

Problem *Let W be the subspace of R^3 spanned by the vectors $(1, 1, 1)$ and $(1, 2, 3)$. Find conditions on x, y, z such that the vector (x, y, z) is in W. (Here W is a plane through the origin, and we are asking for the equation of the plane.)*

Solution *Let* $A = \begin{bmatrix} 1 & 1 & 1 \\ 1 & 2 & 3 \end{bmatrix}$. *We find that* RREF $(A) = \begin{bmatrix} 1 & 0 & -1 \\ 0 & 1 & 2 \end{bmatrix}$.
A basis of $Nullsp(A)$ *is* $(-1, 2, -1)$, *or we can use* $(1, -2, 1)$. *This vector gives us the coefficients of the equation describing* W. *Thus* (x, y, z) *is in* W *if and only if*

$$x - 2y + z = 0.$$

Fact *An orthogonal basis of Rowsp(A) together with an orthogonal basis of Nullsp(A) is an orthogonal basis of* $\mathbf{R}^n$.

We will do some examples of this in the Matlab section.

4.4.1 Matlab

We can use the null(A,'r') command to solve the types of problems discussed in the preceding section because it finds a basis of the null space of A.

Example 4.14 *Find a vector orthogonal to all of the vectors* $(1, 3, 1, 2)$, $(3, -1, 2, 2)$, *and* $(4, 0, 4, 1)$.

```
EDU» A=[1 3 1 2;3 -1 2 2;4 0 4 1]
A =
     1    3   1   2
     3   -1   2   2
     4    0   4   1
EDU» N=null(A,'r')
N =
    -2.0833
    -0.5833
     1.8333
     1.0000
EDU» rats(N)
ans =
    -25/12
     -7/12
     11/6
       1
```

Comment: We can multiply this output by 12 to get rid of fractions, but don't do it using the output of the **rats** command. However, we can do 12*N.

```
EDU» b=12*N
b =
```

$$-25$$
$$-7$$
$$22$$
$$12$$

Comment: We get the vector $(-25, -7, 22, 12)$ as a vector orthogonal to the three given vectors.

EDU» A*b

ans =

0

0 .

0

Comment: This verifies that b is orthogonal to all the rows of A.

Problem *Extend the set* $\{(1, 3, 1, 2), (3, -1, 2, 2), (4, 0, 4, 1)\}$ *to a basis of* R^4.

Solution *All we need is a vector in the null space of the matrix*

$$A = \begin{bmatrix} 1 & 3 & 1 & 2 \\ 3 & -1 & 2 & 2 \\ 4 & 0 & 4 & 1 \end{bmatrix}.$$

We just found one in the preceding example, namely $(-25, -7, 22, 12)$. *Thus the set*

$$\{(1, 3, 1, 2), (3, -1, 2, 2), (4, 0, 4, 1), (-25, -7, 22, 12)\}$$

is a basis for R^4.

Problem *Describe the subspace* $W = sp\{(1, 3, 1, 2), (3, -1, 2, 2), (4, 0, 4, 1)\}$ *by a system of equations.*

Solution *Note that W is the row space of the matrix A from the preceding problem. Recall that* $(-25, -7, 22, 12)$ *is a basis for the null space of A. Let* $B = \begin{bmatrix} -25 & -7 & 22 & 12 \end{bmatrix}$. *Then W is the null space of B. In other words, W is the solution set of the equation*

$$-25x_1 - 7x_2 + 22x_3 + 12x_4 = 0.$$

Example 4.15 *Find a orthonormal basis for* R^4 *such that the first two vectors are in the subspace generated by* $(1, 3, 1, 3)$ *and* $(2, 2, 2, 2)$.

EDU» A=[1 3 1 3;2 2 2 2]

A =

```
      1   3   1   3
      2   2   2   2
EDU» Q=orth(A')
Q =
      0.3549      0.6116
      0.6116     -0.3549
      0.3549      0.6116
      0.6116     -0.3549
```

Comment: The columns of Q are an orthonormal basis for rowsp(A).

```
EDU» N=null(A)
N =
     -0.7071            0
      0.0000     -0.7071
      0.7071       0.000
     -0.0000       0.7071
```

Comment: The columns of N are an orthonormal basis for nullsp(A).

```
EDU» T=[Q N]
T =
      0.3549      0.6116     -0.7071            0
      0.6116     -0.3549      0.0000     -0.7071
      0.3549      0.6116      0.7071       0.000
      0.6116     -0.3549     -0.0000       0.7071
```

Comment: The columns of T are the desired orthonormal basis.of R^4.

```
EDU» T'*T
ans =
      1.0000     -0.0000     0.0000            0
     -0.0000      1.0000     0.0000     0.0000
      0.0000      0.0000     1.0000     0.0000
           0      0.0000     0.0000     1.0000
```

Comment: This verifies that the colums of T are orthonormal.

4.4.2 Exercises

In problems 1-5, find vectors that extend each of the given sets of vectors
to a basis of R^3.

1. $(1, 4, 2)$

2. $(4, 4, 2)$

3. $(1, 4, 2), (4, 4, 2)$

4. $(3, -1, 5), (2, 2, -3)$

5. $(1, -3, -2) , (-2, 3, 1)$

   In problems 5-8, extend each of the given sets of vectors to a basis of R^4.

6. $(1, 1, 3, 2) , (2, 2, 3, 2)$

7. $(3, -2, 2, 4) , (4, 1, 3, 3)$

8. $(1, 0, 2, 2) , (1, 2, 2, 2) , (2, 2, 2, 2)$

   In problems 9-16, find a vector that is orthogonal to all of the given vectors.

9. $(1, 4, 2)$

10. $(4, 4, 2)$

11. $(1, 4, 2) , (4, 4, 2)$

12. $(3, -1, 5) , (2, 2, -3)$

13. $(1, -3, -2) , (-2, 3, 1)$

14. $(1, 1, 3, 2) , (2, 2, 3, 2)$

15. $(3, -2, 2, 4) , (4, 1, 3, 3)$

16. $(1, 0, 2, 2) , (1, 2, 2, 2) , (2, 2, 2, 2)$

    In problems 17-24, find a system of homogeneous equations that describes the subspace spanned by the given vectors

17. $(1, 4, 2)$

18. $(4, 4, 2)$

19. $(1, 4, 2) , (4, 4, 2)$

20. $(3, -1, 5) , (2, 2, -3)$

21. $(1, -3, -2) , (-2, 3, 1)$

22. $(1, 1, 3, 2) , (2, 2, 3, 2)$

23. $(3, -2, 2, 4) , (4, 1, 3, 3)$

24. $(1, 0, 2, 2) , (1, 2, 2, 2) , (2, 2, 2, 2)$

25. Find two vectors, both orthogonal to $(1, 4, 2)$ and also orthogonal to each other.

Appendix

Answers to Exercises 1.1.1

The RREFs are:

1. $\begin{bmatrix} 1 & 0 & -3 \\ 0 & 1 & 0 \\ 0 & 0 & 0 \end{bmatrix}$
2. $\begin{bmatrix} 1 & 0 & 0 \\ 0 & 1 & 0 \\ 0 & 0 & 1 \end{bmatrix}$
3. $\begin{bmatrix} 1 & 0 & -1 & 0 \\ 0 & 1 & 2 & 3 \\ 0 & 0 & 0 & 0 \end{bmatrix}$

4. $\begin{bmatrix} 1 & 2 & 0 & 0 & 0 \\ 0 & 0 & 1 & 0 & 0 \\ 0 & 0 & 0 & 1 & 0 \\ 0 & 0 & 0 & 0 & 1 \end{bmatrix}$
5. $\begin{bmatrix} 1 & 0 & -1 & 0 \\ 0 & 1 & 2 & 0 \\ 0 & 0 & 0 & 1 \end{bmatrix}$

6. $\begin{bmatrix} 1 & 0 & 0 & 1 \\ 0 & 1 & 0 & 1 \\ 0 & 0 & 1 & 1 \end{bmatrix}$
7. $\begin{bmatrix} 1 & 0 & -1 \\ 0 & 1 & -1 \\ 0 & 0 & 0 \end{bmatrix}$

8. $\begin{bmatrix} 1 & 2 & 4 & 0 & 0 \\ 0 & 0 & 0 & 1 & 0 \\ 0 & 0 & 0 & 0 & 1 \end{bmatrix}$
9. $\begin{bmatrix} 1 & 0 & 0 & 0 & 4 \\ 0 & 0 & 1 & 0 & 0 \\ 0 & 0 & 0 & 1 & 0 \end{bmatrix}$

10. $\begin{bmatrix} 1 & 0 & -1 & -2 \\ 0 & 1 & 2 & 3 \\ 0 & 0 & 0 & 0 \end{bmatrix}$
11. $\begin{bmatrix} 1 & 0 & 0 \\ 0 & 1 & 0 \\ 0 & 0 & 1 \end{bmatrix}$

12. $\begin{bmatrix} 1 & 0 & 0 & 2 & 1 \\ 0 & 1 & 0 & 1 & -\frac{3}{2} \\ 0 & 0 & 1 & -1 & \frac{1}{2} \end{bmatrix}$
13. $\begin{bmatrix} 0 & 1 & 0 & 0 & \frac{3}{2} \\ 0 & 0 & 1 & 0 & 0 \\ 0 & 0 & 0 & 1 & -\frac{5}{2} \end{bmatrix}$

14. $\begin{bmatrix} 1 & 0 & -\frac{11}{7} \\ 0 & 1 & \frac{10}{7} \\ 0 & 0 & 0 \end{bmatrix}$

15. Not in RREF. RREF is $\begin{bmatrix} 1 & 5 & 0 \\ 0 & 0 & 1 \\ 0 & 0 & 0 \end{bmatrix}$.

16. Is in RREF.

17. Not in RREF. RREF is $\begin{bmatrix} 1 & 0 & 0 \\ 0 & 1 & 0 \\ 0 & 0 & 1 \end{bmatrix}$.

18. Is in RREF.

19. Is in RREF.

20. Not in RREF. RREF is $\begin{bmatrix} 1 & 0 & 0 & 0 & 1 & 8 & 5 \\ 0 & 1 & 0 & 3 & -1 & -8 & 2 \\ 0 & 0 & 1 & 5 & -1 & 1 & 1 \end{bmatrix}$.

21. Not in RREF. RREF is $\begin{bmatrix} 1 & 2 & 5 & 0 \\ 0 & 0 & 0 & 1 \\ 0 & 0 & 0 & 0 \end{bmatrix}$.

22. Not in RREF. RREF is $\begin{bmatrix} 1 & 0 & 0 & 16 & 0 \\ 0 & 1 & 0 & 4 & 0 \\ 0 & 0 & 1 & -2 & 0 \\ 0 & 0 & 0 & 0 & 1 \end{bmatrix}$.

23. Is in RREF.

24. Not in RREF. RREF is $\begin{bmatrix} 0 & 1 & 0 & 0 & 0 & -3 \\ 0 & 0 & 1 & 0 & 0 & -4 \\ 0 & 0 & 0 & 1 & 0 & 2 \\ 0 & 0 & 0 & 0 & 1 & 6 \end{bmatrix}$.

Answers to Matlab Exercises 1.1.3

1. $\begin{bmatrix} 1 & 2 & 0 \\ 0 & 0 & 1 \end{bmatrix}$

2. $\begin{bmatrix} 1 & 0 & \frac{1}{5} & \frac{1}{5} \\ 0 & 1 & \frac{1}{5} & \frac{6}{5} \\ 0 & 0 & 0 & 0 \\ 0 & 0 & 0 & 0 \end{bmatrix}$

3. $\begin{bmatrix} 1 & 0 & 0 & \frac{45}{44} & -\frac{3}{22} \\ 0 & 1 & 0 & -\frac{69}{110} & \frac{31}{55} \\ 0 & 0 & 1 & -\frac{139}{220} & \frac{21}{110} \end{bmatrix}$

4. $\begin{bmatrix} 1 & 0 & 1 & -\frac{150}{7} \\ 0 & 1 & \frac{1}{3} & \frac{145}{7} \end{bmatrix}$

5. $\begin{bmatrix} 1 & 0 & \frac{17}{2} & \frac{9}{2} \\ 0 & 1 & -11 & -4 \end{bmatrix}$

Answers to Exercises 1.2.1

Solving systems of linear nonhomogeneous equations:

1. Augmented matrix is $\begin{bmatrix} 1 & 2 & 3 & 6 \\ 4 & 5 & 6 & 15 \\ 7 & 8 & 9 & 24 \end{bmatrix}$, RREF is $\begin{bmatrix} 1 & 0 & -1 & 0 \\ 0 & 1 & 2 & 3 \\ 0 & 0 & 0 & 0 \end{bmatrix}$.

Infinitely many solutions, all of the form $\begin{bmatrix} x \\ y \\ z \end{bmatrix} = \begin{bmatrix} t \\ 3 - 2t \\ t \end{bmatrix}$.

2. Augmented matrix is $\begin{bmatrix} 1 & 1 & 1 & 3 \\ 2 & 3 & 4 & 9 \\ 5 & 6 & 7 & 12 \end{bmatrix}$, RREF is $\begin{bmatrix} 1 & 0 & -1 & 0 \\ 0 & 1 & 2 & 0 \\ 0 & 0 & 0 & 1 \end{bmatrix}$.

No solutions.

3. Augmented matrix is $\begin{bmatrix} 1 & 1 & 1 & 3 \\ 1 & 2 & 4 & 7 \\ 1 & 3 & 9 & 13 \end{bmatrix}$, RREF is $\begin{bmatrix} 1 & 0 & 0 & 1 \\ 0 & 1 & 0 & 1 \\ 0 & 0 & 1 & 1 \end{bmatrix}$.

Unique solution is $\begin{bmatrix} x \\ y \\ z \end{bmatrix} = \begin{bmatrix} 1 \\ 1 \\ 1 \end{bmatrix}$.

4. Augmented matrix is $\begin{bmatrix} 1 & 1 & 2 & 1 & 7 \\ 2 & -1 & 3 & -2 & 3 \\ 4 & -3 & 4 & -3 & 3 \end{bmatrix}$,

RREF is $\begin{bmatrix} 1 & 0 & 0 & 2 & 4 \\ 0 & 1 & 0 & \frac{9}{5} & \frac{19}{5} \\ 0 & 0 & 1 & -\frac{7}{5} & -\frac{2}{5} \end{bmatrix}$.

Infinitely many solutions, all of the form $\begin{bmatrix} w \\ x \\ y \\ z \end{bmatrix} = \begin{bmatrix} 4 - 2t \\ \frac{19}{5} - \frac{9}{5}t \\ -\frac{2}{5} + \frac{7}{5}t \\ t \end{bmatrix}$.

5. Augmented matrix is $\begin{bmatrix} 1 & 1 & -3 & 2 & 1 & 4 \\ 3 & 3 & -5 & 1 & -3 & 5 \\ 0 & 0 & 1 & 4 & -2 & 3 \end{bmatrix}$,

RREF is $\begin{bmatrix} 1 & 1 & 0 & 0 & -\frac{11}{3} & \frac{1}{3} \\ 0 & 0 & 1 & 0 & -\frac{34}{21} & -\frac{13}{21} \\ 0 & 0 & 0 & 1 & -\frac{2}{21} & \frac{19}{21} \end{bmatrix}$.

Infinitely many solutions, all of the form $\begin{bmatrix} v \\ w \\ x \\ y \\ z \end{bmatrix} = \begin{bmatrix} \frac{1}{3} - s + \frac{11}{3}t \\ s \\ -\frac{13}{21} + \frac{34}{21}t \\ \frac{19}{21} + \frac{2}{21}t \\ t \end{bmatrix}$.

6. Augmented matrix is $\begin{bmatrix} 1 & 2 & 3 & 4 & 5 & 3 \\ 2 & 4 & 4 & 3 & 9 & 6 \\ 0 & 0 & 1 & 2 & 2 & 5 \end{bmatrix}$,

RREF is $\begin{bmatrix} 1 & 2 & 0 & 0 & -7 & -32 \\ 0 & 0 & 1 & 0 & 8 & 25 \\ 0 & 0 & 0 & 1 & -3 & -10 \end{bmatrix}$.

Infinitely many solutions, all of the form $\begin{bmatrix} v \\ w \\ x \\ y \\ z \end{bmatrix} = \begin{bmatrix} -32 - 2s + 7t \\ s \\ 25 - 8t \\ -10 + 3t \\ t \end{bmatrix}$.

7. Augmented matrix $\begin{bmatrix} 2 & 1 & 1 & 4 \\ 1 & 3 & 2 & 6 \\ 3 & -2 & 2 & 4 \\ -1 & -1 & 5 & 3 \end{bmatrix}$, RREF is $\begin{bmatrix} 1 & 0 & 0 & 0 \\ 0 & 1 & 0 & 0 \\ 0 & 0 & 1 & 0 \\ 0 & 0 & 0 & 1 \end{bmatrix}$.

No solutions.

8. Augmented matrix is $\begin{bmatrix} 1 & 1 & -3 & -5 & 7 & 12 \\ 0 & 1 & 2 & 0 & -5 & 7 \end{bmatrix}$,

RREF is $\begin{bmatrix} 1 & 0 & -5 & -5 & 12 & 5 \\ 0 & 1 & 2 & 0 & -5 & 7 \end{bmatrix}$.

Infinitely many solutions, all of the form $\begin{bmatrix} v \\ w \\ x \\ y \\ z \end{bmatrix} = \begin{bmatrix} 5 + 5r + 5s - 12t \\ 7 - 2r + 5t \\ r \\ s \\ t \end{bmatrix}$.

9. Augmented matrix is $\begin{bmatrix} 1 & 5 & -4 & 1 & 10 \\ 3 & -1 & 1 & -3 & 7 \\ 9 & 13 & -10 & -3 & 42 \end{bmatrix}$,

RREF is $\begin{bmatrix} 1 & 0 & \frac{1}{16} & -\frac{7}{8} & 0 \\ 0 & 1 & -\frac{13}{16} & \frac{3}{8} & 0 \\ 0 & 0 & 0 & 0 & 1 \end{bmatrix}$

No solutions.

10. Augmented matrix is $\begin{bmatrix} 2 & 1 & 1 & 1 & 5 \\ 3 & 2 & -1 & -1 & 7 \\ 16 & 9 & 3 & 3 & 35 \\ 1 & 2 & 1 & 1 & 5 \\ 1 & 1 & 2 & -1 & 6 \end{bmatrix}$,

RREF is $\begin{bmatrix} 1 & 0 & 0 & 0 & 0 \\ 0 & 1 & 0 & 0 & 0 \\ 0 & 0 & 1 & 0 & 0 \\ 0 & 0 & 0 & 1 & 0 \\ 0 & 0 & 0 & 0 & 1 \end{bmatrix}$. No solutions.

11. Augmented matrix is $\begin{bmatrix} 1 & -1 & 1 & -1 & 3 \\ 1 & 1 & 1 & 1 & 5 \\ 1 & 2 & 4 & 8 & 15 \\ 1 & 3 & 9 & 27 & 41 \end{bmatrix}$,

RREF is $\begin{bmatrix} 1 & 0 & 0 & 0 & \frac{7}{2} \\ 0 & 1 & 0 & 0 & -\frac{1}{4} \\ 0 & 0 & 1 & 0 & \frac{1}{2} \\ 0 & 0 & 0 & 1 & \frac{5}{4} \end{bmatrix}$. Unique solution is $\begin{bmatrix} w \\ x \\ y \\ x \end{bmatrix} = \begin{bmatrix} \frac{7}{2} \\ -\frac{1}{4} \\ \frac{1}{2} \\ \frac{5}{4} \end{bmatrix}$.

12. Augmented matrix is $\begin{bmatrix} 4 & -3 & 2 & -1 & 2 \\ 1 & 2 & 3 & 4 & 3 \\ 2 & -1 & 1 & -2 & 6 \end{bmatrix}$,

RREF is $\begin{bmatrix} 1 & 0 & 0 & -5 & 13 \\ 0 & 1 & 0 & -3 & 10 \\ 0 & 0 & 1 & 5 & -10 \end{bmatrix}$.

Infinitely many solutions, all of the form $\begin{bmatrix} w \\ x \\ y \\ z \end{bmatrix} = \begin{bmatrix} 13 + 5t \\ 10 + 3t \\ -10 - 5t \\ t \end{bmatrix}$.

Repeating each problem for the homogeneous system with the same coefficient matrix as the given system.

1. Augmented matrix is $\begin{bmatrix} 1 & 2 & 3 & 0 \\ 4 & 5 & 6 & 0 \\ 7 & 8 & 9 & 0 \end{bmatrix}$, RREF is $\begin{bmatrix} 1 & 0 & -1 & 0 \\ 0 & 1 & 2 & 0 \\ 0 & 0 & 0 & 0 \end{bmatrix}$.

Infinitely many solutions, all of the form $\begin{bmatrix} x \\ y \\ z \end{bmatrix} = \begin{bmatrix} t \\ -2t \\ t \end{bmatrix}$.

2. Augmented matrix is $\begin{bmatrix} 1 & 1 & 1 & 0 \\ 2 & 3 & 4 & 0 \\ 5 & 6 & 7 & 0 \end{bmatrix}$, RREF is $\begin{bmatrix} 1 & 0 & -1 & 0 \\ 0 & 1 & 2 & 0 \\ 0 & 0 & 0 & 0 \end{bmatrix}$.

Infinitely many solutions, all of the form $\begin{bmatrix} x \\ y \\ z \end{bmatrix} = \begin{bmatrix} t \\ -2t \\ t \end{bmatrix}$

3. Augmented matrix is $\begin{bmatrix} 1 & 1 & 1 & 0 \\ 1 & 2 & 4 & 0 \\ 1 & 3 & 9 & 0 \end{bmatrix}$, RREF is $\begin{bmatrix} 1 & 0 & 0 & 0 \\ 0 & 1 & 0 & 0 \\ 0 & 0 & 1 & 0 \end{bmatrix}$.

Unique solution is $\begin{bmatrix} x \\ y \\ z \end{bmatrix} = \begin{bmatrix} 0 \\ 0 \\ 0 \end{bmatrix}.$

4. Augmented matrix is $\begin{bmatrix} 1 & 1 & 2 & 1 & 0 \\ 2 & -1 & 3 & -2 & 0 \\ 4 & -3 & 4 & -3 & 0 \end{bmatrix},$

RREF is $\begin{bmatrix} 1 & 0 & 0 & 2 & 0 \\ 0 & 1 & 0 & \frac{9}{5} & 0 \\ 0 & 0 & 1 & -\frac{7}{5} & 0 \end{bmatrix}.$

Infinitely many solutions, all of the form $\begin{bmatrix} w \\ x \\ y \\ z \end{bmatrix} = \begin{bmatrix} -2t \\ -\frac{9}{5}t \\ \frac{7}{5}t \\ t \end{bmatrix}.$

5. Augmented matrix is $\begin{bmatrix} 1 & 1 & -3 & 2 & 1 & 0 \\ 3 & 3 & -5 & 1 & -3 & 0 \\ 0 & 0 & 1 & 4 & -2 & 0 \end{bmatrix},$

RREF is $\begin{bmatrix} 1 & 1 & 0 & 0 & -\frac{11}{3} & 0 \\ 0 & 0 & 1 & 0 & -\frac{34}{21} & 0 \\ 0 & 0 & 0 & 1 & -\frac{2}{21} & 0 \end{bmatrix}.$

Infinitely many solutions, all of the form $\begin{bmatrix} v \\ w \\ x \\ y \\ z \end{bmatrix} = \begin{bmatrix} -s + \frac{11}{3}t \\ s \\ \frac{34}{21}t \\ \frac{2}{21}t \\ t \end{bmatrix}.$

6. Augmented matrix is $\begin{bmatrix} 1 & 2 & 3 & 4 & 5 & 0 \\ 2 & 4 & 4 & 3 & 9 & 0 \\ 0 & 0 & 1 & 2 & 2 & 0 \end{bmatrix},$

RREF is $\begin{bmatrix} 1 & 2 & 0 & 0 & -7 & 0 \\ 0 & 0 & 1 & 0 & 8 & 0 \\ 0 & 0 & 0 & 1 & -3 & 0 \end{bmatrix}.$

Infinitely many solutions, all of the form $\begin{bmatrix} v \\ w \\ x \\ y \\ z \end{bmatrix} = \begin{bmatrix} -2s + 7t \\ s \\ -8t \\ 3t \\ t \end{bmatrix}.$

7. Augmented matrix $\begin{bmatrix} 2 & 1 & 1 & 0 \\ 1 & 3 & 2 & 0 \\ 3 & -2 & 2 & 0 \\ -1 & -1 & 5 & 0 \end{bmatrix}$, RREF is $\begin{bmatrix} 1 & 0 & 0 & 0 \\ 0 & 1 & 0 & 0 \\ 0 & 0 & 1 & 0 \\ 0 & 0 & 0 & 0 \end{bmatrix}$.

Unique solution is $\begin{bmatrix} x \\ y \\ z \end{bmatrix} = \begin{bmatrix} 0 \\ 0 \\ 0 \end{bmatrix}$.

8. Augmented matrix is $\begin{bmatrix} 1 & 1 & -3 & -5 & 7 & 0 \\ 0 & 1 & 2 & 0 & -5 & 0 \end{bmatrix}$,

RREF is $\begin{bmatrix} 1 & 0 & -5 & -5 & 12 & 0 \\ 0 & 1 & 2 & 0 & -5 & 0 \end{bmatrix}$.

Infinitely many solutions, all of the form $\begin{bmatrix} v \\ w \\ x \\ y \\ z \end{bmatrix} = \begin{bmatrix} 5r + 5s - 12t \\ -2r + 5t \\ r \\ s \\ t \end{bmatrix}$.

9. Augmented matrix is $\begin{bmatrix} 1 & 5 & -4 & 1 & 0 \\ 3 & -1 & 1 & -3 & 0 \\ 9 & 13 & -10 & -3 & 0 \end{bmatrix}$,

RREF is $\begin{bmatrix} 1 & 0 & \frac{1}{16} & -\frac{7}{8} & 0 \\ 0 & 1 & -\frac{13}{16} & \frac{3}{8} & 0 \\ 0 & 0 & 0 & 0 & 0 \end{bmatrix}$

Infinitely many solutions, all of the form $\begin{bmatrix} w \\ x \\ y \\ z \end{bmatrix} = \begin{bmatrix} -\frac{1}{16}s + \frac{7}{8}t \\ \frac{13}{16}s - \frac{3}{8}t \\ s \\ t \end{bmatrix}$.

10. Augmented matrix is $\begin{bmatrix} 2 & 1 & 1 & 1 & 0 \\ 3 & 2 & -1 & -1 & 0 \\ 16 & 9 & 3 & 3 & 0 \\ 1 & 2 & 1 & 1 & 0 \\ 1 & 1 & 2 & -1 & 0 \end{bmatrix}$,

RREF is $\begin{bmatrix} 1 & 0 & 0 & 0 & 0 \\ 0 & 1 & 0 & 0 & 0 \\ 0 & 0 & 1 & 0 & 0 \\ 0 & 0 & 0 & 1 & 0 \\ 0 & 0 & 0 & 0 & 0 \end{bmatrix}$. Unique solution is $\begin{bmatrix} w \\ x \\ y \\ z \end{bmatrix} = \begin{bmatrix} 0 \\ 0 \\ 0 \\ 0 \end{bmatrix}$.

11. Augmented matrix is $\begin{bmatrix} 1 & -1 & 1 & -1 & 0 \\ 1 & 1 & 1 & 1 & 0 \\ 1 & 2 & 4 & 8 & 0 \\ 1 & 3 & 9 & 27 & 0 \end{bmatrix}$,

RREF is $\begin{bmatrix} 1 & 0 & 0 & 0 & 0 \\ 0 & 1 & 0 & 0 & 0 \\ 0 & 0 & 1 & 0 & 0 \\ 0 & 0 & 0 & 1 & 0 \end{bmatrix}$. Unique solution is $\begin{bmatrix} w \\ x \\ y \\ x \end{bmatrix} = \begin{bmatrix} 0 \\ 0 \\ 0 \\ 0 \end{bmatrix}$.

12. Augmented matrix is $\begin{bmatrix} 4 & -3 & 2 & -1 & 0 \\ 1 & 2 & 3 & 4 & 0 \\ 2 & -1 & 1 & -2 & 0 \end{bmatrix}$,

RREF is $\begin{bmatrix} 1 & 0 & 0 & -5 & 0 \\ 0 & 1 & 0 & -3 & 0 \\ 0 & 0 & 1 & 5 & 0 \end{bmatrix}$.

Infinitely many solutions, all of the form $\begin{bmatrix} w \\ x \\ y \\ z \end{bmatrix} = \begin{bmatrix} 5t \\ 3t \\ -5t \\ t \end{bmatrix}$.

Answers to Exercises 1.3.1

The inverses are:

1. $\begin{bmatrix} -3 & 2 \\ 2 & -1 \end{bmatrix}$ 2. $\begin{bmatrix} -5 & 6 \\ 6 & -7 \end{bmatrix}$ 3. $\begin{bmatrix} -1 & 2 \\ 3 & -5 \end{bmatrix}$

4. $\begin{bmatrix} 1 & -2 & 1 \\ 1 & 3 & -2 \\ -1 & -1 & 1 \end{bmatrix}$ 5. Not invertible.

6. $\begin{bmatrix} 3 & -3 & 1 \\ -\frac{5}{2} & 5 & -\frac{3}{2} \\ \frac{1}{2} & -1 & \frac{1}{2} \end{bmatrix}$ 7. $\begin{bmatrix} \frac{2}{5} & \frac{3}{5} & -\frac{7}{5} & -\frac{3}{5} \\ 0 & 0 & 1 & 0 \\ -\frac{1}{5} & \frac{1}{5} & \frac{1}{5} & \frac{4}{5} \\ \frac{1}{5} & -\frac{1}{5} & -\frac{1}{5} & \frac{1}{5} \end{bmatrix}$

8. $\begin{bmatrix} \frac{4}{5} & -\frac{1}{5} & -\frac{1}{5} & -\frac{1}{5} \\ -\frac{1}{5} & \frac{4}{5} & -\frac{1}{5} & -\frac{1}{5} \\ -\frac{1}{5} & -\frac{1}{5} & \frac{4}{5} & -\frac{1}{5} \\ -\frac{1}{5} & -\frac{1}{5} & -\frac{1}{5} & \frac{4}{5} \end{bmatrix}$ 9. Not invertible.

10. $\begin{bmatrix} 1 & -\frac{1}{2} & -\frac{1}{6} & -\frac{2}{3} \\ 0 & \frac{1}{2} & -\frac{1}{6} & \frac{1}{3} \\ 0 & 0 & \frac{1}{3} & -\frac{1}{6} \\ 0 & 0 & 0 & \frac{1}{2} \end{bmatrix}$

11. $X = A^{-1}B = \begin{bmatrix} -3 & 2 \\ 2 & -1 \end{bmatrix} \begin{bmatrix} 5 \\ -3 \end{bmatrix} . = \begin{bmatrix} -21 \\ 13 \end{bmatrix}$

12. $X = A^{-1}B = \begin{bmatrix} 1 & -2 & 1 \\ 1 & 3 & -2 \\ -1 & -1 & 1 \end{bmatrix} \begin{bmatrix} 5 \\ -2 \\ 5 \end{bmatrix} . = \begin{bmatrix} 14 \\ -11 \\ 2 \end{bmatrix}$

13. $X = A^{-1}B = \begin{bmatrix} 3 & -3 & 1 \\ -\frac{5}{2} & 5 & -\frac{3}{2} \\ \frac{1}{2} & -1 & \frac{1}{2} \end{bmatrix} \begin{bmatrix} 1 \\ 0 \\ 1 \end{bmatrix} . = \begin{bmatrix} 4 \\ -4 \\ 1 \end{bmatrix}$

14. $X = A^{-1}B = \begin{bmatrix} -3 & 2 \\ 2 & -1 \end{bmatrix} \begin{bmatrix} 7 & 6 \\ 6 & 5 \end{bmatrix} = \begin{bmatrix} -9 & -8 \\ 8 & 7 \end{bmatrix}$

$Y = BA^{-1} = \begin{bmatrix} 7 & 6 \\ 6 & 5 \end{bmatrix} \begin{bmatrix} -3 & 2 \\ 2 & -1 \end{bmatrix} = \begin{bmatrix} -9 & 8 \\ -8 & 7 \end{bmatrix}$

No, $X \neq Y$.

15. $X = A^{-1}B = \begin{bmatrix} -3 & 2 \\ 2 & -1 \end{bmatrix} \begin{bmatrix} 5 & 2 \\ 3 & 1 \end{bmatrix} = \begin{bmatrix} -9 & -4 \\ 7 & 3 \end{bmatrix}$

$Y = BA^{-1} = \begin{bmatrix} 5 & 2 \\ 3 & 1 \end{bmatrix} \begin{bmatrix} -3 & 2 \\ 2 & -1 \end{bmatrix} = \begin{bmatrix} -11 & 8 \\ -7 & 5 \end{bmatrix}$

No, $X \neq Y$.

16. $X = A^{-1}B = \begin{bmatrix} 1 & -2 & 1 \\ 1 & 3 & -2 \\ -1 & -1 & 1 \end{bmatrix} \begin{bmatrix} 2 & 3 & 4 \\ 1 & 1 & 1 \\ 5 & 8 & 11 \end{bmatrix} = \begin{bmatrix} 5 & 9 & 13 \\ -5 & -10 & -15 \\ 2 & 4 & 6 \end{bmatrix}$

$Y = BA^{-1} = \begin{bmatrix} 2 & 3 & 4 \\ 1 & 1 & 1 \\ 5 & 8 & 11 \end{bmatrix} \begin{bmatrix} 1 & -2 & 1 \\ 1 & 3 & -2 \\ -1 & -1 & 1 \end{bmatrix} = \begin{bmatrix} 1 & 1 & 0 \\ 1 & 0 & 0 \\ 2 & 3 & 0 \end{bmatrix}$

No, $X \neq Y$.

Answers to Matlab Exercises 1.3.3

1. $X = inv(A) * B = \begin{bmatrix} 21.5000 \\ -15.5000 \\ -12.5000 \end{bmatrix}$

2. $X = inv(A) * B = \begin{bmatrix} 0.4194 \\ -0.0194 \\ -1.3611 \end{bmatrix}$

3. $X = inv(A) * B = \begin{bmatrix} 0.7463 \\ 3.6507 \\ 2.1029 \\ -1.9559 \\ 1.1434 \end{bmatrix}$

4. $X = inv(A) * B = \begin{bmatrix} 2.5714 & 1.8571 & 2.1429 \\ 0.2857 & 0.4286 & 1.5714 \\ -0.7143 & -0.5714 & -2.4286 \end{bmatrix}$

5. No solution exists. A is not invertible, and computing rref[A B], a leading 1 in the fourth column shows that the first column of B cannot be written as a linear combination of the columns of A. Thus $AX = B$ has no solution.

6. $X = \begin{bmatrix} 1 & 1 & 2 \\ 1 & 0 & -1 \\ 0 & 0 & 0 \end{bmatrix}$ is one solution. Once again A is not invertible, so we attack the problem using rref[A B]. The last three columns of this matrix are the matrix X given here as an answer. This time there are infinitely many answers because there are infinitely many ways to write the columns of B as linear combinations of the columns of A.

You can check that $\begin{bmatrix} 1-t & 1-t & 2-t \\ 1+t & t & -1+t \\ t & t & t \end{bmatrix}$ is a solution for all values of t. Column 1 is the general solution to $AX =$ first column of B, column 2 is the general solution of $AX =$ second column of B, and column 3 is the general solution of $AX =$ third column of B.

Answers to Exercises 1.4.1

The determinants are:

1. 0   2. 120   3. 0   4. −71

5. 0   6. 54   7. 0   8. −9

9. 0   10. 0   11. −96   12. 2

13. −5   14. 5   15. 0   16. 60

17. $a^4 - 3a^2$ 18. $-9k - 6k^2 - k^3$

19. $512 - 448k + 144k^2 - 20k^3 + k^4$

20. $54 - 51k + 14k^2 - k^3$

21. Numbers 1, 3, 5, 7, 9, 10, and 15 are not invertible.

22. #17 fails to be invertible for $a = 0$, $\sqrt{3}$, and $-\sqrt{3}$.
#18 fails to be invertible for $k = 0$ and -3.
#19 fails to be invertible for $k = 8$ and 4.
#20 fails to be invertible for $k = 2, 3$, and 9.

23. $y = 3$

24. $x = 1$

Answers to Matlab Exercises 1.4.3

In problems 1-4, Matlab returns the following:

1. 72   2. $-1.3411e + 003$ or -1341.1

3. 117,100   4. $-8.1336e - 013$, or 8.1336×10^{-13}, which means 0 to 12 decimal places!

5. We would have confidence that all but number 5 are invertible. Number 5 probably has determinant identically zero, and we are just seeing roundoff error.

6. $y = -\frac{22}{15}$

7. $z = 1$

8. $w = 2$

Answers to Exercises 2.1.2

1. $(3, 4) = -1(1, 2) + 2(2, 3)$

2. $(1, 1, 2) = \frac{3}{4}(1, 1, 1) + \frac{1}{8}(1, -1, 1) + \frac{1}{8}(1, 3, 9)$

3. $(1, 0, 4, 5) = -\frac{8}{11}(2, 0, 8, 1) + \frac{9}{11}(3, 0, 12, 7) + 0(4, 0, 16, 3)$

4. Not possible.

5. $(4,3,2,1) = 5\,(1,1,1,1) + \frac{1}{12}\,(1,-1,1,-1) - \frac{4}{3}\,(1,2,4,8) + \frac{1}{4}\,(1,3,9,27).$

About problems 6-20: In the linearly dependent case the dependence relation and how you express it are not unique. The relation depends on which vector you solve for. Also, there could be more than one linear dependence relation between the vectors. We just give one possible answer for the dependence relations.

6. Linearly dependent. $(2,8) = 2(1,4).$

7. Linearly independent.

8. Linearly dependent. $(2,-1,6) = -13\,(1,2,3) + 5\,(3,5,9).$

9. Linearly dependent. $(3,4,5) = (1,1,1) + (2,3,4).$

10. Linearly independent. $(1,-1,1), (1,2,4), (1,3,9).$

11. Linearly dependent. $(1,3,9) = -2\,(1,1,1) + \frac{1}{3}\,(1,-1,1) + \frac{8}{3}\,(1,2,4).$

12. Linearly independent.

13. Linearly dependent. $(2,2,2) = \frac{8}{3}\,(1,2,3) - \frac{7}{3}\,(2,1,3) + (4,-1,1).$

14. Linearly dependent. $(4,2,4,6) = 2(2,1,2,3).$

15. Linearly dependent.
    $(-3,1,1,1) = -\,(1,-3,1,1) - (1,1,-3,1) - (1,1,1,-3).$

16. Linearly dependent.
    $(4,2,4,2) = (2,1,-1,1) + (5,3,6,0) + (-3,-2,-1,1).$

17. Linearly independent.

18. Linearly independent.

19. Linearly dependent. $(1,8,-13,14) = 3\,(2,1,-1,3) - 5\,(1,-1,2,-1).$

20. Linearly dependent. $(-3,2,-3,0,-1) = 2\,(0,1,0,0,1) - 3\,(1,0,1,0,1).$

About problems 21-35: A basis of the column space is not unique. The one we give is the one you get by finding the RREF of the given matrix, and choosing the columns corresponding to columns in the RREF with leading 1's.

21. $\begin{bmatrix} 1 \\ 3 \\ -2 \end{bmatrix}, \begin{bmatrix} 2 \\ 8 \\ 9 \end{bmatrix}$

22. $\begin{bmatrix} 1 \\ 2 \\ 3 \end{bmatrix}, \begin{bmatrix} 3 \\ -4 \\ -3 \end{bmatrix}, \begin{bmatrix} 9 \\ 8 \\ 3 \end{bmatrix}$. We could also choose $\begin{bmatrix} 1 \\ 0 \\ 0 \end{bmatrix}, \begin{bmatrix} 0 \\ 1 \\ 0 \end{bmatrix}, \begin{bmatrix} 0 \\ 0 \\ 1 \end{bmatrix}$

since the column space is three-dimensional and therefore is all of R^3.

23. $\begin{bmatrix} 2 \\ 3 \\ 4 \end{bmatrix}, \begin{bmatrix} 3 \\ 4 \\ 5 \end{bmatrix}$

24. $\begin{bmatrix} 1 \\ 3 \\ 4 \\ 2 \end{bmatrix}, \begin{bmatrix} 4 \\ 1 \\ 2 \\ 0 \end{bmatrix}, \begin{bmatrix} -6 \\ 0 \\ 1 \\ 0 \end{bmatrix}, \begin{bmatrix} 8 \\ -1 \\ 0 \\ 1 \end{bmatrix}$, column space is all of R^4.

25. $\begin{bmatrix} 1 \\ 2 \\ -3 \end{bmatrix}, \begin{bmatrix} 2 \\ 3 \\ -4 \end{bmatrix}, \begin{bmatrix} 6 \\ 9 \\ 0 \end{bmatrix}$, column space is all of R^3.

26. $\begin{bmatrix} 4 \\ 1 \\ 1 \end{bmatrix}, \begin{bmatrix} 1 \\ 4 \\ 1 \end{bmatrix}, \begin{bmatrix} 1 \\ 1 \\ 4 \end{bmatrix}$, column space is all of R^3.

27. $\begin{bmatrix} -2 \\ 1 \\ 1 \end{bmatrix}, \begin{bmatrix} 1 \\ -2 \\ 1 \end{bmatrix}$

28. $\begin{bmatrix} 1 \\ 3 \\ 5 \end{bmatrix}, \begin{bmatrix} 0 \\ 1 \\ -1 \end{bmatrix}, \begin{bmatrix} 1 \\ 0 \\ -1 \end{bmatrix}$, column space is all of R^3.

29. $\begin{bmatrix} 1 \\ 3 \\ 2 \end{bmatrix}, \begin{bmatrix} 2 \\ 4 \\ 6 \end{bmatrix}, \begin{bmatrix} 3 \\ 5 \\ 8 \end{bmatrix}$, column space is all of R^3.

30. $\begin{bmatrix} 2 \\ 3 \\ 4 \end{bmatrix}, \begin{bmatrix} 3 \\ 4 \\ 5 \end{bmatrix}$

31. $\begin{bmatrix} 2 \\ 3 \\ 4 \end{bmatrix}, \begin{bmatrix} 2 \\ -3 \\ 8 \end{bmatrix}, \begin{bmatrix} 2 \\ 3 \\ 12 \end{bmatrix}$, column space is all of R^3.

32. $\begin{bmatrix} \frac{1}{2} \\ \frac{1}{4} \\ \frac{1}{3} \\ \frac{1}{4} \end{bmatrix}, \begin{bmatrix} \frac{1}{2} \\ -\frac{1}{4} \\ -\frac{1}{3} \\ \frac{1}{2} \end{bmatrix}, \begin{bmatrix} \frac{1}{2} \\ \frac{1}{4} \\ \frac{1}{3} \\ 1 \end{bmatrix}$, column space is all of R^3.

33. $\begin{bmatrix} 5 \\ 1 \\ 8 \end{bmatrix}, \begin{bmatrix} 4 \\ -1 \\ 6 \end{bmatrix}, \begin{bmatrix} 3 \\ 1 \\ 4 \end{bmatrix}$, column space is all of R^3.

34. $\begin{bmatrix} 8 \\ 7 \\ 6 \end{bmatrix}, \begin{bmatrix} 7 \\ 0 \\ 5 \end{bmatrix}, \begin{bmatrix} 6 \\ 5 \\ 0 \end{bmatrix}$, column space is all of R^3.

35. $\begin{bmatrix} 2 \\ 3 \\ 5 \end{bmatrix}, \begin{bmatrix} 5 \\ 4 \\ 9 \end{bmatrix}$

In problems 36-45, put the given spanning set as the columns of a matrix and find the RREF. This allows you to select a basis and express the remaining vectors as linear combinations of basis vectors as done in the examples in this section. The answer is not always unique (for example, reordering the columns of the matrix may produce different correct answers). We give one possible correct answer.

36. Basis is $\{(1,0,2),(2,3,4)\}$, and $(3,4,6) = \frac{1}{3}(1,0,2) + \frac{4}{3}(2,3,4)$.

37. Basis is $\{(1,1,1),(1,-1,1)\}$ and $(2,3,2) = \frac{5}{2}(1,1,1) - \frac{1}{2}(1,-1,1)$.

38. Basis is $\{(1,1,1),(1,-1,1),(1,2,4)\}$ and $(2,3,5) = (1,1,1) + (1,2,4)$.

39. Basis is $\{(1,0,3,4),(0,2,3,4),(1,2,0,4),(1,2,3,0)\}$.

40. Basis is $\{(2,3,4,5),(3,4,5,6)\}$ and

$(4,5,6,7) = -(2,3,4,5) + 2(3,4,5,6),$

$(5,6,7,8) = -2(2,3,4,5) + 3(3,4,5,6).$

41. Basis is $\{(1,0,0,2),(1,0,5,6),(0,0,1,-1),(2,-1,-2,3)\}$

and $(1,0,1,2) = \frac{8}{9}(1,0,0,2) + \frac{1}{9}(1,0,5,6) + \frac{4}{9}(0,0,1,-1)$

42. Basis is $\{(1,2,4,0,1),(3,6,12,1,0),(5,10,20,-1,-1),(1,3,2,5,6)\}$.

43. Basis is
$\{(1,2,1,2,1),(1,0,1,0,2),(0,1,1,5,0),(0,0,1,2,3),(0,1,2,0,3)\}$.

44. Basis is $\{(1,2,0,3,4),(1,1,1,1,1),(0,1,0,1,2),(0,0,1,2,3)\}$

and $(2,4,2,7,10) = (1,2,0,3,4)+(1,1,1,1,1)+(0,1,0,1,2)+(0,0,1,2,3)$.

45. Basis is $\{(1,2,1,0,-1),(1,3,1,-1,1),(2,1,0,-1,-2),(0,0,0,1,2)\}$.

46. Yes.   47. No.   48. Yes.   49. Yes.   50. No.

51. $[v]_B = \begin{bmatrix} -1 \\ -\frac{9}{2} \\ \frac{15}{2} \end{bmatrix}$ 52. $[v]_B = \begin{bmatrix} 6 \\ 3 \\ 0 \end{bmatrix}$ 53. $[v]_B = \begin{bmatrix} -\frac{26}{3} \\ -\frac{19}{3} \\ 8 \end{bmatrix}$

54. $[v]_B = \begin{bmatrix} 2 \\ 0 \\ -1 \\ 0 \end{bmatrix}$ 55. $[v]_B = \begin{bmatrix} \frac{17}{2} \\ -\frac{1}{2} \\ -\frac{1}{4} \\ \frac{11}{12} \end{bmatrix}$

Answers to Exersises 2.2.2

In problems 1-12, for each matrix we give the RREF, a basis of the row space, and a basis of the column space.

1. $\begin{bmatrix} 1 & -1 & -2 \\ 2 & -2 & 9 \\ 3 & -3 & 7 \end{bmatrix} \sim \begin{bmatrix} 1 & -1 & 0 \\ 0 & 0 & 1 \\ 0 & 0 & 0 \end{bmatrix}$, $(1,-1,0),(0,0,1)$, $\begin{bmatrix} 1 \\ 2 \\ 3 \end{bmatrix}, \begin{bmatrix} -2 \\ 9 \\ 7 \end{bmatrix}$.

2. $\begin{bmatrix} 1 & 2 & 4 \\ 2 & 4 & 8 \\ 3 & 3 & -1 \end{bmatrix} \sim \begin{bmatrix} 1 & 0 & -\frac{14}{3} \\ 0 & 1 & \frac{13}{3} \\ 0 & 0 & 0 \end{bmatrix}$, $(1,0,-\frac{14}{3}),(0,1,\frac{13}{3})$, $\begin{bmatrix} 1 \\ 2 \\ 3 \end{bmatrix}, \begin{bmatrix} 2 \\ 4 \\ 3 \end{bmatrix}$.

3. $\begin{bmatrix} 1 & 3 & -1 \\ 5 & 3 & 7 \\ 9 & 2 & 16 \end{bmatrix} \sim \begin{bmatrix} 1 & 0 & 2 \\ 0 & 1 & -1 \\ 0 & 0 & 0 \end{bmatrix}$, $(1,0,2),(0,1,-1)$, $\begin{bmatrix} 1 \\ 5 \\ 9 \end{bmatrix}, \begin{bmatrix} 3 \\ 3 \\ 2 \end{bmatrix}$.

4. $\begin{bmatrix} 1 & 0 & 1 & 5 \\ 2 & 0 & 3 & 4 \\ 4 & 0 & -1 & -8 \\ 5 & 0 & 1 & 1 \end{bmatrix} \sim \begin{bmatrix} 1 & 0 & 0 & 0 \\ 0 & 0 & 1 & 0 \\ 0 & 0 & 0 & 1 \\ 0 & 0 & 0 & 0 \end{bmatrix}$,

$(1,0,0,0),(0,0,1,0),(0,0,0,1)$, $\begin{bmatrix} 1 \\ 2 \\ 4 \\ 5 \end{bmatrix}, \begin{bmatrix} 1 \\ 3 \\ -1 \\ 1 \end{bmatrix}, \begin{bmatrix} 5 \\ 4 \\ -8 \\ 1 \end{bmatrix}$.

5. $\begin{bmatrix} 2 & 3 & 4 & 5 \\ 3 & 4 & 5 & 6 \\ 4 & 5 & 6 & 7 \\ 5 & 6 & 7 & 8 \end{bmatrix} \sim \begin{bmatrix} 1 & 0 & -1 & -2 \\ 0 & 1 & 2 & 3 \\ 0 & 0 & 0 & 0 \\ 0 & 0 & 0 & 0 \end{bmatrix}$,

$(1,0,-1,-2), (0,1,2,3), \quad \begin{bmatrix} 2 \\ 3 \\ 4 \\ 5 \end{bmatrix}, \begin{bmatrix} 3 \\ 4 \\ 5 \\ 6 \end{bmatrix}.$

6. $\begin{bmatrix} 1 & -3 & 2 & 4 \\ 5 & -15 & 3 & 6 \\ 4 & -12 & 4 & 8 \\ 0 & 0 & 5 & 10 \end{bmatrix} \sim \begin{bmatrix} 1 & -3 & 0 & 0 \\ 0 & 0 & 1 & 2 \\ 0 & 0 & 0 & 0 \\ 0 & 0 & 0 & 0 \end{bmatrix}$,

$(1,-3,0,0), (0,0,1,2), \quad \begin{bmatrix} 1 \\ 5 \\ 4 \\ 0 \end{bmatrix}, \begin{bmatrix} 2 \\ 3 \\ 4 \\ 5 \end{bmatrix}.$

7. $\begin{bmatrix} 1 & 4 & 1 & 2 & 8 \\ 2 & 8 & 2 & 3 & 12 \\ 3 & 12 & 3 & -1 & -4 \\ 4 & 16 & -1 & -4 & -16 \end{bmatrix} \sim \begin{bmatrix} 1 & 4 & 0 & 0 & 0 \\ 0 & 0 & 1 & 0 & 0 \\ 0 & 0 & 0 & 1 & 4 \\ 0 & 0 & 0 & 0 & 0 \end{bmatrix}$,

$(1,4,0,0,0), (0,0,1,0,0), (0,0,0,1,4), \quad \begin{bmatrix} 1 \\ 2 \\ 3 \\ 4 \end{bmatrix}, \begin{bmatrix} 1 \\ 2 \\ 3 \\ -1 \end{bmatrix}, \begin{bmatrix} 2 \\ 3 \\ -1 \\ -4 \end{bmatrix}.$

8. $\begin{bmatrix} 1 & 5 & 6 & 1 & 3 \\ 2 & 10 & 12 & 5 & 9 \\ 3 & 15 & 18 & 6 & 12 \\ 0 & 0 & 0 & 4 & 7 \end{bmatrix} \sim \begin{bmatrix} 1 & 5 & 6 & 0 & 0 \\ 0 & 0 & 0 & 1 & 0 \\ 0 & 0 & 0 & 0 & 1 \\ 0 & 0 & 0 & 0 & 0 \end{bmatrix}$,

$(1,5,6,0,0), (0,0,0,1,0), (0,0,0,0,1), \quad \begin{bmatrix} 1 \\ 2 \\ 3 \\ 0 \end{bmatrix}, \begin{bmatrix} 1 \\ 5 \\ 6 \\ 4 \end{bmatrix}, \begin{bmatrix} 3 \\ 9 \\ 12 \\ 7 \end{bmatrix}.$

9. $\begin{bmatrix} 1 & 3 & 2 & 0 & 2 & 4 \\ 5 & 15 & 12 & 0 & -1 & -2 \\ 8 & 17 & 3 & 0 & 3 & 6 \end{bmatrix} \sim \begin{bmatrix} 1 & 0 & 0 & 0 & -\frac{325}{14} & -\frac{325}{7} \\ 0 & 1 & 0 & 0 & \frac{169}{14} & \frac{169}{7} \\ 0 & 0 & 1 & 0 & -\frac{11}{2} & -11 \end{bmatrix}$,

$\left(1,0,0,0,-\frac{325}{14},-\frac{325}{7}\right), \left(0,1,0,0,\frac{169}{14},\frac{169}{7}\right), \left(0,0,1,0,-\frac{11}{2},-11\right)$

$$\begin{bmatrix} 1 \\ 5 \\ 8 \end{bmatrix}, \begin{bmatrix} 3 \\ 15 \\ 17 \end{bmatrix}, \begin{bmatrix} 2 \\ 12 \\ 3 \end{bmatrix}.$$

10. $\begin{bmatrix} 1 & 2 & 0 & 4 & 5 & 6 \\ 2 & 3 & 4 & 0 & 6 & 7 \\ 4 & 0 & 6 & 7 & 8 & 9 \end{bmatrix} \sim \begin{bmatrix} 1 & 0 & 0 & \frac{64}{13} & \frac{41}{13} & \frac{48}{13} \\ 0 & 1 & 0 & -\frac{6}{13} & \frac{12}{13} & \frac{15}{13} \\ 0 & 0 & 1 & -\frac{55}{26} & -\frac{10}{13} & -\frac{25}{26} \end{bmatrix},$

$\left(1,0,0,\frac{64}{13},\frac{41}{13},\frac{48}{13}\right), \left(0,1,0,-\frac{6}{13},\frac{12}{13},\frac{15}{13}\right), \left(0,0,1,-\frac{55}{26},-\frac{10}{13},-\frac{25}{26}\right)'$

$$\begin{bmatrix} 1 \\ 2 \\ 4 \end{bmatrix}, \begin{bmatrix} 2 \\ 3 \\ 0 \end{bmatrix}, \begin{bmatrix} 0 \\ 4 \\ 6 \end{bmatrix}.$$

11. $\begin{bmatrix} -4 & 1 & 1 & 1 & 1 \\ 1 & -4 & 1 & 1 & 1 \\ 1 & 1 & -4 & 1 & 1 \\ 1 & 1 & 1 & -4 & 1 \\ 1 & 1 & 1 & 1 & -4 \end{bmatrix} \sim \begin{bmatrix} 1 & 0 & 0 & 0 & -1 \\ 0 & 1 & 0 & 0 & -1 \\ 0 & 0 & 1 & 0 & -1 \\ 0 & 0 & 0 & 1 & -1 \\ 0 & 0 & 0 & 0 & 0 \end{bmatrix},$

$(1,0,0,0,-1),(0,1,0,0,-1),(0,0,1,0,-1),(0,0,0,1,-1),$

$$\begin{bmatrix} -4 \\ 1 \\ 1 \\ 1 \\ 1 \end{bmatrix}, \begin{bmatrix} 1 \\ -4 \\ 1 \\ 1 \\ 1 \end{bmatrix}, \begin{bmatrix} 1 \\ 1 \\ -4 \\ 1 \\ 1 \end{bmatrix}, \begin{bmatrix} 1 \\ 1 \\ 1 \\ -4 \\ 1 \end{bmatrix}.$$

12. $\begin{bmatrix} 1 & 1 & 1 & 1 & 1 & 1 \\ 1 & -1 & 1 & -1 & 1 & -1 \\ 1 & 3 & 4 & 8 & 16 & 32 \\ 4 & 1 & 7 & 7 & 19 & 31 \end{bmatrix} \sim \begin{bmatrix} 1 & 0 & 0 & 0 & -4 & -8 \\ 0 & 1 & 0 & 0 & 0 & 0 \\ 0 & 0 & 1 & 0 & 5 & 8 \\ 0 & 0 & 0 & 1 & 0 & 1 \end{bmatrix},$

$(1,0,0,0,-4,-8),(0,1,0,0,0,0),(0,0,1,0,5,8)(0,0,0,1,0,1),$

$$\begin{bmatrix} 1 \\ 1 \\ 1 \\ 4 \end{bmatrix}, \begin{bmatrix} 1 \\ -1 \\ 3 \\ 1 \end{bmatrix}, \begin{bmatrix} 1 \\ 1 \\ 4 \\ 7 \end{bmatrix}, \begin{bmatrix} 1 \\ -1 \\ 8 \\ 7 \end{bmatrix}.$$

In problems 13-23, put the given vectors in R^n as either the rows or columns and find the rank of the resulting matrix. The vectors span R^n if and only if the rank of the resulting matrix is n.

13. Do not span R^3.

14. Do not span R^3.

15. Span R^3.

16. Do not span R^3.

17. Do not span R^4.

18. Span R^4.

19. Span R^4.

20. Do not span R^4.

21. Span R^5.

22. Span R^5.

In problems 23-25, determine if the given subspaces are identical.

23. $S \neq T$

24. $S = T$

25. $S \neq T$

Answers to Exercises 2.3.1

For each of the following matrices we give the Hermite form, a basis of the null space, and all solutions of the associated system of linear homogeneous equations.

1. $A = \begin{bmatrix} 1 & 2 \\ 2 & 4 \end{bmatrix}$. Hermite form is $\begin{bmatrix} 1 & 2 \\ 0 & 0 \end{bmatrix}$. Null space basis is $\begin{bmatrix} 2 \\ -1 \end{bmatrix}$.
All solutions of $AX = 0$ are of the form $\begin{bmatrix} 2s \\ -s \end{bmatrix}$.

2. $A = \begin{bmatrix} 1 & 0 & 3 \\ 0 & 2 & 0 \\ 3 & 0 & 1 \end{bmatrix}$. Hermite form is $\begin{bmatrix} 1 & 0 & 0 \\ 0 & 1 & 0 \\ 0 & 0 & 1 \end{bmatrix}$. The null space is the
zero subspace $\{(0)\}$, which has no basis. (0) is the only solution of $AX = 0$.

3. $A = \begin{bmatrix} 2 & 1 & 5 \\ 1 & 3 & 10 \\ 2 & 3 & 11 \end{bmatrix}$. Hermite form is $\begin{bmatrix} 1 & 0 & 1 \\ 0 & 1 & 3 \\ 0 & 0 & 0 \end{bmatrix}$. Null space basis is
$\begin{bmatrix} 1 \\ 2 \\ -1 \end{bmatrix}$. All solutions of $AX = 0$ are of the form $\begin{bmatrix} s \\ 3s \\ -s \end{bmatrix}$.

4. $A = \begin{bmatrix} 1 & 2 & 5 & 0 & 8 \\ 3 & 6 & 1 & 0 & 5 \\ 4 & 8 & 1 & 0 & 3 \end{bmatrix}$. Hermite form is $\begin{bmatrix} 1 & 2 & 0 & 0 & 0 \\ 0 & 0 & 0 & 0 & 0 \\ 0 & 0 & 1 & 0 & 0 \\ 0 & 0 & 0 & 0 & 0 \\ 0 & 0 & 0 & 0 & 1 \end{bmatrix}$.

Null space basis is $\begin{bmatrix} 2 \\ -1 \\ 0 \\ 0 \\ 0 \end{bmatrix}, \begin{bmatrix} 0 \\ 0 \\ 0 \\ -1 \\ 0 \end{bmatrix}$.

All solutions of $AX = 0$ are of the form $s \begin{bmatrix} 2 \\ -1 \\ 0 \\ 0 \\ 0 \end{bmatrix} + t \begin{bmatrix} 0 \\ 0 \\ 0 \\ -1 \\ 0 \end{bmatrix}$.

5. $A = \begin{bmatrix} 1 & -2 & 1 & 1 \\ 1 & 1 & -2 & 1 \\ -2 & 1 & 1 & -2 \end{bmatrix}$. Hermite form is $\begin{bmatrix} 1 & 0 & -1 & 1 \\ 0 & 1 & -1 & 0 \\ 0 & 0 & 0 & 0 \\ 0 & 0 & 0 & 0 \end{bmatrix}$.

Null space basis is $\begin{bmatrix} -1 \\ -1 \\ -1 \\ 0 \end{bmatrix}, \begin{bmatrix} 1 \\ 0 \\ 0 \\ -1 \end{bmatrix}$.

All solutions of $AX = 0$ are of the form $s \begin{bmatrix} -1 \\ -1 \\ -1 \\ 0 \end{bmatrix} + t \begin{bmatrix} 1 \\ 0 \\ 0 \\ -1 \end{bmatrix}$.

6. $A = \begin{bmatrix} -4 & 1 & 1 & 1 \\ 1 & -4 & 1 & 1 \\ 1 & 1 & -4 & 1 \\ 1 & 1 & 1 & -4 \end{bmatrix}$. Hermite form is $\begin{bmatrix} 1 & 0 & 0 & 0 \\ 0 & 1 & 0 & 0 \\ 0 & 0 & 1 & 0 \\ 0 & 0 & 0 & 1 \end{bmatrix}$.

Null space is $\{(0)\}$.

7. $A = \begin{bmatrix} 1 & 2 & 4 & 1 & 1 \\ -2 & -4 & -8 & 1 & 1 \\ 3 & 6 & 12 & 0 & 0 \end{bmatrix}$. Hermite form is $\begin{bmatrix} 1 & 2 & 4 & 0 & 0 \\ 0 & 0 & 0 & 0 & 0 \\ 0 & 0 & 0 & 0 & 0 \\ 0 & 0 & 0 & 1 & 1 \\ 0 & 0 & 0 & 0 & 0 \end{bmatrix}$.

Null space basis is $\begin{bmatrix} 2 \\ -1 \\ 0 \\ 0 \\ 0 \end{bmatrix}, \begin{bmatrix} 4 \\ 0 \\ -1 \\ 0 \\ 0 \end{bmatrix}, \begin{bmatrix} 0 \\ 0 \\ 0 \\ 1 \\ -1 \end{bmatrix}.$

All solutions of $AX = 0$ are of the form

$$r \begin{bmatrix} 2 \\ -1 \\ 0 \\ 0 \\ 0 \end{bmatrix} + s \begin{bmatrix} 4 \\ 0 \\ -1 \\ 0 \\ 0 \end{bmatrix} + t \begin{bmatrix} 0 \\ 0 \\ 0 \\ 1 \\ -1 \end{bmatrix}.$$

8. $A = \begin{bmatrix} 0 & 1 & 2 & 1 & 1 \\ 1 & 0 & 0 & 3 & 3 \\ 1 & 2 & 4 & 5 & 5 \end{bmatrix}$. Hermite form is $\begin{bmatrix} 1 & 0 & 0 & 3 & 3 \\ 0 & 1 & 2 & 1 & 1 \\ 0 & 0 & 0 & 0 & 0 \\ 0 & 0 & 0 & 0 & 0 \\ 0 & 0 & 0 & 0 & 0 \end{bmatrix}.$

Null space basis is $\begin{bmatrix} 0 \\ 2 \\ -1 \\ 0 \\ 0 \end{bmatrix}, \begin{bmatrix} 3 \\ 1 \\ 0 \\ -1 \\ 0 \end{bmatrix}, \begin{bmatrix} 3 \\ 1 \\ 0 \\ 0 \\ -1 \end{bmatrix}.$

All solutions of $AX = 0$ are of the form $r \begin{bmatrix} 0 \\ 2 \\ -1 \\ 0 \\ 0 \end{bmatrix} + s \begin{bmatrix} 3 \\ 1 \\ 0 \\ -1 \\ 0 \end{bmatrix} + t \begin{bmatrix} 3 \\ 1 \\ 0 \\ 0 \\ -1 \end{bmatrix}.$

9. $A = \begin{bmatrix} 1 & 1 & 1 & 1 \\ 1 & 2 & 3 & 4 \\ 2 & 3 & 4 & 5 \\ 3 & 4 & 5 & 6 \\ 4 & 5 & 6 & 7 \end{bmatrix}$. Hermite form is $\begin{bmatrix} 1 & 0 & -1 & -2 \\ 0 & 1 & 2 & 3 \\ 0 & 0 & 0 & 0 \\ 0 & 0 & 0 & 0 \end{bmatrix}.$

Null space basis is $\begin{bmatrix} -1 \\ 2 \\ -1 \\ 0 \end{bmatrix}, \begin{bmatrix} -2 \\ 3 \\ 0 \\ -1 \end{bmatrix}.$

All solutions of $AX = 0$ are of the form $s \begin{bmatrix} -1 \\ 2 \\ -1 \\ 0 \end{bmatrix} + t \begin{bmatrix} -2 \\ 3 \\ 0 \\ -1 \end{bmatrix}.$

10. $A = \begin{bmatrix} 1 & 2 & 3 & 4 & 5 \\ 5 & 4 & 3 & 2 & 1 \\ 1 & 1 & 1 & 1 & 1 \\ 0 & 0 & 0 & 0 & 0 \end{bmatrix}$. Hermite form is $\begin{bmatrix} 1 & 0 & -1 & -2 & -3 \\ 0 & 1 & 2 & 3 & 4 \\ 0 & 0 & 0 & 0 & 0 \\ 0 & 0 & 0 & 0 & 0 \\ 0 & 0 & 0 & 0 & 0 \end{bmatrix}$.

Null space basis is $\begin{bmatrix} -1 \\ 2 \\ -1 \\ 0 \\ 0 \end{bmatrix}, \begin{bmatrix} -2 \\ 3 \\ 0 \\ -1 \\ 0 \end{bmatrix}, \begin{bmatrix} -3 \\ 4 \\ 0 \\ 0 \\ -1 \end{bmatrix}$.

All solutions of $AX = 0$ are of the form $r \begin{bmatrix} -1 \\ 2 \\ -1 \\ 0 \\ 0 \end{bmatrix} + s \begin{bmatrix} -2 \\ 3 \\ 0 \\ -1 \\ 0 \end{bmatrix} + t \begin{bmatrix} -3 \\ 4 \\ 0 \\ 0 \\ -1 \end{bmatrix}$.

Answers to Matlab Exercises 2.3.3

For the given matrices, we give the rank, nullity, and a basis of the null space using Matlab.

1. Rank is 3, nullity is 1, basis of null space is $\begin{bmatrix} 6.5 \\ -2.5 \\ 1 \\ 0 \end{bmatrix}$ or $\begin{bmatrix} \frac{13}{2} \\ -\frac{5}{2} \\ 1 \\ 0 \end{bmatrix}$.

.2. Rank is 4, nullity is 2, basis of null space is $\begin{bmatrix} -2 \\ 1 \\ 1 \\ 0 \\ 0 \\ 0 \end{bmatrix}, \begin{bmatrix} 0 \\ -1 \\ 0 \\ -1 \\ 1 \\ 0 \end{bmatrix}$.

3. Rank is 2, nullity is 2, basis of null space is $\begin{bmatrix} -14 \\ -9 \\ 1 \\ 0 \end{bmatrix}, \begin{bmatrix} -13 \\ -8 \\ 0 \\ 1 \end{bmatrix}$.

4. Rank is 2, nullity is 2, basis of null space is $\begin{bmatrix} -\frac{4}{3} \\ \frac{3}{3} \\ 1 \\ 0 \end{bmatrix}, \begin{bmatrix} 3 \\ -3 \\ 0 \\ 1 \end{bmatrix}$.

5. Rank is 2, nullity is 2, basis of null space is $\begin{bmatrix} -\frac{17}{2} \\ 11 \\ 1 \\ 0 \end{bmatrix}, \begin{bmatrix} -\frac{9}{2} \\ 4 \\ 0 \\ 1 \end{bmatrix}$.

6. Rank is 2, nullity is 1, basis of null space is $\begin{bmatrix} 7 \\ 12 \\ -1 \end{bmatrix}$.

Answers to Exercises 2.4.2

In the following problems we give a particular solution to $AX = B$, a basis of the null space of A, and use these to express all solutions of $AX = B$.

1. $[A\,B] \sim \begin{bmatrix} 1 & 0 & -2 & 1 \\ 0 & 1 & 4 & 3 \end{bmatrix}$. Putting the A part in Hermite form gives

$$\begin{bmatrix} 1 & 0 & -2 & 1 \\ 0 & 1 & 4 & 3 \\ 0 & 0 & 0 & 0 \end{bmatrix}.$$

One particular solution is $X = \begin{bmatrix} 1 \\ 3 \\ 0 \end{bmatrix}$. A basis of null space A is $\begin{bmatrix} -2 \\ 4 \\ -1 \end{bmatrix}$.

All solutions are of the form $X = \begin{bmatrix} 1 \\ 3 \\ 0 \end{bmatrix} + s \begin{bmatrix} -2 \\ 4 \\ -1 \end{bmatrix}$.

2. $[A\,B] \sim \begin{bmatrix} 1 & 2 & 0 & -1 & 5 \\ 0 & 0 & 1 & 3 & 7 \\ 0 & 0 & 0 & 0 & 0 \end{bmatrix}$. Puting the A part in Hermite form gives

$$\begin{bmatrix} 1 & 2 & 0 & -1 & 5 \\ 0 & 0 & 0 & 0 & 0 \\ 0 & 0 & 1 & 3 & 7 \\ 0 & 0 & 0 & 0 & 0 \end{bmatrix}.$$

One particular solution is $X = \begin{bmatrix} 5 \\ 0 \\ 7 \\ 0 \end{bmatrix}$. A basis of null space A is $\begin{bmatrix} 2 \\ -1 \\ 0 \\ 0 \end{bmatrix}, \begin{bmatrix} -1 \\ 0 \\ 3 \\ -1 \end{bmatrix}$.

All solutions are of the form $X = \begin{bmatrix} 5 \\ 0 \\ 7 \\ 0 \end{bmatrix} + s \begin{bmatrix} 2 \\ -1 \\ 0 \\ 0 \end{bmatrix} + t \begin{bmatrix} -1 \\ 0 \\ 3 \\ -1 \end{bmatrix}$.

3. $[A \, B] \sim \begin{bmatrix} 1 & 0 & 2 & 3 & 0 & 2 \\ 0 & 1 & -1 & -4 & 0 & 5 \\ 0 & 0 & 0 & 0 & 1 & 4 \end{bmatrix}$. Putting A part in Hermite form

gives $\begin{bmatrix} 1 & 0 & 2 & 3 & 0 & 2 \\ 0 & 1 & -1 & -4 & 0 & 5 \\ 0 & 0 & 0 & 0 & 0 & 0 \\ 0 & 0 & 0 & 0 & 0 & 0 \\ 0 & 0 & 0 & 0 & 1 & 4 \end{bmatrix}$.

One solution is $X = \begin{bmatrix} 2 \\ 5 \\ 0 \\ 0 \\ 4 \end{bmatrix}$. A basis of null space A is $\begin{bmatrix} 2 \\ -1 \\ -1 \\ 0 \\ 0 \end{bmatrix}, \begin{bmatrix} 3 \\ -4 \\ 0 \\ -1 \\ 0 \end{bmatrix}$.

All solutions are of the form $X = \begin{bmatrix} 2 \\ 5 \\ 0 \\ 0 \\ 4 \end{bmatrix} + s \begin{bmatrix} 2 \\ -1 \\ -1 \\ 0 \\ 0 \end{bmatrix} + t \begin{bmatrix} 3 \\ -4 \\ 0 \\ -1 \\ 0 \end{bmatrix}$.

4. $[A \, B] \sim \begin{bmatrix} 1 & -2 & 3 & 6 \\ 0 & 0 & 0 & 0 \\ 0 & 0 & 0 & 0 \end{bmatrix}$. Putting A part in Hermite form gives

$\begin{bmatrix} 1 & -2 & 3 & 6 \\ 0 & 0 & 0 & 0 \\ 0 & 0 & 0 & 0 \end{bmatrix}$.

One solution is $X = \begin{bmatrix} 6 \\ 0 \\ 0 \end{bmatrix}$. A basis of null space A is $\begin{bmatrix} -2 \\ -1 \\ 0 \end{bmatrix}, \begin{bmatrix} 3 \\ 0 \\ -1 \end{bmatrix}$.

All solutions are of the form $X = \begin{bmatrix} 6 \\ 0 \\ 0 \end{bmatrix} + s \begin{bmatrix} -2 \\ -1 \\ 0 \end{bmatrix} + t \begin{bmatrix} 3 \\ 0 \\ -1 \end{bmatrix}$.

5. $[A \, B] \sim \begin{bmatrix} 1 & 0 & 2 & 3 & 2 \\ 0 & 1 & -1 & -4 & 5 \\ 0 & 0 & 0 & 0 & 0 \end{bmatrix}$. Putting A part in Hermite form gives

$\begin{bmatrix} 1 & 0 & 2 & 3 & 2 \\ 0 & 1 & -1 & -4 & 5 \\ 0 & 0 & 0 & 0 & 0 \\ 0 & 0 & 0 & 0 & 0 \end{bmatrix}$.

One solution is $X = \begin{bmatrix} 2 \\ 5 \\ 0 \\ 0 \end{bmatrix}$. A basis of null space A is $\begin{bmatrix} 2 \\ -1 \\ -1 \\ 0 \end{bmatrix}, \begin{bmatrix} 3 \\ -4 \\ 0 \\ -1 \end{bmatrix}$.

All solutions are of the form $X = \begin{bmatrix} 2 \\ 5 \\ 0 \\ 0 \end{bmatrix} + s \begin{bmatrix} 2 \\ -1 \\ -1 \\ 0 \end{bmatrix} + t \begin{bmatrix} 3 \\ -4 \\ 0 \\ -1 \end{bmatrix}$.

6. $[A\,B] \sim \begin{bmatrix} 1 & 0 & 3 & 0 \\ 0 & 1 & 2 & 0 \\ 0 & 0 & 0 & 1 \\ 0 & 0 & 0 & 0 \end{bmatrix}$. This system has no solutions.

7. $[A\,B] \sim \begin{bmatrix} 1 & 2 & 0 & 4 \\ 0 & 0 & 1 & 5 \end{bmatrix}$.

Putting A part in Hermite form gives $\begin{bmatrix} 1 & 2 & 0 & 4 \\ 0 & 0 & 0 & 0 \\ 0 & 0 & 1 & 5 \end{bmatrix}$.

One solution is $X = \begin{bmatrix} 4 \\ 0 \\ 5 \end{bmatrix}$. A basis for null space of A is $\begin{bmatrix} 2 \\ -1 \\ 0 \end{bmatrix}$.

All solutions are of the form $X = \begin{bmatrix} 4 \\ 0 \\ 5 \end{bmatrix} + s \begin{bmatrix} 2 \\ -1 \\ 0 \end{bmatrix}$.

8. $[A\,B] \sim \begin{bmatrix} 1 & 0 & 3 \\ 0 & 1 & 2 \\ 0 & 0 & 0 \\ 0 & 0 & 0 \end{bmatrix}$.

Putting A part in Hermite form gives $\begin{bmatrix} 1 & 0 & 3 \\ 0 & 1 & 2 \end{bmatrix}$.

The unique solution is $X = \begin{bmatrix} 3 \\ 2 \end{bmatrix}$. The null space of A is the zero subspace.

9. $[A\,B] \sim \begin{bmatrix} 1 & 0 & 2 & 0 & 4 \\ 0 & 1 & -3 & 0 & -\frac{1}{2} \\ 0 & 0 & 0 & 0 & 0 \\ 0 & 0 & 0 & 1 & 2 \end{bmatrix}$. One solution is $X = \begin{bmatrix} 4 \\ -\frac{1}{2} \\ 0 \\ 2 \end{bmatrix}$.

A basis of null space A is $\begin{bmatrix} 2 \\ -3 \\ -1 \\ 0 \end{bmatrix}$.

All solutions are of the form $X = \begin{bmatrix} 4 \\ -\frac{1}{2} \\ 0 \\ 2 \end{bmatrix} + s \begin{bmatrix} 2 \\ -3 \\ -1 \\ 0 \end{bmatrix}$.

10. $[A \, B] \sim \begin{bmatrix} 1 & 0 & 2 & -\frac{1}{5} & \frac{1}{2} \\ 0 & 1 & 3 & 4 & 2 \\ 0 & 0 & 0 & 0 & 0 \\ 0 & 0 & 0 & 0 & 0 \end{bmatrix}$. One solution is $X = \begin{bmatrix} \frac{1}{2} \\ 2 \\ 0 \\ 0 \end{bmatrix}$.

A basis of null space A is $\begin{bmatrix} 2 \\ 3 \\ -1 \\ 0 \end{bmatrix}, \begin{bmatrix} -\frac{1}{5} \\ 4 \\ 0 \\ -1 \end{bmatrix}$.

All solutions are of the form $X = \begin{bmatrix} \frac{1}{2} \\ 2 \\ 0 \\ 0 \end{bmatrix} + s \begin{bmatrix} 2 \\ 3 \\ -1 \\ 0 \end{bmatrix} + t \begin{bmatrix} -\frac{1}{5} \\ 4 \\ 0 \\ -1 \end{bmatrix}$.

Answers to Exercises 3.1.1

1. In this problem:

   (a) The eigenvalues are -2 and 5.

   (b) For $k = -2$, a basis of the eigenspace is $\begin{bmatrix} 2 \\ -1 \end{bmatrix}$.

   For $k = 5$, a basis of the eigenspace is $\begin{bmatrix} 1 \\ 3 \end{bmatrix}$.

   (c) The algebraic multiplicity of each eigenvalue is 1.

   The geometric multiplicity of each eigenvalue is 1.

2. In this problem:

   (a) The eigenvalues are -4 and 1.

   (b) For $k = -4$, a basis of the eigenspace is $\begin{bmatrix} 1 \\ -3 \end{bmatrix}$.

For $k = 1$, a basis of the eigenspace is $\begin{bmatrix} 1 \\ 2 \end{bmatrix}$

(c) The algebraic multiplicity of each eigenvalue is 1.

The geometric multiplicity of each eigenvalue is 1.

3. The characteristic polynomial is $k^2 + 4$. The matrix has no real eigenvalues.

4. In this problem:

(a) The eigenvalues are 4 and 9.

(b) For $k = 4$, a basis of the eigenspace is $\begin{bmatrix} 1 \\ -3 \end{bmatrix}$.

For $k = 9$, a basis of the eigenspace is $\begin{bmatrix} 1 \\ 2 \end{bmatrix}$.

(c) The algebraic multiplicity of each eigenvalue is 1.

The geometric multiplicity of each eigenvalue is 1.

5. In this problem:

(a) The only eigenvalue is 3.

(b) For $k = 3$, a basis for the eigenspace is $\begin{bmatrix} 1 \\ 0 \end{bmatrix}$.

(c) The algebraic multiplicity of 3 is 2.

The geometric multiplicity of 3 is 1.

6. In this problem:

(a) The eigenvalues are 2 and 4.

(b) For $k = 2$, a basis of the eigenspace is $\begin{bmatrix} 1 \\ -1 \end{bmatrix}$.

For $k = 4$, a basis of the eigenspace is $\begin{bmatrix} 1 \\ 1 \end{bmatrix}$.

(c) The algebraic multiplicity of each eigenvalue is 1.

The geometric multiplicity of each eigenvalue is 1.

7. In this problem:

(a) The only eigenvalue is 3.

(b) For $k = 3$, a basis of the eigenspace is $\begin{bmatrix} 2 \\ 1 \end{bmatrix}$.

(c) The algebraic multiplicity of 3 is 2.

The geometric multiplicity of 3 is 1.

8. The characteristic polynomial is $k^2 - 3k + 8$. The matrix has no real eigenvalues.

9. In this problem:

   (a) The eigenvalues are 3 and 5.

   (b) For $k = 3$, a basis for the eigenspace is $\begin{bmatrix} 1 \\ 0 \\ 0 \end{bmatrix}$.

   For $k = 5$, a basis for the eigenspace is $\begin{bmatrix} 17 \\ 4 \\ 1 \end{bmatrix}$.

   (c) For $k = 3$, the algebraic multiplicity is 2, the geometric multiplicity is 1.

   For $k = 5$, both algebraic and geometric multiplicity equal 1.

10. In this problem:

    (a) The eigenvalues are 3 and 9.

    (b) For $k = 3$, a basis of the eigenspace is $\begin{bmatrix} 1 \\ -1 \\ 0 \end{bmatrix}$, $\begin{bmatrix} 1 \\ 0 \\ -1 \end{bmatrix}$.

    For $k = 9$, a basis for the eigenspace is $\begin{bmatrix} 1 \\ 1 \\ 1 \end{bmatrix}$.

    (c) for $k = 3$ both algebraic and the geometric multiplicity equal 2.

    for $k = 9$ both algebraic and the geometric multiplicity equal 1.

11. In this problem:

    (a) the eigenvalues are 3, -3, and 9.

    (b) For $k = 3$, a basis for the eigenspace is $\begin{bmatrix} 2 \\ -1 \\ -1 \end{bmatrix}$.

For $k = -3$, a basis for the eigen space is $\begin{bmatrix} 0 \\ 1 \\ -1 \end{bmatrix}$.

For $k = 9$, a basis for the eigenspace is $\begin{bmatrix} 1 \\ 1 \\ 1 \end{bmatrix}$.

(c) For each eigenvalue both algebraic and geometric multiplicity equal 1.

12. In this problem:

(a) The only real eigenvalue is 9.

(b) For $k = 9$, a basis for the eigenspace is $\begin{bmatrix} 1 \\ 1 \\ 1 \end{bmatrix}$.

(c) For $k = 9$, both algebraic and geometric multiplicity equal 1.

13. In this problem:

(a) The eigenvalues are 2 and 8.

(b) For $k = 2$, a basis for the eigenspace is $\begin{bmatrix} 1 \\ 3 \\ 0 \end{bmatrix}$, $\begin{bmatrix} 2 \\ 0 \\ -3 \end{bmatrix}$.

For $k = 8$, a basis for the eigenspace is $\begin{bmatrix} 1 \\ 1 \\ 2 \end{bmatrix}$.

(c) For $k = 2$, both algebraic and geometric multiplicity equal 2.

For $k = 8$, both algebraic and geometric multiplicity equal 1.

14. In this problem:

(a) The eigenvalues are 2 and 13.

(b) For $k = 2$, a basis for the eigenspace is $\begin{bmatrix} 3 \\ -1 \\ 0 \end{bmatrix}$, $\begin{bmatrix} 2 \\ 0 \\ 1 \end{bmatrix}$.

For $k = 13$, a basis for the eigenspace is $\begin{bmatrix} 1 \\ 2 \\ -2 \end{bmatrix}$.

(c) For $k = 2$, both algebraic and geometric multiplicity equal 2.

For $k = 13$, both algebraic and geometric multiplicity equal 1.

15. In this problem:

(a) The eigenvalues are $-1, 3$, and 7.

(b) For $k = -1$, a basis of the eigenspace is $\begin{bmatrix} -1 \\ 1 \\ -1 \end{bmatrix}$.

For $k = 3$, a basis for the eigenspace is $\begin{bmatrix} 1 \\ -1 \\ -1 \end{bmatrix}$.

For $k = 7$, a basis of the eigenspace is $\begin{bmatrix} 1 \\ -9 \\ -15 \end{bmatrix}$.

(c) Each of the eigenvalues has both algebraic and geometric multiplicity equal to 1.

16. In this problem:

(a) The eigenvalues are 3 and -3.

(b) For $k = 2$, a basis of the eigenspace is $\begin{bmatrix} 2 \\ 1 \\ 0 \\ 0 \end{bmatrix}, \begin{bmatrix} 1 \\ 0 \\ 1 \\ 0 \end{bmatrix}, \begin{bmatrix} 0 \\ 0 \\ 0 \\ 1 \end{bmatrix}$.

For $k = 4$, a basis of the eigenspace is $\begin{bmatrix} -1 \\ 2 \\ 1 \\ 0 \end{bmatrix}$.

(c) For $k = 3$, the algebraic multiplicity is 3 and the geometric multiplicity is 3.

For $k = -3$, both algebraic and geometric multiplicity equal 1.

17. In this problem:

(a) The eigenvalues are 2 and 1.

(b) For $k = 2$, a basis of the eigenspace is $\begin{bmatrix} 1 \\ 2 \\ 3 \end{bmatrix}$.

For $k = 1$, a basis of the eigenspace is $\begin{bmatrix} 1 \\ 4 \\ 6 \end{bmatrix}$.

(c) For $k = 2$, the algebraic multiplicity is 2 and the geometric multiplicity is 1.

For $k = 1$, both algebraic and geometric multiplicity equal 1.

18. In this problem:

  (a) The only real eigenvalue is 5.

  (b) For $k = 5$, a basis of the eigenspace is $\begin{bmatrix} 0 \\ 1 \\ 1 \end{bmatrix}$.

  (c) For $k = 5$, both algebraic and geometric multiplicity equal 1.

19. In this problem:

  (a) The eigenvalues are $2, 3$, and 1.

  (b) For $k = 2$, a basis for the eigenspace is $\begin{bmatrix} 1 \\ 2 \\ 3 \end{bmatrix}$.

     For $k = 3$, a basis for the eigenspace is $\begin{bmatrix} 1 \\ 4 \\ 6 \end{bmatrix}$.

     For $k = 1$, a basis for the eigenspace is $\begin{bmatrix} 1 \\ 1 \\ 1 \end{bmatrix}$.

  (c) For each eigenvalue both algebraic and geometric multiplicity equal 1.

20. In this problem:

  (a) The eigenvalues are 2 and 15.

  (b) For $k = 2$, a basis of the eigenspace is $\begin{bmatrix} 2 \\ -3 \\ 0 \end{bmatrix}, \begin{bmatrix} 2 \\ 0 \\ -3 \end{bmatrix}$.

     For $k = 15$, a basis of the eigenspace is $\begin{bmatrix} 1 \\ 2 \\ 3 \end{bmatrix}$.

(c) For $k = 2$, both algebraic and geometric multiplicity are 2.

   For $k = 15$, both algebraic and geometric multiplicity are 1.

Answers to Matlab Exercises 3.1.3

These exercises are the same as in Exercises 3.1.1, except done by Matlab, so the answers are given above. Recall that a basis for a subspace is not unique.

Answers to Optional Matlab Exercises 3.1.5

1. Only rational root is -4.

2. Rational roots are -4 and 2.

3. No rational roots.

4. No rational roots.

5. Rational roots are -1, 3, and -5.

6. No rational roots.

7. Only rational root is -5.

8. Only rational root is 3

9. No rational roots.

10. Only rational root is -5.

Answers to Exercises 3.2.1

Remember that the diagonalizing matrix P is not unique.

1. Diagonalizable. $P = \begin{bmatrix} 2 & 1 \\ -1 & 3 \end{bmatrix}$.

2. Diagonalizable. $P = \begin{bmatrix} 1 & 1 \\ -3 & 2 \end{bmatrix}$.

3. Not diagonalizable.

4. Diagonalizable. $P = \begin{bmatrix} 1 & 1 \\ -3 & 2 \end{bmatrix}$.

5. Not diagonalizable.

6. Diagonalizable. $P = \begin{bmatrix} 1 & 1 \\ -1 & 1 \end{bmatrix}$.

7. Not diagonalizable.

8. Not diagonalizable.

9. Not diagonalizable.

10. Diagonalizable. $P = \begin{bmatrix} 1 & 1 & 1 \\ -1 & 0 & 1 \\ 0 & -1 & 1 \end{bmatrix}$.

11. Diagonalizable. $P = \begin{bmatrix} 2 & 0 & 1 \\ -1 & 1 & 1 \\ -1 & -1 & 1 \end{bmatrix}$.

12. Not diagonalizable.

13. Diagonalizable. $P = \begin{bmatrix} 1 & 2 & 1 \\ 3 & 0 & 1 \\ 0 & -3 & 2 \end{bmatrix}$.

14. Diagonalizable. $P = \begin{bmatrix} 3 & 2 & 1 \\ -1 & 0 & 2 \\ 0 & 1 & -2 \end{bmatrix}$.

15. Diagonalizable. $P = \begin{bmatrix} -1 & 1 & 1 \\ 1 & -1 & -9 \\ -1 & -1 & -15 \end{bmatrix}$.

16. Diagonalizable. $P = \begin{bmatrix} 2 & 1 & 0 & -1 \\ 1 & 0 & 0 & 2 \\ 0 & 1 & 0 & 1 \\ 0 & 0 & 1 & 0 \end{bmatrix}$.

17. Not diagonalizable.

18. Not diagonalizable.

19. Diagonalizable. $P = \begin{bmatrix} 1 & 1 & 1 \\ 2 & 4 & 1 \\ 3 & 6 & 1 \end{bmatrix}$.

20. Diagonalizable. $P = \begin{bmatrix} 2 & 2 & 1 \\ -3 & 0 & 2 \\ 0 & -3 & 3 \end{bmatrix}$.

21. Diagonalizable (Has three distinct real eigenvalues.)

22. Not diagonalizable.
    (Eigenvalue 3 has geometric multiplicity < algebraic multiplicity.)

23. Diagonalizable.
    (Has three distinct real roots.)

24. Not diagonalizable.
    (Eigenvalue 2 has geometric multiplicity < algebraic multiplicity.)

25. Not diagonalizable
    (Eigenvalue 3 has geometric multiplicity < algebraic multiplicity.)

26. Diagonalizable. (Has three distinct real eigenvalues.)

27. Not diagonalizable. (Has some complex eigenvalues.)

28. Not diagonalizable.
    (Eigenvalue 4 has geometric multiplicity < algebraic multiplicity.)

29. Diagonalizable.
    (Geometric multiplicity = algebraic multiplicity for all eigenvalues.)

30. Not diagonalizable.
    (Eigenvalue 4 has geometric multiplicity < algebraic multiplicity.)

Answers to Matlab Exercises 3.2.3

1. Eigenvalues are 6 and 2. Matrix is diagonalizable. One P that will work is $P = \begin{bmatrix} 1 & -1 \\ 1 & 3 \end{bmatrix}$. The [P,D]=eig(A) command gives $P = \begin{bmatrix} 0.7071 & -0.3162 \\ 0.7071 & 0.9487 \end{bmatrix}$, $D = \begin{bmatrix} 6 & 0 \\ 0 & 2 \end{bmatrix}$. The given P is a decimal approximation of $\begin{bmatrix} \frac{1}{\sqrt{2}} & -\frac{1}{\sqrt{10}} \\ \frac{1}{\sqrt{2}} & \frac{3}{\sqrt{10}} \end{bmatrix}$.

2. Eigenvalues are $-1, -1$, and 3. Diagonalizable.

   One P that will work is $\begin{bmatrix} 0 & 1 & 2 \\ 1 & 0 & 2 \\ 0 & 1 & 1 \end{bmatrix}$.

The [P,D]=eig(A) command gives

$$P = \begin{bmatrix} 0 & .6667 & .0452 \\ 1 & .6667 & .9998 \\ 0 & .3333 & .0452 \end{bmatrix}, D = \begin{bmatrix} -1 & 0 & 0 \\ 0 & 3 & 0 \\ 0 & 0 & -1 \end{bmatrix}.$$

3. Eigenvalues are $1, 3$, and 5. Diagonalizable. One P that will work is

$$P = \begin{bmatrix} -1 & 0 & 1 \\ -2 & -1 & 2 \\ 2 & 1 & 2 \end{bmatrix}.$$ The [P,D]=eig(A) command gives

$$P = \begin{bmatrix} -.3333 & 0 & .3333 \\ -.6667 & .7071 & .6667 \\ .6667 & -.7071 & .6667 \end{bmatrix}, D = \begin{bmatrix} 1 & 0 & 0 \\ 0 & 3 & 0 \\ 0 & 0 & 5 \end{bmatrix}.$$

4. Eigenvalues are $3, 3$, and 2. Not diagonalizable.

5. Eigenvalues are 3 and 312. Diagonalizable. One P that will work is

$$P = \begin{bmatrix} -1 & 1 & -1 \\ 1 & 0 & -1 \\ 0 & 4 & 1 \end{bmatrix}.$$

6. Eigenvalues are $-5, 2$, and 2. Not diagonalizable.

7. Eigenvalues are $\sqrt{2}$ and $-\sqrt{2}$ (or approximately 1.4142 and -1.4142) Diagonalizable. $P = \begin{bmatrix} 0.8165 & -0.1865 \\ 0.5774 & 0.5774 \end{bmatrix}.$

8. Eigenvalues are $4, \sqrt{3},$ and $-\sqrt{3}$ (or approximately $4, 1.7321$ and -1.7321)

Diagonalizable. $P = \begin{bmatrix} -0.6882 & -0.1294 & 0.4830 \\ -0.6882 & 0.9659 & -0.2588 \\ -0.2294 & 0.2241 & 0.8365 \end{bmatrix}$

9. Eigenvalues are -1, $1 + \frac{\sqrt{192}}{2}$, and $1 - \frac{\sqrt{192}}{2}$ (or approximately -1,

7.9282, and -5.9282). Diagonalizable. $P = \begin{bmatrix} 0 & 0.8224 & -0.1032 \\ 1 & 0.5089 & 0.8896 \\ 0 & 0.2544 & 0.4448 \end{bmatrix}.$

10. Eigenvalues are approximately $-3.8922, 2.8004$, and 0.0917. Diago-

nalizable. $P = \begin{bmatrix} -0.6768 & 0.1200 & -0.2363 \\ 0.5786 & 0.4815 & 0.1550 \\ 0.4552 & 0.8682 & 0.9592 \end{bmatrix}.$

11. Eigenvalues are approximately 4.2466, −1.6697, and 0.4231. Diago-
nalizable. $P = \begin{bmatrix} 0.5620 & 0.4953 & -0.2250 \\ 0.6691 & -0.2443 & -0.3831 \\ 0.4863 & -0.8336 & 0.8959 \end{bmatrix}$

12. Eigenvalues are approximately 7.8121, 1.8718, and −0.6839. Diago-
nalizable. $P = \begin{bmatrix} -0.6936 & -0.6081 & -0.3364 \\ -0.6350 & 0.7739 & 0.0144 \\ -0.3401 & 0.1772 & 0.9416 \end{bmatrix}$

13. Eigenvalues are 4, 4, and 1. Not diagonalizable.

14. Eigenvalues are 0, 0, −2, and 18. Diagonalizable.

Answers to Exercises 3.3.1

Keep in mind that the answers here are not unique, so that your answer
may be correct even though it is different from the answer given here.

1. $(0, 1, 0), (1, 0, 2)$

2. $(2, 1, 1), (-1, 2, 0)$

3. $(1, 3, 1, 1), (4, -3, 1, 4)$

4. $(1, 0, 1, 0), (0, 1, 0, 0), (-1, 0, 1, 1)$

5. Normalizing the vectors, we have

   (a) $(0, 1, 0), \frac{1}{\sqrt{5}}(1, 0, 2)$
   (b) $\frac{1}{\sqrt{6}}(2, 1, 1), \frac{1}{\sqrt{5}}(-1, 2, 0)$
   (c) $\frac{1}{\sqrt{12}}(1, 3, 1, 1), \frac{1}{\sqrt{42}}(4, -3, 1, 4)$
   (d) $\frac{1}{\sqrt{2}}(1, 0, 1, 0), (0, 1, 0, 0), \frac{1}{\sqrt{3}}, (-1, 0, 1, 1)$

6. $(0, 1, -1), (4, -1, -1)$

7. $(0, 1, -2), (5, 2, 1)$

8. $(-1, 3, -1, 0), (4, -1, -7, -11)$

9. $(0, 1, 0, 0), (0, 0, 1, -1), (4, 0, -1, -1)$

10. $(1, 0, 0, -1), (0, 1, -1, 0), (2, -1, -1, 2)$

11. Normalizing the vectors, we have

   (a) $\frac{1}{\sqrt{2}}(0,1,-1), \frac{1}{\sqrt{18}}(4,-1,-1)$

   (b) $\frac{1}{\sqrt{5}}(0,1,-2), \frac{1}{\sqrt{30}}(5,2,1)$

   (c) $\frac{1}{\sqrt{11}}(-1,3,-1,0), \frac{1}{\sqrt{187}}(4,-1,-7,-11)$

   (d) $(0,1,0,0), \frac{1}{\sqrt{2}}(0,0,1,-1), \frac{1}{\sqrt{18}}(4,0,-1,-1)$

   (e) $\frac{1}{\sqrt{2}}(1,0,0,-1), \frac{1}{\sqrt{2}}(0,1,-1,0), \frac{1}{\sqrt{10}}(2,-1,-1,2)$

Answers to Matlab Exercises 3.3.3

For problems 1-5 the basis vectors are the columns of Q=orth(A), where A is a matrix with columns the given spanning set.

1. $(0.3098, 0.4064, 0.6507, 0.5616), (0.7137, 0.4783, -0.4757, -0.1886),$
   $(0.7137, 0.4783, -0.4757, -0.1886)$

2. $(-0.0970, 0.4467, 0.8894), (-0.7170, -0.6511, 0.2488)$

3. $(0.1325, 0.5298, -0.2649, 0.7947), (0.5345, 0.2673, 0.80180)$

4. $(0.5020, 0.2999, -0.2595, 0.6891, 0.3403)$
   $(-0.4658, -0.0910, -0.4048, 0.5162, -0.5868)$
   $(-0.7287, 0.2648, 0.0800, 0.1448, 0.6095)$

5. $(0.6120, 0.6707, 0.4191), (0.0661, -0.5715, 0.8180)$
   For problems 6-10 the basis vectors are the columns of N=null(A), where A is the given matrix.

6. $(-0.9541, 0.0376, 0.2442, 0.1690), (0, -0.8157, 0.4088, -0.4093)$
   $(0, -0.5647, -0.4093, 0.7167)$

7. $(-0.8864, -0.1612, 0.4029, 0.1612), (0, 0.8704, 0.4381, -0.2248)$
   $(0, 0.3482, -0.2248, 0.9101)$

8. $(-0.8845, 0.2488, 0.2164, -0.2759, 0.1812),$
   $(0, 0.5235, -0.2556, 0.6183, 0.5276)$
   $(0, -0.2998, 0.8186, 0.4676, 0.1460)$

9. $(-0.8944, 0.2236, 0.2236, 0.2236, 0.2236),$
   $(0, -0.5000, 0.8333, -0.1667, -0.1667)$
   $(0, -0.5000, -0.1667, 0.8333, -0.1667),$
   $(0, -0.5000, -0.1667, -0.1667, 0.8333)$

10. $(-1.0000, 0, 0, 0), (0, 0, 1.0000, 0), (0, -0.8944, 0, 0.4472)$

Answers to Exercises 3.4.1

Recall that P is not unique, so the given P is not the only correct answer.

1. Eigenvalues are 1 and 6. $P = \begin{bmatrix} \frac{2}{\sqrt{5}} & -\frac{1}{\sqrt{5}} \\ \frac{1}{\sqrt{5}} & \frac{2}{\sqrt{5}} \end{bmatrix}$.

2. Eigenvalues are 1 and 5. $P = \begin{bmatrix} -\frac{1}{\sqrt{2}} & \frac{1}{\sqrt{2}} \\ \frac{1}{\sqrt{2}} & \frac{1}{\sqrt{2}} \end{bmatrix}$.

3. Eigenvalues are -1, 1, and 5. $P = \begin{bmatrix} -\frac{1}{\sqrt{3}} & 0 & \frac{2}{\sqrt{6}} \\ \frac{1}{\sqrt{3}} & -\frac{1}{\sqrt{2}} & \frac{1}{\sqrt{6}} \\ \frac{1}{\sqrt{3}} & \frac{1}{\sqrt{2}} & \frac{1}{\sqrt{6}} \end{bmatrix}$.

4. Eigenvalues are 4, 4 and 10. $P = \begin{bmatrix} -\frac{1}{\sqrt{2}} & \frac{1}{\sqrt{6}} & \frac{1}{\sqrt{3}} \\ \frac{1}{\sqrt{2}} & \frac{1}{\sqrt{6}} & \frac{1}{\sqrt{3}} \\ 0 & -\frac{2}{\sqrt{6}} & \frac{1}{\sqrt{3}} \end{bmatrix}$.

5. Eigenvalues are 3, 3, and -3. $P = \begin{bmatrix} \frac{1}{\sqrt{2}} & \frac{1}{\sqrt{3}} & \frac{1}{\sqrt{6}} \\ 0 & \frac{1}{\sqrt{3}} & -\frac{2}{\sqrt{6}} \\ \frac{1}{\sqrt{2}} & -\frac{1}{\sqrt{3}} & -\frac{1}{\sqrt{6}} \end{bmatrix}$.

6. Eigenvalues are 6, 6,and -3. $P = \begin{bmatrix} \frac{2}{\sqrt{5}} & \frac{2}{\sqrt{45}} & \frac{1}{3} \\ -\frac{1}{\sqrt{5}} & \frac{4}{\sqrt{45}} & \frac{2}{3} \\ 0 & \frac{5}{\sqrt{45}} & -\frac{2}{3} \end{bmatrix}$.

7. Eigenvalues are -1, 2, and 0. $P = \begin{bmatrix} 1 & 0 & 0 \\ 0 & \frac{1}{\sqrt{2}} & -\frac{1}{\sqrt{2}} \\ 0 & \frac{1}{\sqrt{2}} & \frac{1}{\sqrt{2}} \end{bmatrix}$.

8. Eigenvalues are 3, 4, and 0. $P = \begin{bmatrix} 1 & 0 & 0 \\ 0 & \frac{1}{\sqrt{2}} & -\frac{1}{\sqrt{2}} \\ 0 & \frac{1}{\sqrt{2}} & \frac{1}{\sqrt{2}} \end{bmatrix}$.

9. Eigenvalues are 9, 9, and 6. $P = \begin{bmatrix} \frac{1}{\sqrt{2}} & -\frac{1}{\sqrt{6}} & \frac{1}{\sqrt{3}} \\ 0 & \frac{2}{\sqrt{6}} & \frac{1}{\sqrt{3}} \\ \frac{1}{\sqrt{2}} & \frac{1}{\sqrt{6}} & -\frac{1}{\sqrt{3}} \end{bmatrix}$.

10. Eigenvalues are 8, 8, 8, and 4. $P = \begin{bmatrix} \frac{1}{\sqrt{2}} & 0 & \frac{1}{2} & \frac{1}{2} \\ -\frac{1}{\sqrt{2}} & 0 & \frac{1}{2} & \frac{1}{2} \\ 0 & -\frac{1}{\sqrt{2}} & -\frac{1}{2} & \frac{1}{2} \\ 0 & \frac{1}{\sqrt{2}} & -\frac{1}{2} & \frac{1}{2} \end{bmatrix}.$

11. Eigenvalues are 1, 1, 3 and 7. $P = \begin{bmatrix} -\frac{1}{\sqrt{2}} & 0 & \frac{1}{\sqrt{2}} & 0 \\ \frac{1}{\sqrt{2}} & 0 & \frac{1}{\sqrt{2}} & 0 \\ 0 & -\frac{1}{\sqrt{2}} & 0 & \frac{1}{\sqrt{2}} \\ 0 & \frac{1}{\sqrt{2}} & 0 & \frac{1}{\sqrt{2}} \end{bmatrix}.$

12. Eigenvalues are 7, −5, and 1. $P = \begin{bmatrix} \frac{2}{\sqrt{6}} & 0 & -\frac{1}{\sqrt{3}} \\ \frac{1}{\sqrt{6}} & -\frac{1}{\sqrt{2}} & \frac{1}{\sqrt{3}} \\ \frac{1}{\sqrt{6}} & \frac{1}{\sqrt{2}} & \frac{1}{\sqrt{3}} \end{bmatrix}.$

Answers to Matlab Exercises 3.4.3

1. Eigenvalues are 1, 4, and 7. $P = \begin{bmatrix} 0.6667 & -0.6667 & 0.3333 \\ -0.6667 & -0.3333 & 0.6667 \\ 0.3333 & 0.6667 & 0.6667 \end{bmatrix}.$

2. Eigenvalues are −5, −5, and 16. $P = \begin{bmatrix} 0.4644 & -0.1496 & 0.8729 \\ 0.6059 & -0.6651 & -0.4364 \\ -0.6459 & -0.7316 & 0.2182 \end{bmatrix}.$

3. Eigenvalues are 3, 3, and −6. $P = \begin{bmatrix} 0.9333 & -0.1333 & 0.3333 \\ 0.1333 & -0.7333 & -0.6667 \\ -0.3333 & -0.6667 & 0.6667 \end{bmatrix}.$

4. Eigenvalues are 4.4142 and 1.5858. $P = \begin{bmatrix} -0.9239 & 0.3827 \\ -0.3827 & -0.9239 \end{bmatrix}.$

5. Eigenvalues are −1.5311 and 6.5311. $P = \begin{bmatrix} 0.7497 & 0.6618 \\ -0.6618 & 0.7497 \end{bmatrix}.$

6. Eigenvalues are −1, 5, and −1. $P = \begin{bmatrix} 0.8944 & 0.4082 & -0.1826 \\ -0.4472 & 0.8165 & -0.3651 \\ 0 & -0.4082 & -0.9129 \end{bmatrix}.$

7. Eigenvalues are 6, 3, and 0. $P = \begin{bmatrix} 0.6667 & 0.6667 & 0.3333 \\ -0.6667 & 0.3333 & 0.6667 \\ -0.3333 & 0.6667 & -0.6667 \end{bmatrix}.$

8. Eigenvalues are 1, -1, and 5.0833. $P = \begin{bmatrix} 0.9104 & 0.1010 & -0.4013 \\ 0.2483 & -0.9091 & 0.3344 \\ 0.3310 & 0.4041 & 0.8527 \end{bmatrix}$.

9. Eigenvalues are -2, -0.1962, and 10.1962.

$$P = \begin{bmatrix} 0.3015 & -0.8822 & 0.3618 \\ -0.9045 & -0.1447 & 0.4011 \\ 0.3015 & 0.4482 & 0.8416 \end{bmatrix}.$$

10. Eigenvalues are 3, 3, -3, and 3.

$$P = \begin{bmatrix} 0.7616 & -0.5034 & -0.4082 & 0 \\ 0.0580 & -0.5744 & 0.8165 & 0 \\ 0.6455 & 0.6455 & 0.4082 & 0 \\ 0 & 0 & 0 & 1.0000 \end{bmatrix}.$$

11. Eigenvalues are 4, 4, 4, and 16.

$$P = \begin{bmatrix} 0.8476 & 0.8476 & 0.8476 & 0.5000 \\ -0.4391 & 0.4911 & 0.5621 & 0.5000 \\ -0.2553 & -0.8241 & 0.0757 & 0.5000 \\ -0.1532 & 0.2768 & -0.8062 & 0.5000 \end{bmatrix}.$$

Answers to Exercises 4.1.2

1. $x(t) = -c_1 e^{5t} + c_2 e^{2t}$

   $y(t) = c_1 e^{5t} + 2c_2 e^{2t}$

2. $x(t) = c_1 e^{-3t} + 2c_2 e^{2t} - c_3 e^t$

   $y(t) = 2c_1 e^{-3t} - c_2 e^{2t}$

   $z(t) = c_1 e^{-3t} + 2c_2 e^{2t} + c_3 e^t$

3. $x(t) = 600 e^{4t} - 100 e^{-3t}$

   $y(t) = 100 e^{4t} + 100 e^{-3t}$

4. $x(t) = e^{2t} - 2e^{3t}$

   $y(t) = e^t + 2e^{2t} - 2e^{3t}$

   $z(t) = -2e^{2t} + 2e^{3t}$

5. $x(t) = 2c_1 e^{10t} - 3c_2 e^{3t}$

   $y(t) = c_1 e^{10t} + 2c_2 e^{3t}$

6. $x(t) = -c_1 e^t - 2c_2 e^t + c_3 e^{5t}$
   $y(t) = c_1 e^t - c_3 e^{5t}$
   $z(t) = c_2 e^t + c_3 e^{5t}$

7. $x(t) = -5c_1 e^{5t} - 4c_3 e^{3t}$
   $y(t) = -c_1 e^{5t} - c_2 e^{-5t} + c_3 e^{3t}$
   $z(t) = c_1 e^{5t} + c_2 e^{-5t} + 3c_3 e^{3t}$

8. $x(t) = -c_1 e^t + c_3 e^{5t}$
   $y(t) = -2c_1 e^t - c_2 e^{3t} + 2c_3 e^{5t}$
   $z(t) = 2c_1 e^t + c_2 e^{3t} + 2c_3 e^{5t}$

9. $x(t) = c_1 e^t + c_2 e^{2t} + c_3 e^{-2t}$

10. $x(t) = c_1 e^t + c_2 e^{2t} + c_3 e^{-t}$

11. $x(t) = c_1 e^t + c_2 e^{2t} + c_3 e^{3t}$

Answers to Exercises Section 4.2.1

1. $y = 2.9x + 2$

2. $y = x + 6.5$

3. $y = 1.1x + 3.5$

4. $y = x + \frac{11}{3}$

5. $y = \frac{43}{35}x - \frac{18}{35}$

6. $y = -1.8x + 5.8$

7. $v = \left(\frac{19}{26}, \frac{31}{26}\right)$

8. $\left(\frac{25}{13}, \frac{44}{13}, \frac{31}{13}, \frac{25}{13}\right)$

9. $\left(\frac{41}{3}, \frac{19}{3}, -\frac{35}{6}\right)$

10. $\left(-\frac{2}{7}, -\frac{1}{7}, \frac{4}{7}\right)$

Answers to Matlab Exercises 4.2.3

1. $y = 1.8x + 2.8$

2. $y = .9x + 1.2$

3. $y = 1.9x + .6$

4. $y = 1.6x + 2$

5. $y = 2.9x + 6.1$

6. $(3, 2)$

7. $(1, 0, 3)$

8. $\left(-\frac{13}{30}, \frac{3}{5}\right)$

9. $\left(\frac{41}{30}, -\frac{4}{15}, \frac{1}{6}\right)$

10. $\left(\frac{19}{7}, \frac{59}{14}, \frac{27}{14}, \frac{19}{7}\right)$

Answers to Optional Matlab Exercises 4.2.5

1. $\begin{bmatrix} 125 & 25 & 5 & 1 \\ 27 & 9 & 3 & 1 \\ -8 & 4 & -2 & 1 \\ 64 & 16 & 4 & 1 \end{bmatrix}$

2. 420

3. $y = 4x^2 - 18x + 19$

4. $y = -4x^2 + 18x - 12$

5. $y = -0.5667x^2 + 4.7667x - 4.2000$, or
   $y = -\frac{17}{30}x^2 + \frac{143}{30}x - \frac{21}{5}$

6. $y = -3.6x + 3 \ \ (d = 4.2)$

7. $y = -0.5x^2 - 3.1x + 0.8 \ \ (d = 3.2)$

8. $p(x) = 1.3333x^3 - 2.5x^2 - 4.8333x + 2$

9. $p(x) = 2.5x^2 - 1.5x + 4$ (The points lie on a parabola, so the exact fit polynomial of degree 3 or less is actually of degree 2.)

10. $y = 3.1x + 3.5 \ \ (d = 1.1)$

11. $p(x) = -0.0833x^4 + 0.1667x^3 + 0.5833x^2 + 2.3333x + 3$

12. $y = -3.1x + 11.8$ $(d = 1.1)$

13. $p(x) = -0.0714x^2 - 2.8143x + 11.6571$ $(d = 1.0286)$

14. $p(x) = -0.2500x^3 + 1.4286x^2 - 4.9643x + 11.9571$ $(d = 0.1286)$

15. $p(x) = 0.1250x^4 - 1.2500x^3 + 3.8750x^2 - 6.7500x + 12$

Answers to Exercises 4.3.2

1. The matrices are:

   (a) Regular. $(A^2$ has no zeros.$)$
   (b) Not regular. (Last column always the same.)
   (c) Regular. $(A^4$ has no zeros.$)$
   (d) Regular. $(A^2$ has no zeros.$)$

2. The transition matrix is

$$
\begin{array}{cc}
 & \begin{array}{cc} rainy & sunny \end{array} \\
\begin{array}{c} rainy \\ sunny \end{array} & \begin{bmatrix} \frac{2}{3} & \frac{1}{3} \\ \frac{1}{3} & \frac{1}{2} \end{bmatrix}
\end{array} .
$$

The steady-state vector is

$$
\begin{bmatrix} \frac{3}{5} \\ \frac{2}{5} \end{bmatrix} .
$$

In the long run, 3 out of every 5 days are rainy and 2 out of every 5 days are sunny.

3. The transition matrix is

$$
\begin{array}{c}
 & \begin{array}{ccc} oat & bran & corn \end{array} \\
\begin{array}{c} oatmeal \\ bran\,flakes \\ corn\,flakes \end{array} & \begin{bmatrix} 0 & \frac{1}{3} & 1 \\ \frac{1}{2} & 0 & 0 \\ \frac{1}{2} & \frac{2}{3} & 0 \end{bmatrix}
\end{array} .
$$

The steady-state vector is

$$
\begin{bmatrix} \frac{6}{14} \\ \frac{3}{14} \\ \frac{5}{14} \end{bmatrix} .
$$

4. The steady-state vectors are:

(a) $\begin{bmatrix} \frac{7}{11} \\ \frac{4}{11} \end{bmatrix}$

(b) $\begin{bmatrix} \frac{9}{16} \\ \frac{7}{16} \end{bmatrix}$

(c) $\begin{bmatrix} \frac{34}{164} \\ \frac{59}{164} \\ \frac{71}{164} \end{bmatrix}$

(d) $\begin{bmatrix} \frac{41}{107} \\ \frac{42}{107} \\ \frac{24}{107} \end{bmatrix}$

Answers to Exercises 4.4.2

The answers are not unique; we give one correct answer.

1. $(4, -1, 0), (2, 0, -1)$

2. $(1, -1, 0), (1, 0, -2)$

3. $(0, 1, -2)$

4. $(5, -17, -8)$

5. $(1, 1, -1)$

6. $(1, -1, 0, 0), (0, 0, 2, -3)$

7. $(8, 1, -11, 0), (10, -7, 0, -11)$

8. $(0, 0, 1, -1)$

9. $(4, -1, 0)$

10. $(1, -1, 0)$

11. $(0, 1, -2)$

12. $(5, -17, -8)$

13. $(1, 1, -1)$

14. $(1, -1, 0, 0)$

15. $(8, 1, -11, 0)$

16. $(0, 0, 1, -1)$

17. $4x - y = 0$
    $2x - z = 0$

18. $x - y = 0$
    $x - 2z = 0$

19. $y - 2z = 0$

20. $5x - 17y - 8z = 0$

21. $x + y - z = 0$

22. $x_1 - x_2 = 0$
    $2x_3 - 3x_4 = 0$

23. $8x_1 + x_2 - 11x_3 = 0$
    $10x_1 - 7x_2 - 11x_4 = 0$

24. $x_3 - x_4 = 0$

25. $(4, -1, 0), (2, 8, -17)$